# Israel Horovitz

## Plays: 1

### The Indian Wants the Bronx, Line, The Widow's Blind Date, Park Your Car in Harvard Yard, Cat Lady

*The Indian Wants the Bronx*: An East Indian, lost in the Bronx, finds himself in a chilling world of isolation and fear.

*Line*: Five strangers waiting in line, each willing to do anything to be first.

*The Widow's Blind Date*: Two workmen trade macho stories. When Margy arrives for her date, a series of terrifying revelations and events is initiated.

*Park Your Car in Harvard Yard*: A hilarious and deeply moving tale about the final year in the life of the meanest teacher from Gloucester High School and the ex-student hired to look after him.

*Cat Lady*: Alone with her memories, an old woman searches for her last companion in this poignant elegy to loss and isolation.

**Israel Horovitz** was born in Wakefield, Massachusetts, in 1939. He first lived in London in 1961–3 as a drama student at the Royal Academy of Dramatic Art. In 1965, he returned to London as playwright-in-residence at the Royal Shakespeare Company's Aldwych Theatre. Since 1967, he has had more than fifty plays produced in New York City, many of them translated and performed around the world. Among his best-known are *Line* (off-Broadway's longest-running play), *The Indian Wants the Bronx* (which introduced Al Pacino), *Rats, North Shore Fish, It's Called the Sugar Plum, Morning, The Primary English Class, The Wakefield Plays* (a seven-play cycle), *Lebensraum, My Old Lady*, and his cycle of Massachusetts-based plays which includes *Park Your Car in Harvard Yard* and *The Widow's Blind Date*. Other recent plays include *Sins of the Mother, Security, Fast Hands, Compromise, 50 Years of Caddieing*, and *The Secret of Mme. Bonnard's Bath*. BBC radio plays include *Stations of the Cross, Phone Tag, The Chips Are Down, Fighting Over Beverley*, and *Man In Snow*, for which Horovitz won the Sony Radio Academy Award. His screenplays include *3 Weeks after Paradise, The Strawberry Statement*, for which he won the Prix du Jury, Festival de Cannes, *Author! Author!, A Man in Love, James Dean, Believe in Me*, and *Sunshine*, for which he won the European Film Academy Award (Best Screenwriter). Other awards include the OBIE (twice), the NY Drama Desk Award, the Prix de Plaisir du Théâtre, the Prix Italia, the Writers Guild of Canada (Best Screenwriter) Award, the Drama Desk Award, an Award in Literature of the American Academy of Arts and Letters, and many others. He is founder and Artistic Director of Gloucester Stage Company, and of the New York Playwrights Lab.

ISRAEL HOROVITZ

# Plays: 1

**The Indian Wants the Bronx**
**Line**
**The Widow's Blind Date**
**Park Your Car in Harvard Yard**
**Cat Lady**

*with an introduction by Israel Horovitz*

Methuen Drama

Published by Methuen Drama 2006

1 3 5 7 9 10 8 6 4 2

First published in Great Britain in 2006 by
Methuen Drama
A & C Black Publishers Limited
38 Soho Square
London W1D 3HB

A CIP catalogue record for this book is available from the British Library

ISBN 0 413 77489 9
978 0 413 77489 7

Typeset by SX Composing DTP, Rayleigh, Essex

**Caution**

# Contents

# Israel Horovitz:
# A Select Chronology

1958  *The Comeback* (Emerson Theatre, Boston)

1967  *Line* (Café LaMama, New York)

1968  *The Indian Wants the Bronx* (Astor Place Theatre, New
York)
*It's Called the Sugar Plum* (Astor Place Theatre, New
York)
*Rats* (Café au Go-Go, New York)

1969  *Leader* (Gramercy Arts Theatre, New York)
*The Honest to God Schnozzola* (Gramercy Arts Theatre,
New York)

1971  *Acrobats* (Theatre de Lys, New York)

1972  *Shooting Gallery* (WPA Theatre, New York)
*Alfred the Great* (American Cultural Center, Paris)

1973  *Our Father's Failing* (Eugene O'Neill Theatre Center,
Conneticutt)

1974  *Spared* (American Cultural Center, Paris)

1975  *The Primary English Class* (Circle in the Square
Theatre, New York)
*Uncle Snake* (Central Park, New York)

1976  *Stage Directions* (Actors Studio, New York)

1977  *The Former One-on-One Basketball Champion* (Actors
Studio, New York)
*Hopscotch* (Public Theatre, New York)
*The 75th* (Public Theatre, New York)

1978    *A Christmas Carol: Scrooge and Marley* (Center Stage,
Baltimore)
*The Widow's Blind Date* (Actors Studio, New York)

1979    *The Good Parts* (Actors Studio, New York)
*The Great Labor Day Classic* (Actors Theatre of
Louisville)

1980    *Sunday Runners in the Rain* (Actors Playhouse, New
York)

1983    *Park Your Car in Harvard Yard* (Los Angeles Theatre
Center)

1985    *Henry Lumper* (Gloucester Stage, Boston)

1986    *A Rosen by Any Other Name* (American Jewish Theatre,
New York)
*North Shore Fish* (Gloucester Stage, Boston)
*Year of the Duck* (Gloucester Stage, Boston)

1993    *Fighting Over Beverley* (Gloucester Stage, Boston)

1996    *Lebensraum* (Gloucester Stage, Boston)
*My Old Lady* (Gloucester Stage, Boston)

1997    *One Under* (Gloucester Stage, Boston)

2004    *Cat Lady* (Boston Playwright's Theatre)

# Preface

Israel Horovitz is a young man, really nice, really charming – a tender American hoodlum. Sweet. As soon as you see him, you can't help but love him. Like all the tender ones, like all the sweet ones, he writes the cruelest things one can imagine. And these are the works that ring the truth.

Israel Horovitz is both a sentimentalist and a realist. One can only imagine, therefore, to what degree he can be ferocious.

I'm not going to present to you – *explain* to you – his play *Line*. Rest assured. I'll only say that it's unique – that there's no action – nothing happens, nothing but everything.

Everything? What? Well, *Line* illustrates the themes of conflict. More precisely, competition. Put two men together – strangers . . . then three, then four, then five – then, introduce a woman among them. Conflict will erupt.

These strangers know each other at heart, and because they know each other, they hate each other – they *despise* each other! They'll battle for first place, which, of course, they'll lose and regain and re-lose – because of the woman, who is, of course, *also* fighting for first place. I think that they would even be willing to kill each other, and that they would even be willing to die in the first place, if there is no other way to end up first. Of course, first place is an illusion. There's no head to any line. We need to believe that there's a first place. Otherwise, how could we possibly have competition?

In this play, Israel tells us all, which means he says nothing. I won't tell you how much I love this play. I will let you discover it on your own. Because we might not agree – especially if I were the first one to have said it!

Eugène Ionesco

# Introduction

Although *The Indian Wants the Bronx* seems to be born on
the streets of New York, the play, in fact, has its roots
in England.

In the early 1960s, I lived in London, where I was
studying at the Royal Academy of Dramatic Art . . . and, of
course, writing plays. To say I was poor, back then, is to say
the sky had possibilities. The labor laws in England were
absurdly biased against foreigners and I was only allowed to
take work that no Englishman would accept. I found such
an odious job, as a bartender, in an American Air Force
non-commissioned officers' club in West Ruislip, six miles
west of the BBC. For my forty-five hours of labor, each
week, I took home the equivalent of $35 . . . which was
precisely what I needed to pay the rent, and not a
penny more.

I should add that I was by then supporting a family of
three . . . my daughter Rachael (now a film producer) was
already alive and eating food on a regular basis.

I offer all this as background to my particular state of
mind during the conception and writing of *The Indian
Wants the Bronx*. I was not what you might call a
frivolous guy.

Several times a week I ate the odd meal (on my way to or
from school and/or work) in the cafeteria at the
Commonwealth Institute on Kensington High Street.
Between normal mealtimes, slightly out-of-date, over-
cooked food was less expensive to buy in the restaurant
there than it was to buy in a food market. It was less than
wonderful. Early-morning breakfasts at the Commonwealth
Institute often featured the previous night's unserved meals.
Curried eggs and veal chops sort of thing.

One particular morning, when I got to the
Commonwealth Institute, the cafeteria was still shut and
locked. At the door, there was already a substantial line of
hungry people, waiting to buy a cheap meal. We were a mix
of students and older down-and-outers, all colorless, in tan
or olive-drab raincoats. Because of his turban and native

dress, one young Indian student – a Hindu, twentyish, my age – was considerably more visible than the rest of us.

We all stood together silently, no chat, as Londoners are wont to do, for several minutes . . . until the silence was exploded by a carful of Teddy boys (*c*.1963 version of Skinheads) screaming racist insults at the young Hindu . . . such as: 'Hey, Sahib, move your fookin' elephant!'

None of us knew what to do, exactly. We stood there dumbfounded, listening to heckling that grew more and more obscene, more and more violent, as the Teddy boys tried to outdo one another.

And then, one by one, we saw that the young Hindu was anything but upset. He was laughing . . . nodding . . . waving to his verbal assassins. In fact, his friendliness undid the Teddy boys, who drove off, annoyed and unsatisfied.

We all stood together silently, watching the Teddy boys' car disappear into the clot of morning traffic – and then watching the young Hindu calm his happy giggles down to embarrassed smiles.

We all had the same question burning in our minds: What the hell just happened?

Insofar as finding an answer was concerned, the Brits did nothing. I was American, so I leaned in and asked him: 'What the hell just happened?' He replied with the most amazing gibberish: flawless Hindi. He didn't speak a word of English. Not a word. He must have been a country boy. He must have arrived in London the night before, or that morning, with one address: the Commonwealth Institute. So profound was the young Hindu's loneliness, he was thrilled to have human contact, even from cruel and dangerous aggressors.

When I finished drama school I left London and moved to New York for the first time in my life. I'd grown up in a small town in Massachusetts and New York City seemed to me like twenty-five Londons. I was lonely and I was terrified.

My second child, Matthew (a novelist), was now alive and eating food regularly. I had two full-time jobs. (Yes, America was indeed the land of opportunity.) In the middle of the night I wrote plays. *The Indian Wants the Bronx* was the first new play I finished after returning to America. It was somehow quite easy to imagine myself a Hindu, lost in Manhattan, trying to reach a child. The first draft came together quickly and surely. I knew exactly what I was writing about and why.

Al Pacino was acting in a play in somebody's living room uptown on Central Park West. The play was called (I think) *Y Is a Crooked Letter*. It was impenetrable. Pacino was great. I was one of eight in the packed audience. There was no question that Pacino was the right actor for my play. I introduced myself and gave him the script, which he read that night. The next day we had our first meeting. He was a janitor in a run-down building in the West Sixties. (Maybe it wasn't run-down when Al took the job?) His apartment was in the basement. I remember drinking coffee from old orange-juice cans.

I also remember doing a performance of *The Indian Wants the Bronx* in a 3,000-seat ballroom-theatre on Long Island during our search for a commercial producer to bring our show in to New York. Only three people were in the audience – ladies, extremely old, in picture hats. Midway through the show they left. Al stopped acting, looked out front: 'What do we do now, Israel?' he said.

At risk of turning this already too-long short introduction to *The Indian Wants the Bronx* into a full-length autobiography, I'll offer one more story and then stop.

When Pacino auditioned for the commercial producer we'd finally turned up for an off-Broadway production, she didn't want him. She'd actually never seen Pacino perform the play. She'd only met him. She thought he was too short and not handsome. So, on audition day, she brought in the actor she wanted: blond, blue-eyed, tall, untalented. I said no, absolutely no. She said, fine, OK, she wouldn't produce the play. I said let both actors audition for us and then we'll decide, calmly, intelligently. I told Al exactly what was going on. He was furious with me for putting such pressure on him.

Pacino was made to audition during an open call, as he

wasn't yet a member of Actors Equity. The play had made
the rounds of NYC talent agents and it seemed like every
young non-union actor in NYC showed up that day . . . in
addition to the actors who'd auditioned previously and were
call-backs. First, we endured the Producer's Choice. He
was, in a word, boring. Then it was Pacino's turn. (I'd
gotten the producer to agree to audition the two front
runners back to back, for what I'd promised her would be
easy comparison.)

The theatre was packed with hopeful young actors sitting
in the audience, waiting their turns, when Pacino auditioned
for the role of Murph in *The Indian Wants the Bronx*. He came
out singing . . . and then he moved downstage, center,
looked straight through the fourth wall into the house and
bellowed the first lines of the play . . . directly into the
producer's smiling face:

'Hey, Pussyface, can you hear us? Can you hear your
babies singin' to ya'?'

The producer was startled, terrified. I grabbed her arm.

'OK, OK, you see it, right? . . . You can see he's better,
right?'

She said yes, meekly. I ran on to the stage, in front of all
the other hopeful actors, still waiting to audition, and
hugged Pacino.

'You got the part, Al! She said yes!'

The rest is history. Pacino and John Cazale both did the
play off-Broadway. And they were both brilliant. We all
won OBIES – Al won as Best Actor; John won as
Distinguished Actor ( John won for *Line*, as well as *Indian* . . .
he'd graced two of my plays that first glorious season in New
York); and I won for Best Play.

In the summer of 1968 we took *The Indian Wants the Bronx*
to the Spoleto Festival in Italy, where we were reviewed
by a great number of European critics. In a word, our
careers *happened*.

*Line* was my first play to be produced in New York City.
Thanks to Leonard Melfi, who talked Ellen Stewart into
taking me and my play on faith, *Line* was scheduled to run

for six consecutive nights at Café LaMama at its original
original location on 2nd Avenue. In those days LaMama
was, arguably, the hottest showcase in the country for a
beginning playwright. If you had a play on at LaMama it
was reviewed. And you were either In or Out.

Thus, the premiere of *Line* was, simply, terrifying. James
Hammerstein and I assembled a sublime cast of talented
friends . . . all willing to work without pay. Each production
was given a budget of $80, in cash, handed over by Ellen
Stewart (LaMama herself), who said, 'The money's yours,
honey. If you don't spend it all on scenery and props, you
can keep the difference.' I'd brought John Cazale and Ann
Wedgeworth into the cast; Jimmy brought the others.
Cazale and I had grown up in neighboring Massachusettts
towns: he in Winchester, me in Wakefield. I'd stage-
managed a Tennessee Williams play with Ann Wedgeworth
at the Paper Mill Playhouse in New Jersey two years before.
Except for Hammerstein, who had worked on Broadway,
none of us had had any particular prior success in NYC. We
all took *Line* and LaMama very, very seriously. We
rehearsed endlessly.

Our dress rehearsal was wonderful . . . hilarious and
frightening. We seemed to be, in a word, unstoppable. And
then the bomb fell. The young actor who was playing
Stephen announced – *after* the dress rehearsal – that he'd
gotten a role in a TV series pilot and was going from the
theatre to the airport, where he would fly away for ever. He
did all of the above.

I turned to Hammerstein and told him that it was obvious
that he would have to take over the role. In those days
LaMama was booked solid for a year. I was certain that
postponing *Line* would mean postponing our careers – for
a year.

James Hammerstein, talented and dear, was and is six
feet eight inches tall, feet stockinged or unstockinged. There
was no way he'd fit into the little quitter's costume. All eyes
were suddenly on me.

We stayed in the theatre, rehearsing through the night
and through the next day. At 8 p.m., I walked out on stage

as Stephen in *Line*, facing an auditorium no longer empty
and safe, but now filled to the brim with NEW YORK
DRAMA CRITICS! . . . One look at their faces and I forgot
who I was, where I was . . .

Horrified, I did what any actor in my shoes (*especially* in
my shoes) would have done: I yelled, 'Line!' Bonnie Frindel
Morris, my lifelong friend and then stage manager, yelled
back at me with the first line of the play: 'Is this a line?' I
then dutifully repeated what she'd said: 'Is this a line?' As it
was the sixties, the audience, understandably, assumed that
*Line* was 'that kind of play'. They laughed at our rapid-fire
exchange of 'lines', and they applauded. My stage fright
soared to uncharted heights. My heart shifted into
Automatic Pilot and I sailed through the rest of the play
word-perfect – almost – until John Cazale, with his flawless
North Shore Massachusetts 'Pahk Yo'r Cah' accent, looked
me straight in the panic-stricken eye, upstage center, and
whispered, proudly, 'Yo'r doin' great, Ah'tie!' (Artie was my
nickname, diminutive for my middle name, Arthur.) As soon
as I heard the word 'Ah'tie', I once again forgot who I was,
where I was . . .

Jerry Tallmer, reviewing *Line* for the *New York Post*, gave
me my first review in New York City . . . as a playwright
and as an actor. The review's headline was WELCOME
MR HOROVITZ.

Two years later a commercial production of *Line* in NYC
fared less well. I'd replaced myself with Richard Dreyfuss, a
then unknown  young actor I'd seen in  Gordon Davidson's
brilliant LA production of *Line* at the Mark Taper Forum.
Richard had played in *Rats* there as well. He was wonderful
in both of my plays. On my return to NYC I was so
enthusiastic about Dreyfuss that Hammerstein agreed to
take him as Stephen in *Line* sight unseen.

Alas, I'd been talked into putting a curtain-raiser with
*Line*, which, on its own, only ran an hour or so. The
reviews for *Line* were stunning. But the reviews for its
curtain-raiser, *Acrobats*, were far less than stunning. In fact,
the word on the street was 'Skip the first play; don't miss
the second play'. . . We ran for only a few months, playing

to half-houses, and then we closed. I had expected much more, and I was devastated.

A few years later Edith O'Hara, who ran the 13th Street Repertory Theatre, asked me if she could do a revival of *Line*. I said yes, but with one condition: that *Line* be done on its own. The 13th Street Repertory Theatre's production of *Line* has been, at this writing, running for nineteen consecutive years and is off-Broadway's longest-running play (as distinguished from *The Fantasticks*, which is off-Broadway's longest-running *musical*).

Eugène Ionesco's introduction to *Line*, the Preface in this edition, represents another kind of turning point in my life. I'd had some plays performed in Paris, with some success, prior to *Line*, but I was totally unprepared for what would happen with *Line* itself. The Paris production opened well after the play's commercial failure in NYC, but before its 13th Street Repertory Theatre revival. Essentially, I worked on the Paris production for the pure fun of being in France and working with French actors. Speaking French that was, like Jean-Paul Sartre, *tout charmant, mais jamais correct*, I co-directed the French-language premiere of *Line*. I was teamed with my friend Michel Fagadau, who'd guided the French premieres of *The Indian Wants the Bronx* and *It's Called the Sugar Plum* two years earlier.

Luckily for me the French translation of *Line* had been done by Claude Roy, who was, and is, two things: an angel and a genius. On the opening night Claude and I went together to a festival of Marx Brothers movies in a tiny cinema on rue d'Ombre. We watched four consecutive hours of Marx Brothers antics. The event was hilarious and humbling, and, as we'd hoped, totally distracting. We passed by the Théâtre de Poche-Montparnasse at 10 p.m., to see if there was any hint of what had happened there earlier. We found Michel alone, waiting for us on the sidewalk in front of the darkened theatre. Cautiously, Claude asked him how it went. We both liked his answer: *Cétait une triomphe!* It seems that Jean-Jacques Gauthier had stood at the end and yelled 'Bravo!' Gauthier was *Le Figaro*'s drama critic, and the most respected drama critic in Paris

during the 1970s. That production ran for eleven years and
*Line* (*Le Premier*) is almost constantly in production in the
French language.

In fact, like *The Indian Wants the Bronx*, *Line* has been
translated into and played in nearly thirty languages
worldwide.

Why one play succeeds and another play does not is
really the mystery of mysteries. I love to hear people explain
successes and failures. I always eavesdrop. It's always funny,
gorgeously pretentious dialogue: 'See, *Line* is cheap to
produce . . . nice acting roles . . .' The truth is that both *The
Indian Wants the Bronx* and *Line* have enjoyed similar success
around the globe, and Lord only knows why. The plays are
as different as different can be. By all that's holy, they
should appeal to totally different audiences.

But, as Euripides so often said, when asked about the
success or failure of any his 126 plays: 'Go figure!'

During the past fifteen or so years I have written a group of
plays that I call my 'blue-collar' plays. This work serves to
create, among other things, a kind of record of what
working-class life was like during my time on my little dot
on the planet Earth. It seemed to me that working-class life
in small-town America was rapidly disappearing. I won't
burden you here with my particular analysis of the whys and
wherefores. My job is to dramatize, make theatrical. So let
me try to make my point, quickly and cleverly, by posing a
couple of essential questions . . . and then I'll move on to
introducing my plays: How would you feel if your
daughter/son became a truck driver? How would you feel if
your daughter/son married a plumber?

Hopefully, the people of my blue-collar plays will explain
themselves through their actions. Like their author, they
won't attempt to offer a tidy polemic, a smug or simple
reason why the world is changing as it is . . . but the
characters of these plays will be quick to *show* you how they
have responded, to let you know how they feel about a
world that has begun to exclude them.

My impulse in limiting my plays to small-town New

England was this: I thought that if I could focus my particular telescope/microscope and get it right, *really* right, for one small New England town, I might possibly have it right for the world. Let me be quick to cite my influences. I had, for one, an excellent mentor in Thornton Wilder and a nearly perfect model in his beautiful play *Our Town*.

In the 1970s, I wrote another cycle of plays, 'The Wakefield Plays'. I was recently out of a Ph.D. program in English Lit. and 'The Wakefield Plays' were brim-full of complex, arcane literary allusion. Martin Esslin called the work 'an American Oresteia'. Thornton Wilder had something else to say.

I had dinner with Mr Wilder from time to time. He was eighty-six years old and not able to get around easily. When we met we talked about playwriting and about life. He read my 'Wakefield Plays' and was extremely flattering in his praise . . . But at the end of it all, Thornton Wilder spoke one sentence that would alter the course of my playwriting for years and years to come. He ended his praise with '. . . Of course, there isn't very much Wakefield in those plays.' Spoken by Thornton Wilder, who had created Grovers Corners, New England's best-known, best-loved small town, that ten-word sentence had for me great meaning, and great impact. If my New England-based plays would be nothing else, they would be brim-full of New England.

Mr Wilder often talked about a notion that 'all knowledge flowed through the trunk of the tree . . .' That was to say that if one thing could be learned to its fullest, then all things could be at the same time learned. Consider a carpenter who is truly a master, an ultimate genius-level joiner. Couldn't this carpenter easily do skillful brain surgery? After all, the essential theories of great carpentry and of great brain surgery are the same: cutting and joining.

In the end, of course, Wilder had *invented* Grovers Corners, and my goal was to somehow use real people, real places, real events, in a mix with dramatic fiction. I began my 'Wakefield Plays' cycle with *Hopscotch*, a one-act play. Unlike the longer, more literary plays of the cycle (*Alfred the*

*Great, Our Father's Failing, Alfred Dies, Spared*), *Hopscotch* used
Andrew Wyeth-like detail . . . something I've come to call
'super-realism' . . . an *over*abundance of real-life detail mixed
with imagined detail . . . observed dialogue that concerns
itself with accent . . . real time, real place, local reference,
local idiom, musicality of local language, etc., etc. Ten pages
into the writing of *Hopscotch*, I knew I would be, like a
hungry fish, hooked. I had stumbled into a style . . . a
method of writing, a method of digging into real life . . .
*psycho-archaeology* . . . And, not incidentally, a way of making
certain inalterable facts of my own particular real life much
more stageworthy, much more special. And the result would
be a full decade of work . . . a dozen full-length plays about
blue-collar New Englanders in a time of crisis . . .

By way of introduction to two of those plays, collected
herein, I have allowed myself (and written down) a series of
memories of the whens and whys (I think) I wrote each of
them . . . in hope that the reader (actor, director, designer,
critic . . .) will gain some special insight into my work that
no doubt eluded me as author: unqualified judge.

Some fifteen years ago I began *The Widow's Blind Date*, a
play that drew heavily on easily remembered detail . . .
and, as it turned out much to my shock, detail not so
easily remembered.

When I was a young boy I worked on Saturdays for my
father's eldest brother Max, in Uncle Max's junk shop in
Stoneham, Massachusetts, a few miles from my birthplace,
Wakefield. My uncle's shop's main function was the creation
of bales of old books, bales of old and new (unread)
newspapers, and bales of old and new magazines, which my
uncle sold to my father, who in turn trucked and sold to
paper mills where old paper was recycled into new paper.
One of my frequent tasks was the tearing of bindings and
covers from the old books, preparing them for the crush of
the book-baling press. I would, single-handedly, rip bindings
and covers from some 2,000 books each Saturday. (I say
'single-handedly', but I did of course use both hands.) From
time to time some book or another would catch my eye, my

attention, and I would stop a while and read. And thus I
had my earliest introduction to English literature.

Years later, when I was teenaged, a friend of mine – a
fine, upstanding lad from a fine, upstanding family –
pointed to a young woman and excitedly blurted out a story
of a gang rape he'd been part of the night before. I turned
and looked at the young girl who had been the object of my
friend's lust. And his friends' lust. Her frightened, defeated
eyes are still etched in my memory.

And some fifteen years after that, through the magic that
is writing, I brought the same young woman back to 'life' to
enter my Uncle Max's shop and to confront two of her
unwanted lovers. And *The Widow's Blind Date* was born. To
my amazement, when my mother saw the play's production
in my own little theatre in Massachusetts she said to me, 'I
didn't think you knew!' . . . 'Knew *what*?' I asked. And she
told me a story of a gang rape that had taken place in my
uncle's junk shop some twenty-five years earlier. A young
woman working in the laundry next door was somehow
enticed into the shop, where she was raped by several of the
men, many of them 'winos' who worked for fifty cents a day.
As a boy I must have overheard these men talking,
bragging, and buried their sordid story somewhere in my
deepest, darkest subconscious. Thus *The Widow's Blind Date*
is partly true and partly invented. But it is also coherent,
organized and conclusive. And in the end these are not
qualities of Life. This is Writing.

*The Widow's Blind Date* was first presented as a staged
reading at the Actors Studio in NYC prior to the world
premiere at the Los Angeles Actors Theatre, and then a
production in my own theatre, Gloucester Stage, in
Gloucester, Massachusetts. The production I directed at
Gloucester Stage transferred to the Circle-in-the-Square in
NYC for its commercial premiere. Since then, *Widow* has
found audiences around the globe. The play is particularly
popular in France, where it was in fact seen *prior* to its
opening in NYC. *Le Figaro*'s drama critic described it as '*du
grand art*'. Yuh, well, perhaps.

In any event, with *The Widow's Blind Date* I found a new

voice, again . . . as I had a decade earlier with *The Indian Wants the Bronx* . . . but this new voice was miles more personal, more satisfying. Sitting in a theatre in France recently, watching *Widow* . . . watching the audience watching *Widow*, I thought to myself, 'I am a lucky man.'

A number of my working-class plays are set in Gloucester, Massachusetts, my adopted home town. Gloucester is thirty-eight miles north of Boston and precisely marathon distance from my birthplace, Wakefield. Gloucester was where my parents took my sister and me on special days.

My first play ever (with a devilishly ironic title: *The Comeback*) opened in Boston about a hundred years ago when I was nineteen. Some years and several plays later, after I'd found the courage actually to leave New York City summers, without fear that my 'New York Playwright' logo would be passed to a younger, fresher out-of-towner, I thought to myself, 'Why not put my life down where special days are spent?' . . . I bought my first (and last) Gloucester house, a tiny wood-framed Victorian with slightly Gothic pretensions. I thought that I'd bought a house for summers and for the odd warm weekend. Then I noticed that I'd stayed in Gloucester for sixteen consecutive months. In 1985 my (twin) children, Hannah and Oliver, were born at the Addison-Gilbert Hospital in Gloucester. They are Gloucester kids.

Gloucester is a place of great natural beauty. Majestic cliffs overlook a Kodak-perfect coastline. Every Gloucester kid knows a half-dozen secret sandy beaches. Every Gloucester kid knows a dozen secret swimmable granite quarries. Tourists in search of cheap lobsters and/or early Americana usually bypass Gloucester, opting for the calendar-cute village of Rockport five miles up the road. And as Brackish says in *Park Your Car in Harvard Yard*, come Labor Day . . . 'the summ'ah people pack up their greasy hot-dog-colored bodies and their grotesque charcoal sketches of Motif No. 1' . . . and we locals smile, because we locals know that September and October are, simply, the best months . . .

When I first began spending time in Gloucester as an adult, I remember quite vividly observing that 'Gloucester's heroes are carpenters and fishermen, not playwrights'. Quite clearly Gloucester, located on an island (Cape Ann), land's end, was to be one of America's final bastions of blue-collar life. The more time I spent in Gloucester, the more I felt the need to have a theatre in town, a place to see plays . . . a place to try my new work first. In 1980, with two friends, I co-founded the Gloucester Stage Company. We started out as a summer theatre, producing one-act plays in the back room at the Blackburn Tavern. From Day One we had an audience.

Although Gloucester had also boasted a tradition of High Art (Winslow Homer, Edward Hopper, Milton Avery, T. S. Eliot, Charles Olson, etc. all lived and worked in Gloucester), it is and was and always will be essentially a working person's town, blue collar, a place for 'fish people' . . . fishermen, lobstermen, lumpers (stevedores), fish cutters. Once a bustling, world-class seaport, Gloucester's best days are either past or deeply buried in secret days ahead. At the moment Gloucester is in trouble. The fish business has all but gone away. The economy is floating belly-up. Drug traffic is unthinkably high. Gloucester people are, in a word, worried.

My first Gloucester-based play, *Mackerel*, was whimsical . . . a sort of Nixon/Bush parable about a Gloucester man, Ed Lemon, who watches a 250,000-pound mackerel crash through the wall of his house. *Mackerel* was written in the 1970s, just after *The Primary English Class*, just before *Hopscotch* . . . As I settled into actually living life in Gloucester, my notion to write blue-collar plays that were set in Gloucester became more serious. As did the plays themselves.

*Park Your Car in Harvard Yard* is probably the most famous of my Gloucester-based plays. Like *Widow*, it was first done at the Los Angeles Actors Theatre in collaboration with Gloucester Stage. Bill Bushnell, LAAT's artistic director, came to Gloucester to work with me on the script, while at the same time working for me at Gloucester Stage, directing

*The Widow's Blind Date. Park Your Car in Harvard Yard* had
been a success at Bushnell's theatre in Los Angeles, but it
was a *triumph* in Gloucester. Local people made quick
identification with the people of my play . . . led easily into
this not-quite-make-believe world by the play's abundance
of detail . . . the new style . . . *super-realism* . . . with people
talking like Gloucester people about real-life Gloucester
events, people and places . . . and with the play's real-life
politics. The Gloucester audience was deeply moved by my
play. And I was deeply moved by my play's audience. There
is no better support system for a playwright than an
appreciative audience. A clap on the back from a teary-eyed
playgoer is for me so much more satisfying than a rave in
the *Times*, Gloucester or otherwise. I mean this. The praise I
remember most from my four decades of being a produced
playwright are moments of direct contact with audience, not
quotes from rave reviews. A pickup truck screeches to a stop
along Gloucester's back shore. I'm out there, running my
daily six. A burly man blocks my path, shakes my hand:
'The play was great!' In the subway in New York City, a
skinny lady asks me if I'm me, tells me the woman in *Park
Your Car* was so much like her mother! . . . And she begins to
weep. And I begin to weep, because I have touched
somebody. And in France, even though it's called *Quelque
Part dans cette Vie*, it still works . . . an impeccably dressed
older couple seek me out and find me at the back of the
theatre, and they embrace me. They are weeping. And I am
so pleased to be a playwright, in spite of all.

*Park Your Car in Harvard Yard* centers on Gloucester High
School's toughest teacher ever, and the housekeeper he
hires to tend to him at the end of his life. But for his
education, Jacob Brackish (the teacher) would be the same
person as Kathleen Hogan (his housekeeper and former
student). In the way that *Park Your Car* contrasts an educated
life with a non-educated life, this play became a kind of
paradigm for me in my writing a dozen plays that, among
other things, dramatize a changing attitude toward working-
class life.

*Cat Lady* is a short play, so it will get a shortish introduction.

New York City's theatre scene is in a sorry state just now. Broadway shows seem to be either produced by Disney, or produced with Disney audiences in mind. In fact, most New Yorkers I know – playwrights included – don't even bother to go to Broadway shows. Broadway seems to be a tourist attraction, a theme park.

As I'm far too young to remember the legendary Broadway of Moss Hart and Clifford Odets, I really can't work up an ounce of sadness. For me, off-Broadway was always comfy. I have had something like fifty-three different plays produced in NYC since *Line*'s premiere at Café LaMama back in November 1967. All but two of them have been produced off-Broadway. (Two were actually produced *on* Broadway, but one was a miracle and the other was a complete misunderstanding.) Granted, some of the fifty-three are short plays, but even at that the number fifty-three seems enormous to me, insanely so.

I guess playwriting is what I'll do when I grow up.

But I digress. Back to NYC theatre's sorry state.

At the moment most NYC theatres produce evenings of ten-minute plays. In fact, it's safe to say that *most* original work shown in NYC theatres these days takes the form of evenings of ten-minutes plays. Why? I suppose little theatres can most easily succeed with omnibus evenings of ten tiny plays, giving them ten 'name' playwrights and ten separate casts, all of whom will sell tickets to loyal friends and family. (Actors in Equity-approved showcases are paid $0. Actually, they're each given two subway tokens. But that's another essay for another time.)

Simply said, last season alone I reckon I was asked by twenty-five different theatres to write a ten-minute play. I said 'yes' to approximately half of the theatres and wrote two new ten-minute plays, which I circulated to worthy askers. One of them is called *The Fat Guy Gets the Girl*, the other is *Cat Lady*. Those two plays were each produced five or six times during the 2004 season in various evenings of ten-minute plays.

Yes, of course I had other larger plays of mine produced

in NYC and around the globe. I am simply reporting why an oddity such as *Cat Lady* came to be written.

In fact, Ann-Katherine Graf, a marvelous Swiss-French director based in Geneva, had adapted a novella of mine called *Nobody Loves Me*, about an unhappy man and his ugly dog. Graf contacted me, asking if I could possibly create a short play for an older woman that she could produce on the same bill with my dog story. Her request came on the same day as two other requests (coincidentally from other women) for ten-minute plays. So *Cat Lady* was written, intercut with *Nobody Loves Me* and took care of, uh, three birds with one, uh, stone.

After Geneva, *Cat Lady* had its USA premiere at the Boston Theatre Marathon – which is an annual twenty-four-hour, non-stop presentation of – you guessed it – ten-minute plays. The play represented my own little theatre in the marathon and the sublime Nancy Carroll gave a genius-level performance in the title role. The Boston critics agreed, and then some.

In fact, I enjoy the form of the ten-minute play. The challenge is to not write a sketch, but a fully realized stage play, with rising-and-falling action, metaphor, social purpose. *Cat Lady* at the very least achieves nine lives in ten minutes. And that seems good value.

Israel Horovitz
NYC, March 2005

# The Indian Wants the Bronx

*The Indian Wants the Bronx* was first presented at the Astor Place Theatre in New York City (along with *It's Called the Sugar Plum*) on 17 January 1968 by Ruth Newton Productions in association with Diana Mathews. It was directed by James Hammerstein and designed by Fred Voelpel. The cast was as follows:

| | |
|---|---|
| **Indian (Gupta)** | John Cazale |
| **Joey** | Matthew Cowles |
| **Murph** | Al Pacino |

## Characters

**Gupta**, *an* **Indian**
**Joey**
**Murph**

## Setting

A bus stop on upper Fifth Avenue in New York City. A chilly September night.

*As the curtains open, the lights fade up, revealing an* **Indian**
(**Gupta**). *He is standing alone, right of center stage, near a 'bus stop'
sign. An outdoor telephone booth is to his left; several city-owned 'litter'
baskets to his right.*

**Gupta** *is in his fifties. Although he is swarthy in complexion, he is
anything but sinister. He is, in fact, meek and visibly frightened by the
city.*

*He is dressed in traditional East Indian garb, appropriately for mid-
September. He crosses right.*

*As* **Gupta** *strains to look for a bus on the horizon, the voices of two
boys can be heard in the distance, singing. They sing a rock 'n' roll
song, flatly, trying to harmonize.*

**Joey** (*entering*)
  I walk the lonely streets at night,
  A 'lookin' for your door,
  I look and look and look and look,
  But, baby, you don't care.
  Baby, you don't care.
  Baby, no one cares.

**Murph** (*following* **Joey**. **Murph** *stops* **Joey**. *Interrupting*)
Wait a minute, Joey. I'll take the harmony. Listen. (*He sings.*)
  But, baby, you don't care,
  Baby, you don't care.
  Baby, no one cares.

(*Confident that he has fully captured the correct harmony, he boasts.*)
See? I've got a knack for harmony. You take the low part.

**Joey** *and* **Murph** (*they sing, together*)
  I walk . . . the lonely, lonely street . . .
  A 'listenin' for your heartbeat,
  Listening for your love.
  But, baby, you don't care.
  Baby, you don't care.
  Baby, no one cares.

*They appear on stage. First boy is* **Joey**. *Second boy is* **Murph**.
**Joey** *is slight, baby-faced, in his early twenties.* **Murph** *is stronger, long-haired, the same age.*

**Murph** (*circles as* **Joey** *crosses to baskets. Singing*)
    . . . The lonely, lonely streets, called out for lovin'
    . . . but there was no one to love . . .
    'cause, baby, you don't care . . .

**Joey** (*joins in the singing*)
    Baby, you don't care . . .

**Murph**
    Baby, you don't care.
    Baby, you don't care.
    Baby, no one cares.
    Baby, no one cares.

(*Calls out into the audience, across to the row of apartment houses opposite the park.*) Hey, Pussyface! Can you hear your babies singing? Pussyface. We're calling you.

**Joey** (*joins in*)    Pussyface. Your babies are serenading your loveliness. (*They laugh.*)

**Murph**    Baby, no one cares.

**Murph** *and* **Joey** (*singing together*)
    Baby, no one cares.
    Baby, no one cares.

**Murph** (*screams*)    Pussyface, you don't care, you goddamned idiot! (**Murph** *notices the* **Indian**.) Hey. Look at the Turk. (**Joey** *stares at the* **Indian** *for a moment, then replies.*)

**Joey** (*foot on litter basket*)    Just another pretty face. Besides. That's no Turk. It's an Indian.

**Murph** (*continues to sing*)
    Baby, no one cares.

(*He dances to his song, strutting in the* **Indian**'s *direction. He then turns back to* **Joey** *during the completion of his stanza and feigns a boxing match.*)

I walk the lonely, lonely streets,
 A'callin' out for loving . . .
But, baby, you don't give a Christ for
Nothin' . . . Not for nothin'.

(*Pretends to swing a punch at* **Joey**, *who backs off laughing.*) You're nuts. It's a Turk!

**Joey** Bet you a ten spot. It's an Indian.

**Murph** It's a Turk, schmuck. Look at his fancy hat. Indians don't wear fancy hats. (*Calls across the street, again.*) Hey, Pussyface. Joey thinks we got an Indian. (*Back to* **Joey**.) Give me a cigarette.

**Joey** You owe me a pack already, Murphy.

**Murph** So I owe you a pack. Give me a cigarette.

**Joey** Say 'please', maybe?

**Murph** Say 'I'll bust your squash if you don't give me a cigarette!'

**Joey** One butt, one noogie.

**Murph** First, the butt.

**Joey** You're a Jap, Murphy. (*As* **Joey** *extends the pack,* **Murph** *grabs it. Ducks around litter baskets.*)

**Murph** You lost your chance, baby. (*To the apartment block.*) Pussyface! Joey lost his chance!

**Joey** We made a deal. A deal's a deal. You're a Jap, Murphy. A rotten Jap. (*To the apartment.*) Pussyface, listen to me! Murphy's a rotten Jap and just Japped my whole pack. That's unethical, Pussyface. He owes me noogies, too!

**Murph** Now I'll give you twenty noogies, so we'll be even. (*He raps* **Joey** *on the arm. The* **Indian** *looks up, as* **Joey** *squeals.*)

**Joey** Hey. The Indian's watching.

**Murph** (*raps* **Joey** *sharply again on the arm*)  Indian's a Turkie.

**Joey** (*grabs* **Murphy**'s *arm and twists it behind his back*) Gimme my pack and it's an Indian, right?

**Murph**  I'll give you your head in a minute, jerkoff.

**Joey**  Indian? Indian? Say, Indian! (**Murph** *twists around. He twists* **Joey**'s *little finger, slowly.* **Joey**'s *in pain.*)

**Murph**  Turkie? Turkie?

**Joey**  Turkie. OK. Let go. (**Murph** *lets him up and laughs.* **Joey** *jumps up and screams.*) Indian! (*He runs a few steps.*) Indian!

**Murph** (*laughing*)  If your old lady would have you on Thanksgiving you'd know what a turkey was, ya' jerk. (*Hits him on the arm again.*) Here's another noogie, turkie-head! (*The* **Indian** *coughs.*)

**Joey**  Hey, look. He likes us. Shall I wink?

**Murph**  You sexy beast, you'd wink at anything in pants.

**Joey**  Come on. Do I look like a Murphy?

**Murph** (*grabs* **Joey** *and twists both of his arms from behind*) Take that back.

**Joey**  Aw! Ya' bastard. I take it back.

**Murph**  You're a Turkie-lover, right?

**Joey**  Right.

**Murph**  Say it.

**Joey**  I'm a Turkie-lover.

**Murph**  You're a Turkie-humper, right?

**Joey**  *You're* a Turkie-humper.

**Murph**  Say, *I'm* a Turkie-humper.

**Joey**  That's what I said. You're a Turkie-humper. (**Murph** *twists his arms a bit further.*) OWW, YA' DIRTY

BASTARD! Alright, I'm a Turkie-humper! Now, leggo!
(**Joey** *pretends to laugh.*)

**Murph**   You gonna hug him and kiss him and love him
up like a mother?

**Joey**   Whose mother?

**Murph**   Your mother. She humps Turkies, right?

**Joey**   Owww! All right. Yeah. She humps Turkies. Now,
leggo!

**Murph** (*he lets go*)   You're free.

**Joey** (*breaks. Changes the game*)   Where's the bus?

**Murph**   Up your mother.

**Joey**   My old lady's gonna kill me. It must be late as hell.

**Murph**   Maybe we'll get our own place. Yeah. How about
that, Joey?

**Joey**   Yeah, sure. I move out on her and she starves. You
know that.

**Murph**   Let her starve, the Turkie-humper.

**Joey** (*hits **Murph** on the arm and laughs*)   That's my mother
you're desecrating, you nasty bastard.

**Murph**   How do you desecrate a whore? Call her a lady?

**Joey**   Why don't you ask your mother?

**Murph** (*hits **Joey** on the arm*)   Big mouth, huh?

**Joey**   Hey! Why don't you pick on som'body your own
size, like Turkie, there.

**Murph**   Leave Turkie out of this. He's got six elephants in
his pocket, probably.

**Joey** (*laughs at the possibility*)   Hey, Turkie, you got six
elephants in your pocket?

**Murph**    Hey, shut up, Joey. (*He glances in the* **Indian***'s direction and the* **Indian** *glances back.*) Shut up.

**Joey**    Ask him for a match.

**Murph**    You ask him.

**Joey**    You got the butts.

**Murph**    Naw.

**Joey**    Chicken. Want some seeds to chew on?

**Murph**    I'll give you somethin' to chew on.

**Joey**    Go on, ask him. I ain't never heard an Indian talk Turkie-talk.

**Murph**    He's a Turkie, I told ya'. Any jerk can see he's a definite Turk!

**Joey**    You're a definite jerk, then. 'Cause I see a definite Indian!

**Murph**    Yeah?

**Joey**    Yeah.

**Murph**    I'll show you. (*He walks toward the* **Indian**, *slowly, taking a full minute to cross the stage. He slithers from side to side and goes through pantomime of looking for matches.*)

**Joey**    Hey, Murph. You comin' for dinner. We're havin' turkey tonight! Hey! Tell your Turkie to bring his elephants.

**Murph**    Schmuck! How's he going to fit six elephants in a rickshaw? Quick!

**Joey** (*flatly*)    Four in front. Three in back. (*He reaches the* **Indian**.)

**Murph**    Excuse me. May I borrow a match? (*Pantomimes looking for matches. Note: The* **Indian** *answers in his own language, Hindi, not English, unless noted otherwise.*)

**Indian**    I cannot speak your language. I don't understand.

**Murph** (*to* **Joey**, *does a terrific 'take', then speaks, incredulous*) He's got to be kidding. (**Joey** *and* **Murph** *laugh.*)

**Indian**    I'm sorry. I don't understand you.

**Murph**    No speak English, huh? (*The* **Indian** *looks at him blankly, louder.*) You can't speak English, huh? (*The* **Indian** *stares at him confused by the increase in volume. The* **Indian** *smiles.*)

**Joey** (*flatly*)    Son of a bitch. Hey, Murph. Guess what? Your Turkie only speaks Indian.

**Murph** (*moves in closer, examining the* **Indian**)    Say something in Indian, big mouth.

**Joey** (*holds up his hand*)    How's your teepee? (*The* **Indian** *stares at him. He laughs.*) See. (*The* **Indian** *welcomes* **Joey**'s *laugh and smiles. He takes their hands and 'shakes' them.*)

**Murph** (*nodding and smiling as he shakes the* **Indian**'s *hand. Catches on as to why the* **Indian** *has joined the smile and feigns a stronger smile until they all laugh aloud.* **Murph** *cuts off the laughter with*)    You're a fairy, right?

**Indian** (*he smiles harder than before*)    I don't understand you. I'm looking for my son's home. We were supposed to meet, but I could not find him. I'm looking for his home. This is his address. Am I headed in the correct direction? (*The* **Indian** *produces a slip of paper with an address typed on it. And a photograph.*)

**Murph** (*takes photo*)    Gupta. In the Bronx. Maybe it is an Indian. Big deal. (*To the* **Indian**.) Indian, right? You an Indian? Indian? (*Pauses.*) He don't know. (**Murph** *shakes his head up and down, smiling. The* **Indian**, *mistaking this signal for approval of direction, shakes his head and smiles as well.*) This picture must be his kid. Looks like you, Joey.

**Joey** (*looks at picture. Steps out of* **Murph**'s *reach*)    Looks Irish to me. (*Hands picture to* **Murph**.)

**Joey** *and* **Murph**    Ohhh.

**Murph**    Yeah. Why'd you rape all those innocent children? (*Pause.*) I think he's the wrong kind of Indian. (*To the* **Indian**.) You work in a restaurant? (*Pauses. Does an overstated 's' sound with:*) It's such a shame to kill these Indians. They do such superb beaded work. (**Murph** *shakes his head up and down again, smiling.*)

**Indian** ( *follows* **Murph**'*s cue*)    I haven't seen my son all day. Your city is so big and so busy.

**Joey**    Ask him to show you his elephants.

**Murph**    You ask. You're the one who speaks Turkie-Indian.

**Joey** (*steps toward them, holds up hand*)    White man fork with tongue. Right? Naw, he don't understand me. You ask. You got the right kind of accent. All you foreigners understand each other good. (*Pulls left.*)

**Murph**    You want another noogie?

**Joey**    Maybe Turkie wants a noogie or six?

**Murph** (*shaking his head*)    You want a noogie, friend?

**Indian** (*agrees*)    I'm sorry. I haven't been here long.

**Murph**    Give him his noogie.

**Joey**    Naw. He's your friend. You give it to him. That's what friends are for.

**Murph** (*looks at paper and photograph, gives them back*)    Jesus, look at that for a face. Prem Gupta. In the Bronx. Jesus, this is terrific. The Indian wants the Bronx.

**Joey**    He ain't gonna' find no Bronx on this bus.

**Murph**    Old Indian, pal. (*Gives the* **Indian** *card.*) You ain't going to find the Bronx on this bus. Now, I've got a terrific idea for fun and profit.

**Indian**    Excuse me?

**Murph** (*leans left on basket. Pauses*)    Why don't you come home and meet my mother? (*No response from the* **Indian**.) Or maybe you'd like to meet Pussyface, huh? (*To* **Joey**.) Should we bring him over to Pussyface?

**Joey**    He don't even know who Pussyface is. You can't just go getting Indians blind dates without giving him a breakdown.

**Murph** (*to the* **Indian**)    OK, Chief. Here's the breakdown on Pussyface. She's a pig. She lives right over there. See that pretty building. (*Points over the audience, to the back row.*) That one. The fancy one. That's Pussyface's hideaway. She's our Social Worker.

**Joey**    That's right.

**Murph**    Pussyface got assigned to us when we were tykes, right, Joe?

**Joey**    Just little fellers.

**Murph**    Pussyface was sent to us by the City. To watch over us. And care for us. And love us like a Mother. Not because she wanted to. But because she was paid to. Because we were bad boys. We stole a car.

**Joey**    We stole two cars.

**Murph**    We stole two cars. And we knifed a kid.

**Joey**    You knifed a kid.

**Murph** (*to* **Joey**)    Tell it to the judge, fella! (*He takes a pocket knife from his pocket and shows it to the* **Indian** *who pulls back in fear.*)

**Joey**    The Chief thinks you're going to cut him up into a totem pole.

**Murph**    Easy, Chief! I've never cut an Indian in my life. (*Puts knife away.*)

**Joey**    You've never *seen* an Indian in your life.

**Murph**    Anyway, you got a choice. My mother – who happens to have a terrific personality. Or Pussyface, our beloved Social lady.

**Joey**    Where's the bus?

**Murph**    It's coming.

**Joey**    So's Christmas.

**Murph**    Hey. Show Turkie my Christmas card for Pussyface. (*To the* **Indian**.) Pussyface gives us fun projects. I had to make Christmas cards last year. (*Back to* **Joey**.) Go on. Show the Chief the card. (**Joey** *fishes through his wallet, finds a 'dog-eared' photostat, gives it to* **Murph**. *He hands it to the* **Indian**, *who accepts curiously.*)

**Indian**    What is this?

**Murph**    I made that with my own two cheeks. Tell him, Joe.

**Joey**    Stupid, he don't speak English.

**Murph**    It don't matter. He's interested, ain't he?

**Joey**    You're a fink-jerk.

**Murph**    Oooo. I'll give you noogies up the kazzooo. This is a Christmas card. I made it. Get me? Pussyface got us Christmas jobs last year. She got me one with the City. With the War on Poverty. I ran the Xerox machine.

**Joey**    Jesus. You really are stupid. He don't understand one word you're saying.

**Murph** (*mimes the entire scene, slowly*)    He's interested, ain't he? That's more than I can say for most of them. (*To the* **Indian**.) Want to know how you can make your own Christmas cards with your simple Xerox 2400? It's easy. I'll show you. Watch. (*Crosses straight upstage centre and begins his act.*) First you lock the door to the stat room, so no one can bust in. Then you turn the machine on. (*Crosses to 'machine',* *turns dial.*) Then you set the dial at the number of people you want to send cards to. Thirty, forty.

**Joey**    Three or four.

**Murph**    Right, fella'. Then you take off your pants. And your underpants. Them's the ones underneath. You sit on the glass. You push the little button. The lights flash. When the picture's developed you write 'Noël' across it! (*Pauses. Crosses to the* **Indian**. *The* **Indian** *hands card to* **Murph**.) That's how you make Christmas cards. (**Murph** *waits for a reaction from the* **Indian**, *then turns back to* **Joey**, *dismayed. To* **Joey**.) He's waiting for the bus. (*Gives him card.*)

**Joey**    Me, too. Jesus. Am I ever late!

**Murph**    Tell her to stuff it. You're a big boy now.

**Joey**    She gets frightened, that's all. She really don't care how late I come in, as long as I tell her when I'm coming. If I tell her one, and I don't get in until one-thirty, she's purple when I finally get in. (*Pauses.*) She's alright. Where's the goddamned bus, huh? (*Calls across the park.*) Pussyface, did you steal the bus, you dirty old whore? Pussyface, I'm calling you! (*Pauses. Looks for bus.*) She's alright, Murph. Christ, she's my mother. I didn't ask for her. She's alright.

**Murph**    Who's alright? That Turkie-humper? (*To the* **Indian**.) His old lady humps Turkies, you know that? (*Smiles, but the* **Indian** *doesn't respond.*) Hey, Turkie's blowin' his cool a little. (*The* **Indian** *looks for bus.*) Least you got som'body waitin'. My old lady wouldn't know if I was gone a year.

**Joey**    What? That Turkie-humper?

**Murph** (*to the* **Indian** *– yells*)    'Hey!' (*The* **Indian** *jumps, startled,* **Murph** *laughs.*) Hey! You got any little Indians runnin' around your teepee? No? Yeah? No? Aw, ya' stupid Indian. Where is the goddamn bus?

**Joey**    Let's walk it.

**Murph**   Screw that. A hundred blocks? Besides, we got ta keep this old Turkie company, right? We couldn't let him stand all alone in this big ole' city. Some nasty boys might come along and chew him up, right?

**Joey**   We can walk it. Let the Indian starve.

**Murph** (*crosses to the* **Indian**)   So walk it, jerk. I'm waiting with the Chief. (**Murph** *stands next to the* **Indian**.)

**Joey**   Come on, we'll grab the subway.

**Murph**   Joe, the trains are running crazy now. Anyway, I'm waitin' with my friend the Chief, here. You wanna' go, go. (*Murmurs.*) Where is it, Chief? Is that it? Here it comes. Huh? (*Looks for the bus, acting it out.*) I think I see it. Sure.

**Joey** (*considers it*)   Yeah, we gotta' watch out for Turkie. (*He stands on the other side of the* **Indian**, *who finally walks, slowly, back to the bus stop area.*)

**Murph**   See that, Turkie, little Joey's gonna' keep us company. That's nice, huh? (*The* **Indian** *looks for the bus. He's still holding the ID card.*) You know, Joey, this Turkie's kinda' a pain in the ass. He don't look at me when I talk to him. (*Takes card, hands it to* **Joey** *in front of the* **Indian**.)

**Joey**   He oughta' be polite. (*Hands card to* **Murph** *behind the* **Indian**. *They pass the card in a game. The* **Indian** *smiles.*)

**Murph**   I don't think he learned many smarts in Indiana. Any slob knows enough to look when they're being talked to. Huh? (*Hands card to* **Joey** *in front of the* **Indian**.)

**Joey**   This ain't just any slob. This is a definite Turkie-Indian slob. (*Hands card to* **Murph** *behind him, as in a magic act. They fool the* **Indian**.)

**Murph**   He's one of them Iraqi slobs, probably. War-mongering bastard. (*Card to* **Joey** *in front of the* **Indian**. *Flatly.*) Saddam, here, rapes all the little kids.

**Joey**   Terrible thing. (*Card to* **Murph**.) Too bad we can't give him some smarts. We'll give 'im plenty of smarts.

(*Crosses upstage. The* **Indian** *follows. Card to the* **Indian**.) Want some smarts, Chief?

**Indian** I can't understand you. Please? When is the bus due here? Am I at the right station? (*He contains his dignity, smiling.*)

**Joey** Hey, look. He's talking out of the side of his mouth. Sure, that's right . . . Hey, Murph. Ain't Indian broads s'posed to have sideways breezers? Sure.

**Murph** (*grins*) You mean Chinks, Joey.

**Joey** Naw. Indian broads too. All them foreign broads. Their breezers are sideways. That's why them foreign cars have the back seats facing the side, right?

**Murph** Is that right, Turkie? Your broads have horizontal snatches?

**Indian** (*stares at him nervously*) I can't understand you.

**Murph** (*repeating him in the same language*) I can't understand you.

**Indian** (*recognizing the language, finally. He speaks with incredible speed*) Yes, that's correct. I can't understand your language. I'm sorry, but I've only been in your country for a few days. I haven't had time to understand your language. Please forgive me. I'm separated from my son. He's been living in your country for six years. When his mother died two months ago, he sent for me. I came immediately. He's a good son to his father. I'm sorry I haven't learned your language yet, but I shall learn.

**Murph** (*does a 'take'. Flatly*) This Turkie's a real pain in the ass.

**Joey** Naw. I think he's pretty interesting. I never saw an Indian before.

**Murph** (*crosses to* **Joey** *and slaps the back of* **Joey**'s *head*) Oh. It's fascinating. It's marvelous. This city's a regular melting pot. Turkies. Kikes like you. (*Pause.*) I even had me a French lady once.

**Joey**    A French lady, huh?

**Murph**    Yep. A real French broad.

**Joey**    You been at your mother again?

**Murph** (*hits him on the arm*)    Wise-ass. Just what nobody likes. A wise-ass.

**Joey**    Where'd you have this French lady, huh?

**Murph**    I found her in the park over there. (*Points.*) Just sitting on a bench. She was great. (*Boasts.*) A real *talent*.

**Joey**    Yeah, sure thing. (*Calls into the park.*) Hello, talent. Hello, talent! (*Pauses.*) I had a French girl, too. (*Turns to avoid* **Murph***'s eyes, caught in a lie.*) Where the hell's that bus?

**Murph**    Sure you did. Like the time you had a mermaid?

**Joey**    You better believe I did. She wasn't really French. She just lived there a long time. I went to first grade with her. Geraldine. She was my first girlfriend. (*Talks very quickly.*) Her old man was in the army or something, 'cause they moved to France. She came back when we were in high school.

**Murph**    Then what happened?

**Joey**    Nothin'. She just came back, that's all.

**Murph**    I thought you said you *had* her?

**Joey**    No, she was just my girlfriend.

**Murph**    In high school?

**Joey**    No, ya' stoop. In the first grade. I just told you.

**Murph**    You had her in the first grade?

**Joey**    Jesus, you're stupid. She was my girlfriend. That's all.

**Murph** (*feigns excitement*)   Hey . . . that's a *sweet little story*, (*Flatly.*) What the hell's wrong with you?

**Joey**   What do ya' mean?

**Murph**   What do you mean, 'what do you mean?' First you say you had a French girl, then you say you had a girlfriend in first grade, who went to France. What the hell kind of story's that?

**Joey**   It's a true one, that's all. Yours is full of crap.

**Murph**   What's full of crap?

**Joey**   About the French lady in the park. You never had any French lady unless you been at your own old lady again. Or maybe you've been at Pussyface?

**Murph**   Jesus, you're lookin' for it, aren't you?

**Joey**   I mean, if you gotta tell lies to your best buddy, you're in bad shape, that's all.

**Murph** (*gives* **Joey** *a 'high-sign'*)   Best buddy? You? (*Noogie gesture to* **Joey**. *The noogie gesture sign to the* **Indian**. *He returns the obscene gesture, thinking it an American sign of welcome.*)

**Joey**   Turkie! Is that how it is in Ceylon, sir?

**Murph**   Say-lon? What the hell is say-long?

**Joey**   See, ya' jerk. Ceylon's part of India. That's where they grow tea.

**Murph**   No kiddin'? Boy, it's terrific what you can learn just standin' on a corner with a schmuck like you. Tea, huh? (*To the* **Indian**, *he screams:*) Hey! (*Looks for bus, crosses to* **Indian**. *The* **Indian** *turns around, startled, but catches* **Murph** *at the game and smiles.* **Murph** *returns the smile and asks:*) How's your teabags? (*No response.*) No? (*To* **Joey**.) Guess you're wrong again. He don't know teabags.

**Joey**   Look at the bags under his eyes.

(*Transition scene:* **Murph** *screams: 'Hey!' – The* **Indian** *smiles.*
*They dance a war-dance around him – beating a rhythm on the trash*
*cans, hissing and cat-calling for a full minute.* **Murph** *scares the*
**Indian** *who retreats.* **Murph** *ends the dance with a final 'Hey!'*
*The* **Indian** *jumps in fear.* **Murph** *works the* **Indian** *around*
*behind the litter baskets. Now that they sense his fear, the comedy has*
*ended.*)

**Murph**    Turkie looks like he's getting bored.

**Joey**    Poor old Indian. Maybe he wants to play a game.

**Murph**    You know any poor old Indian games?

**Joey**    We could burn him at the stake. (*He laughs.*) That
ain't such a terrible idea, you know. Maybe make an Indian
stew.

**Murph**    Naw, we couldn't burn a nice fellow like Turkie.
That's nasty.

**Joey**    We got to play a game. Pussyface always tells us to
play games. (*To the apartment.*) Ain't that right, Pussyface?
You always want us to play games.

**Murph** (*screams*)    Hey! (*The* **Indian** *jumps, startled again.*)
Hey! I know a game. (*Makes false jump at the* **Indian**.) 'Indian
– Indian – Where's the Indian?'

**Joey**    That's a sweet game. I haven't played that for years.

**Murph** (*steps toward* **Joey**)    Wise-ass. You want to play a
game, don't you?

**Joey**    Indian-Indian. Where's the Indian?

**Murph**    Sure. It's just like Ring-a-leave-eo. Only with a
spin.

**Joey**    That sounds terrific.

**Murph** (*crosses to* **Joey**)    Look. I spin the hell out of you
until you're dizzy. Then you run across the street and get
Pussyface. I'll grab the Indian and hide him. Then Pussyface
and you come over here and try to find us.

**Joey**    We're going to spin, huh?

**Murph**    Sure.

**Joey**    Who's going to clean up after you? Remember the Ferris wheel, big shot? All those happy faces staring up at you?

**Murph**    I ain't the spinner. You're the spinner. I'll hide the Chief. Go on. Spin.

**Joey**    How about if we set the Rules as we go along? (*To the* **Indian**.) How does that grab you, Chief?

**Indian**    I'm sorry, but I can't understand your language.

**Murph**    He's talking Indiana again. He don't understand. Go on. Spin. I'll grab the Chief while you're spinning . . . count to ten . . . hide the Chief, while you're after Pussyface. Go on. Spin.

**Joey**    I ain't going to spin. I get sick.

**Murph**    Ain't you going to play?

**Joey**    I'll play. But I can't spin any better than you can. I get sick. You know that. How about if you spin and I hide the Chief? You can get Pussyface. She likes you better than me, anyhow.

**Murph**    Pussyface ain't home. You know that. She's in New Jersey.

**Joey**    Then what the hell's the point of this game, anyway?

**Murph**    It's just a game. We can pretend.

**Joey**    You can play marbles for all I care. I just ain't going to spin, that's all. And neither are you. So let's forget the whole game.

**Murph** (*fiercely*)    Spin! Spin!

**Joey**    You spin.

**Murph** (*slaps* **Joey** *on arm*)   Hey. I told you to spin. (*He squares off against* **Joey**, *menacingly*. **Joey** *looks* **Murph** *straight in the eye for a moment and then says*.)

**Joey**   OK. Big deal. So I'll spin. Then I get Pussyface, right? You ready to get the Chief?

**Murph**   Will you stop talking and start spinning?

**Joey**   Alright. Alright. Here I go. (*He spins himself meekly as* **Murph** *grabs the* **Indian** *and runs for the trash can.* **Joey** *giggles as he spins ever so slowly.* **Murph** *glances at* **Joey** *as* **Joey** *pretends.* **Murph** *is confused*.) There. I spun. Is that OK?

**Murph**   That's a spin?

**Joey**   Well, it wasn't a foxtrot.

**Murph**   I told you to spin! Any slob knows that ain't no spin! Now spin, goddamn it! Spin!

**Joey** (*crosses to* **Murph**)   This is stupid. You want to play games. You want a decent spin. (*Strikes at* **Murph**.) You spin. (*He walks straight to* **Murph** – *a challenge. He slaps* **Murph**. *They freeze*.)

**Murph** (*circles* **Joey** *as if to hit him. He squares off viciously. Raises his arms. Looks at* **Joey** *cruelly and orders*)   Spin me. (**Joey** *brings* **Murph**'s *arms behind* **Murph**'s *back, and holds* **Murph**'s *wrists firmly so* **Murph** *is helpless.* **Joey** *spins him three times. Slowly at first. Then faster. Faster.* **Joey**'s *hostility is released.* **Joey** *laughs*.)

**Joey**   You wanted to spin. Spin. Spin. (*He spins* **Murph** *frantically. The* **Indian** *watches in total horror, not knowing what to do. The* **Indian** *cuddles next to the bus stop sign: his island of safety.* **Murph** *screams*.)

**Murph**   Enough, you little bastard!

**Joey** (*continues to spin him*)   Now YOU get Pussyface. Go on. (*He spins* **Murph** *all the faster as in a grotesque dance gone berserk*.) I'LL hide the Chief. This is your game! This is your game. YOU get Pussyface. I'll hide the Chief. Go on, Murphy.

You want some more spin. (*He has stopped the spinning now, as* **Murph** *is obviously ill.*) You want to spin some more?

**Murph**    Stop it, Joey. I'm sick.

**Joey** (*spins* **Murph** *once more around*)    You want to spin some more or are you going to get Pussyface and come find the Chief and me?

**Murph**    You little bastard.

**Joey** (*spins* **Murph** *once again, still holding* **Murph** *helpless with his arms behind his back*)    I'll hide the Chief. YOU get Pussyface and find us. OK? OK? OK?

**Murph** (*stumbling upstage right*)    OK. You bastard. OK.

**Joey** (*spins* **Murph** *once more*)    Here's one more for good luck, (**Joey** *spins* **Murph** *three more times, fiercely, then shoves him off stage.* **Murphy** *can be heard retching, about to vomit, during the final spins.* **Joey** *first pushes* **Murph** *off stage, then grabs the* **Indian***, who pulls back in terror.* **Murph** *stumbles off as* **Joey** *grabs the* **Indian***, pushes him behind litter baskets.*)

**Indian**    No, please, what are you going to do?

**Joey**    Easy, Chief. (*Slaps the* **Indian**.) It's just a game. Murph spun out on us. It's just a game. I've got to hide you now. (**Murph***'s final puking sounds can be heard well in the distance.*)

**Indian**    No. No. Please, I beg you.

**Joey**    Easy, Chief. Look. I promise you, this ain't for real. This is only a game. A game. Get it? It's all a game! Now I got to count to ten. One. Two. Three. Murphy? (*He laughs.*) Four. Five. Murph? Come get us. Six. Seven. Pussyface is waiting. Eight. Nine. (*Pauses.*) Murphy? Murph? Hey, buddy. (**Joey** *stands up. Speaks.*) Ten. Get up. Up. (*No response.*) Get up, Turkie. (**Joey** *turns, sees the* **Indian** *is already up. The* **Indian** *shakes from fear. Then the* **Indian** *shakes from a chill. There is a moment's silence as* **Joey** *watches.* **Joey** *removes his own sweater and offers it to the* **Indian**.) Here. Here.

Put it on. It's OK. Put it on. (**Joey** *crosses to the* **Indian**, *ties sweater around his neck. The* **Indian** *stares at the sweater.* **Joey** *takes it from his hands and begins to cover the* **Indian**, *who is amazed.*) I hope I didn't hurt you too much. You OK? (*No response.*) You ain't sick too bad, huh? (*Pause.*) Huh? (*Checks the* **Indian** *for cuts.*) You look OK. You're OK, huh? (*No response.*) I didn't mean to rough you up like that, but . . . you know. Huh? (*The* **Indian** *raises his eyes to meet* **Joey**'s. **Joey** *looks down to avoid the stare.*) I hope you ain't mad at me or nothin'. (*Pause.*) Boy, it's gettin' chilly. I mean, it's cold, right? Sure is quiet all of a sudden. Kind of spooky, huh? (*Calls.*) Hey, MURPHY! (**Joey** *laughs aloud.*) Murph ain't a bad guy. He's my best buddy, see? I mean, he gets kinda' crazy sometimes, but that's all. Everybody gets kind of crazy sometimes, right? (*No response.*) Jesus, you're a stupid Indian. Can't you speak any English? No? Why the hell did you come here, anyway? Especially if you can't talk any English. You ought to say something. Can't you even say 'Thank you'? (*The* **Indian** *recognizes those words, finally, and mimics them slowly. Painfully.*)

**Indian** (*in English – very British*)   Thank you.

**Joey** (*crosses to* **Indian**)   I'll be goddamned! You're welcome. (*Slowly, indicating for the* **Indian** *to follow.*) You're welcome. (*Waits.*)

**Indian** (*in English*)   You are welcome.

**Joey**   That's terrific. You are welcome. (**Joey** *smiles, as though all is forgiven. In relief.*) How are you?

**Indian**   You are welcome.

**Joey**   No. How are ya? (*He is excited. The* **Indian** *might be a second friend!*)

**Indian** (*In English – very '***Joey**'*)   How are ya?

**Joey** (*joyously*)   Jesus. You'll be talking like us in no time! You're OK, huh? You ain't bleeding or anything. I didn't wanna' hurt you none. But Murph gets all worked up. You know what I mean. He gets all excited. This ain't the first time, you know. No, sir!

**Indian** (*in English*)   No, sir.

**Joey**   That's right. He's especially crazy around broads.

**Indian** (*in English*)   Broads.

**Joey** (*forgetting that the* **Indian** *is only mimicking*)   That's right. Broads. (*He pauses and remembers, deeply.*) What am I yakking for? Tell me about India, huh? I'd like to go to India some time. Maybe I will. You think I'd like India? India? (*No response.*) That's where you're from, ain't it? Jesus, what a stupid Indian. India! (*Spells the word.*) I.N.D.I.A. Nothin'. Schmuck. India.

**Indian**   India.

**Joey**   Yeah! Tell me about India! (*Long pause as they stand staring at each other.*) No? You're not talking, huh? Well, what do you want to do? Murph oughta' be back soon. (*Discovers coin in his pocket. Crosses to the* **Indian**.) You wanna' flip for quarters? Flip? No? Look, Kennedy half. (*He goes through three magic tricks with the coin: No. 1. He palms the coin, offers the obvious choice of hand, then uncovers the coin in his other hand. The* **Indian** *raises his hand to his turban in astonishment.*) Like that, huh? (*No. 2. Coin slapped on breast.*) Which hand is it under? This hand right? Which hand is it under? Go on, which hand? This hand here! Is it in this hand? This hand. No! It's in this hand. Back to your dumb act? Here's the one you liked! (*Does No. 1. This time the* **Indian** *points to the correct hand instantly.*) You're probably some kind of hustler. OK. Double or nothing. (*Flips.*) Heads, you live. Tails, you die. OK? (*Uncovers the coin.*) I'll be a son-of-a-bitch. You got Indian luck. Here. (*Hands coin to the* **Indian**.)

**Indian** (*stares in question*)   NO?

**Joey** (*considers cheating*)   Take it. You won. No, go ahead. Keep it. (*Offers coin to the* **Indian** *who takes it.*) I ain't no

Indian giver. (*Pause. He laughs at his own joke. No response.*) You ain't got no sense of humor, that's what.

**Indian**    Thank you.

**Joey**    Murph's my best buddy, you know. Me and him were buddies when we were kids. Me and Murph, all the time. And Maggie. His kid sister. (*Pause.*) I had Maggie once. Sort of. Well, kind of. Yeah, I had her. That's right. Murph don't know. Makes no difference now. She's dead, Maggie. Makes no difference when you're dead. (*Sings.*) The worms crawl in. The worms crawl out. (*Speaks.*) What the hell difference does it make? Right?

**Indian** (*steps closer to* **Joey**. *In English*)    No sir.

**Joey** (*without noticing*)    That's why Murph is crazy. That's why he gets crazy, I mean. She dies seventeen, that's all. Seventeen. Just like *that*. Appendix. No one around. There was no one around. His old lady? Forget it! The old man took off years go. All there was really was just Murph and Maggie. That's why he could take it. At home. You think my old lady's bad. She's nothing. His old lady's a pro. You know? She don't even make a living at it, either. That's the bitch of it. Not even a living. She's a dog. I mean, *I* wouldn't even pay her a nickel. Not a nickel. Not that I'd screw around with Murphy's old lady. Oh! Not that she doesn't try. She tries. Plenty. (*His fantasy begins.*) That's why I don't come around to his house much. She tries all the time. She wouldn't charge me anything, probably. But it ain't right screwing your best buddy's old lady, right? I'd feel terrible if I did. She ain't that bad, but it just ain't right. I'd bet she'd even take Murph on. She probably tries it with him, too. That's the bitch of it. She can't even make a living. You think Pussyface is a help? That's the biggest joke yet. (*The* **Indian** *is by now thoroughly confused on all counts. He recognizes the name 'Pussyface' and reacts slightly. Seeing* **Joey**'s *anxiety, he cuddles him. For a brief moment, they embrace: an insane father-and-son tableau. Note: Be careful here. I.H.*) Pussyface. There's a brain. You see what she gave us for Christmas. (*He fishes a*

*knife out of his pocket.*) Knives. Brilliant, huh? Murph's up on a
rap for slicing a kid and she gives us knives for Christmas.
To whittle with. She's crazier than Murphy. Hah. (*He flashes
his open knife at the* **Indian**, *who misinterprets the move as spelling
disaster. The* **Indian** *waits, carefully scrutinizing* **Joey**, *until* **Joey**
*begins to look away.* **Joey** *now wanders to the spot where he pushed*
**Murph** *off stage.*) Hey, Murph! (*The* **Indian** *moves slowly to
the other side of the stage.* **Joey** *sees his move at once and races after
him, thinking the* **Indian** *was running away.*) Hey. Where are
you going? Don't run away. We got to wait for Murphy.
(*The* **Indian** *knows he'll be hit. He tries to explain with mute
gestures and attitude. It's futile.*) You were gonna' run off. Right.
Son of a bitch. You were gonna' tell Murphy. (*He punches the*
**Indian**, *left, right, left, right. The* **Indian** *breaks, runs behind
baskets, and then* **Joey** *chases him, hitting him with a rabbit punch as
the* **Indian** *rushes against* **Murph**, *who has just entered. The*
**Indian** *falls back against booth. The* **Indian** *makes one last effort
to escape and runs the length of the stage, screaming a bloodcurdling
anguished scream.* **Murph** *enters. Stops. Stares incredulously as the*
**Indian** *runs into his open arms.* **Joey** *races to the* **Indian** *and
strikes a karate chop to the back of the* **Indian***'s neck,* **Joey** *is
audibly sobbing. The* **Indian** *drops to the stage as a bull in the ring,
feeling the final thrust of the sword . . .* **Joey** *stands frozen above the*
**Indian**. **Murph** *stares, first at* **Joey**, *then to the* **Indian**.)

**Murph**    Pussyface isn't home yet. She's still in New Jersey.
Ring-a-leave-eo.

**Joey** (*staring at the* **Indian**. *Sobbing, senses his error*)    Indians
are dumb.

**Murph**    Pussyface isn't home. I rang her bell. She don't
answer. I guess she's still on vacation. She ruined our game.

**Joey** (*sobbing*)    Oh, jumping Jesus Christ. Jesus. Jesus. Jesus.
Indians are dumb.

**Murph**    Pussyface ruins everything. She don't really care
about our games. She ruins our games. Just like Indians.
They don't know how to play our games either.

**Joey**    Indians are dumb. Dumb. (*He sobs.*)

**Murph** (*crosses to* **Joey**, *slaps his arm*)    What the hell's going on?

**Joey**    He tried to run. I hit him.

**Murph**    Yeah. I saw that. You hit him alright. (*Stares at the* **Indian**.) Is he alive? (*The* **Indian** *groans. Pulls himself to his knees.*)

**Joey**    He was fighting. I hit him.

**Murph**    OK. You hit him. (*The* **Indian** *groans again. Then he speaks in a plea.*)

**Indian** (**Murph** *turns to look at the* **Indian**)    Please. Don't hurt me any more. What have I done? Please don't hurt me.

**Murph** (*to* **Joey**)    He's begging for something. Maybe he's begging for his life. Maybe he is. Sure, maybe he is.

**Joey** (*crosses to the* **Indian**. *Embarrassed, starts to help the* **Indian** *to his feet*)    C'mon there, Chief. Get up and face the world. C'mon, Chief. Everything's going to be alright.

**Murph**    What's got into you, anyway?

**Joey**    C'mon, Chief. Up at the world. Everything's OK. (*The* **Indian** *ad libs words of pleading and pain.*)

**Murph**    Leave him be. (*But* **Joey** *continues to help the* **Indian**.) Leave him be. What's with you? Hey, Joey! I said 'Leave him be!' (*He pulls* **Joey** *back and the* **Indian** *pulls back with fear.*)

**Joey**    OK, Murph. Enough's enough.

**Murph**    Just tell me what the hell's wrong with you?

**Joey** (*kicks basket*)    He tried to run away, that's all. Change the subject. Change the subject. It ain't important. I hit him, that's all.

**Murph**    OK, so you hit him.

**Joey** (*rises*)   OK! Where were you? Sick. Were you a little bit sick? I mean, you couldn't have been visiting, 'cause there ain't no one to visit, right?

**Murph** (*crosses to* **Joey**)   What *do* you mean?

**Joey**   Where the hell were you? (*Looks at* **Murph** *and giggles*.) You're a little green there, Irish.

**Murph**   You're pretty funny. What the hell's so funny?

**Joey**   Nothing's funny. The Chief and I were just having a little powwow and we got to wondering where you ran off to. Just natural for us to wonder, ain't it? (*To the* **Indian**.) Right, Chief?

**Murph** (*crosses to the* **Indian**, *feels sweater*)   Hey, look at that. Turkie's got a wooly sweater just like yours. Ain't that a terrific coincidence. You two been playing strip poker?

**Joey**   Oh sure. Strip poker. The Chief won my sweater and I won three of his feathers and a broken arrow. (*To the* **Indian**, *he feigns a deep authoritative voice. Crosses to the* **Indian**.) You wonder who I am, don't you? Perhaps this silver bullet will help to identify me? (*He extends his hand. The* **Indian** *peers into* **Joey**'s *empty palm, quizzically. As he does,* **Murph** *quickly taps the underside of* **Joey**'s *hand, forcing the hand to rise and slap the* **Indian**'s *chin, sharply. The* **Indian** *pulls back at the slap.* **Joey** *turns on* **Murph**, *quickly*.) What the hell did you do that for, ya' jerk. The Chief didn't do nothing.

**Murph**   Jesus, you and your Chief are pretty buddy-buddy, ain't you? (*Mimicks* **Joey**.) 'The Chief didn't do nothing.' Jesus. You give him your sweater. Maybe you'd like to have him up for a beer . . .

**Joey** (*grabs sweater*)   Drop it, Murph. You're giving me a pain in the ass.

**Murph** (*crosses to* **Joey**. *Retorts fiercely*)   You little pisser. Who the hell do you think you're talking to? (*The telephone rings in the booth, they are all startled. Especially the* **Indian**, *who senses hope*.)

**Joey** (*after a long wait,* **Joey** *speaks the obvious, flatly*)    It's the phone.

**Murph** (*to the* **Indian**)    The kid's a whiz. He guessed that right away. (*Second ring.*)

**Joey**    Should we answer it?

**Murph**    What for? Who'd be calling here? It's a wrong number. (*The phone rings menacingly. A third time. Suddenly the* **Indian** *darts into the phone booth and grabs the receiver.* **Joey** *and* **Murph** *are too startled to stop him until the* **Indian** *has blurted out his hopeless plea, in his own language.*)

**Indian**    Prem? Is this my son? Prem? Please be Prem. Please help me. I'm frightened. Please help me. Two boys are hurting me. . . I'm frightened. Please. Prem? (*The* **Indian** *stops talking sharply and listens. He crumbles as the voice drones the wrong reply. He drops the receiver and stares with horror at the boys.* **Murph** *realizes the* **Indian**'s *horror and begins to laugh hysterically.* **Joey** *stares silently. The* **Indian** *begins to mumble and weep. He walks from the phone booth. The Voice is heard as a drone from the receiver. The action freezes.*)

**Murph** (*crosses to booth, hangs up receiver. Laughing*)    Hey! (*Kicks him.*) What's the matter, Turkie? Don't you have a dime? (*Steps out of booth.*) Give Turkie a dime, Joe. Give him a dime.

**Joey**    Jesus Christ. I'd hate to be an Indian.

**Murph**    Hey, the paper! C'mon, Joey, get the paper from him. We'll call the Bronx.

**Joey**    Cut it out, Murph. Enough's enough.

**Murph**    Get the frigging piece of paper. What's the matter with you anyway?

**Joey**    I just don't think it's such a terrific idea, that's all.

**Murph**    You're chicken. That's what you are.

**Joey**   Suppose his son has called the police? He knows the old man don't speak any English. He called the police. Right? And they'll trace our call.

**Murph**   You're nuts. They can't trace any phone calls. Anyway, we'll be gone from here. You're nuts.

**Joey**   I don't want to do it.

**Murph**   For Christ's sakes. They can't trace nothing to nobody. Who's going to trace? Get the paper.

**Joey** (*pulls back a step*)   Get it yourself. Go on. Get it yourself. I ain't going to get it.

**Murph**   C'mon, Joey. It's not real. This is just a game. It ain't going to hurt anybody. You know that. It's just a game.

**Joey**   Why don't we call somebody else? We'll call somebody else and have the Indian talk. That makes sense. Imagine if an Indian called you up and talked to you in Indian. I bet the Chief would go for that alright. Jesus, Murphy.

**Murph**   Get the paper and picture.

**Indian**   What are you going to do now? I'm sorry. I thought that was my son, Prem. I thought that it might be Prem calling me on the telephone. Prem. That's who I thought it was. Prem.

**Murph** (*to the* **Indian**)   Prem. That's the name. (*Plays the rhyme.*)

**Indian**   Prem?

**Murph**   Yes, Prem. I want to call Prem. Give me the paper with his name.

**Indian**   What are you saying about Prem? Prem is my son. What have you done to Prem? What do you know about him? Do you know where he is?

**Murph**   Shut up already and give me the paper. (*He drags the* **Indian** *from the booth.*) Easy. I ain't gonna' hurt you. Easy.

**Joey**    Jesus, Murph.

**Murph** (*turning the* **Indian** *around so that they face each other*)
This is ridiculous. (*He searches the* **Indian**, *who resists a bit at
first, and then not at all. Finally,* **Murph** *finds the slip of paper.*) I
got it. I got it. Terrific. 'Prem Gupta.' In the Bronx. In the
frigging Bronx. This is terrific. Here. Hold him. (*The*
**Indian** *follows* **Murph**.)

**Indian** (*crosses to* **Murph**)    What are you doing? Are you
going to call my son?

**Murph**    Shut him up. (**Joey** *grabs the* **Indian**, *holds him.
He fishes for a dime.*) Give me a dime, goddamn it. This is
terrific.

**Joey** (*finds the coins in his pocket*)    Here's two nickels. (*Hands
them over.*) I think this is a rotten idea, that's what I think.
(**Murph** *crosses to booth. Pauses.*) And don't forget to pay me
back those two nickels either.

**Murph** (*from booth*)    Just shut up. (*Dials the 'Information
Operator'.*) Hello. Yeah, I want some information. I want a
number up in the Bronx. Gupta. G.U.P.T.A. An Indian kid.
His first name's Prem. P.R.E.M. No. I can't read the street
right. Wait a minute. (*He reads.*) For Christ's sakes. How
many Indians are up in the Bronx? There must be only one
Indian named Gupta. There are two Indians named Gupta.
(*To the Operator.*) Is the both of them names Prem? (*Pauses.*)
Well, that's what I told you. Jesus. Wait a minute. OK. OK.
Say that again. OK. OK. Right. OK. Thanks. (*Hurries
quickly to return the coins to the slot. The* **Indian** *mumbles. To*
**Joey**.) Don't talk to me. (*He dials.*) Six. Seven-four. Oh.
One. (*Pauses.*) It's ringing. It's ringing. (*Pauses.*) Hello. (*Covers
phone with hand.*) I got him! Hello? Is this Prem Gupta? Oh
swell. How are you? (*To* **Joey**.) I got the kid! (*The* **Indian**
*breaks from* **Joey**'s *arm and runs to the telephone . . .* **Murph** *sticks
out his leg and holds the* **Indian** *off. The* **Indian** *fights but seems
weaker than ever.*)

**Indian** (*breaks partially loose.* **Joey** *restrains him. Screams*)
Please let me talk to my son. (**Murph** *slams the* **Indian** *aside,*
*violently.* **Joey** *stands frozen watching. The* **Indian** *wails and*
*finally talks calmly, as in a trance.*) Please let me talk to my son.
Oh Prem. Please, I beg of you. Please. I'll give you anything
at all. Just tell me what you want of me. Just let me talk with
my son. Won't you, please? (**Murph** *glares at the* **Indian**,
*who no longer tries to interfere, as it becomes obvious that he must listen*
*to even the language he cannot understand.*)

**Murph**    Just listen to me, will you, Gupta. I don't know
where the hell your old man is, that's why I'm calling. We
found an old elephant down here in Miami and we thought
it must be yours. You can't tell for sure whose elephant is
whose. You know what I mean? (**Murph** *is laughing now.*)
What was that? Say that again. I can't hear you too well. All
the distance between us, you know what I mean? It's a long
way down here, you follow me? No. I ain't got no Indian. I
just got an elephant. And he's eating all my peanuts. Gupta,
you're talking too fast. Slow down.

**Indian**    Prem! Prem! Please come and get me. Please let
me talk to my son, mister. Why don't you let me talk to my
son? (*The* **Indian** *runs to booth,* **Murph** *shoves him,* **Joey** *pushes*
*the* **Indian** *to floor holding him.* **Joey** *lies on top of the* **Indian**.)

**Murph**    That was the waiter. I'm in an Indian restaurant.
(*Pauses.*) Whoa. Slow down, man. That was nobody. That
was just a myth. Your imagination. (*Pauses. Screams into*
*receiver.*) Shut up, damn you! And listen. OK? OK. Are you
listening? (**Murph** *tastes the moment. He silently clicks the receiver*
*back to the hook. To* **Joey**.) He was very upset. (*To the* **Indian**.)
He was very upset. (*Pauses.*) Well, what the hell's the matter
with you? I only told him we found an elephant, that's all. I
thought maybe he lost his elephant. (*The* **Indian** *whimpers.*)

**Indian**    Why have you done this? What have you said to
my son?

**Murph** (*to the* **Indian**)    You don't have to thank me,
Turkie. I only told him your elephant was OK. He was

probably worried sick about your elephant. (**Murph** *laughs. Crosses to* **Joey**.) This is terrific, Joey. Terrific. You should have heard the guy jabber. He was so excited he started talking in Indian just like the Chief. He said that Turkie here and him got separated today. Turkie's only been in the city one day. You're pretty stupid, Turkie. One day in the city . . . and look at the mess you've made. You're pretty stupid. We'll call again. Sure. (**Murph** *goes into the phone booth.*) Sure. (*The* **Indian** *leaps on* **Murph***, who throws him off maniacally pounding the booth four times, screaming.*) Get him off of me! (**Murph** *takes a dime from his pocket, shows it to* **Joey***. He dials number again and waits for reply.* **Joey** *puts one-half nelson on the* **Indian**.) Hello? Is this Gupta again? Oh, hello there. I'm calling back to complain about your elephant. Hey, slow down, will you? Let me do the talking. OK? Your elephant is a terrific pain in the balls to me. Get it. Huh? Do you follow me so far? (*Pauses.*) I don't know what you're saying, man. How about if I do the talking, alright. Your elephant scares the hell out of me and my pal here. We don't like to see elephants on the street. Spiders and snakes are OK, but elephants scare us. Elephants. Yeah, that's right. Don't you get it, pal? Look, we always see spiders and snakes. But we never expect to see an elephant. What do you mean? 'I'm crazy'? I don't know nothing about your old man. I'm talking about your elephant. Your elephant offends the hell out of me. So why don't you be a nice Indian kid and come pick him up? That's right. Wait a minute. I'll have to check the street sign. (*Covers the receiver.*) This is terrific. (*Talks again into the telephone.*) Jesus, I'm sorry about that. There don't seem to be no street sign. That's a bitch. I guess you lose your elephant. Well, what do you expect me to do, bring your elephant all the way up to the Bronx? Come off it, pal. You wouldn't ever bring my elephant home. I ain't no kid, you know! I've lost a couple of elephants in my day. (*Listens.*) Jesus, you're boring me now. I don't know what the hell you're talking about. Maybe you want to talk to your elephant. Huh? (*Turns to the* **Indian**.) Here, come talk to your 'papoose'. (*Offers the telephone. The* **Indian** *stares in* *disbelief then grabs the phone from* **Murph**'s *hands and begins to chatter wildly.*)

**Indian**    Prem? Oh, Prem. Please come and take me away. What? I don't know where I am. Please come and take me to your house. Please? There are two bad people. Two young men. They are dangerous. I cannot protect myself from them. Please. You must come and get me. (**Murph** *takes his knife from his pocket, cuts the line.*)

**Murph**    You've had enough, Chief. (*He laughs aloud, showing the* **Indian** *the dangling cord.*)

**Indian**    (*not at once realizing the line must be connected, continues to talk into the telephone, in Hindi*)    Prem. Prem. Please come here. The street sign reads . . . (*He now realizes he has been cut off and stares dumbly at the severed receiver as* **Murph** *waves the severed cord in his face. To* **Murph**.) What have you done?

**Murph**    There it is, Turkie Who you talkin' to?

**Indian**    (*to* **Joey**, *screaming a father's fury and disgust*)    Why have you done this? Please. Please help me. (**Joey** *has been standing throughout the entire scene, frozen in terror and disgust.* **Joey** *bolts from the stage, muttering one continuous droning sob, as* **Murph** *kicks the* **Indian** *straight at* **Joey**.)

**Murph**    Go ahead, Joey. Love him. Like a mother. Hey? Joey? What the hell's the matter? C'mon, buddy? (*He turns to the* **Indian**, *takes his hand, upstage, and cuts the* **Indian**'s *hand, so blood is on the knife.*) Sorry, Chief. This is for my buddy, Joey. And for Pussyface. (*He calls off stage.*) Joey! Buddy! What the hell's the matter? (*He races from the stage after* **Joey**.) Joey! Wait up. Joey! I killed the Indian! (*He exits. The* **Indian** *stares dumbly at his hand, dripping blood. He then looks to the receiver and talks into it.*)

**Indian**    Prem. Prem. (*He walks center stage, well away from the telephone booth.*) Why can I not hear my son, Prem? Why have you done this to me? (*Suddenly, the telephone rings again. Once. Twice. The* **Indian** *is startled. He talks into the receiver, while he holds the dead line in his bleeding hand.*) Prem? Is that you? Prem?

(*The telephone rings a third time.*) Prem. Prem? Is that you? (*A fourth ring. The* **Indian** *knows the telephone is dead.*) Prem. Prem. Help me. Prem. (*As the telephone rings once more, in the silence of the night, the sounds of two boys' singing is heard:*)

**Joey**
I walk the lonely streets at night . . .
A'lookin' for your door . . .

**Murph**
I look and look and look and look . . .

**Together**
But, baby, you don't care . . .
But, baby, no one cares . . .
But, baby, no one cares . . .

*Their song continues to build, as they repeat the lyrics, so the effect is one of many, many voices. The telephone continues its unanswered ring.*

**Indian** (*in English. He speaks the only words he has learned*)
How are you? You're welcome. You're welcome. How are you? How are you? Thank you. (*To the front.*) Thank you!

*Lights switch to black.*

## Hindi Translations of Indian's Speeches

1. MAI TOOM-HAREE BO-LEE NAH-HEE BOL SAK-TAH. MAI TUM-HAH REE BAH-SHA NAH-HEE SAH-MAJ-TAH.
2. MOO-JHAY MAHAF KAR-NAH MAI TOOM-HAH-REE BAH-ART NAH-HEE SAH-MAJ SAK-TAH.
3. MAI TOOM-HAREE BAH-AT NAH-HEE SAH-MAJ-TAH. MAI AP-NAY LAR-KAY KAH GHA-R DHOO-ND RAH-HAH HOOH. OOS-NAY MOO-JHAY MIL-NAH TAR PAHR NAH-JAH-NAY WOH CAH-HAH HAL. MAI OOS-KAH MAH-KAN DHOO-ND RAH-HAH HOON. OOS-KAH PAH-TAH YEH RAH-HAH K-YAH MAI SAH-HEE RAH-STAY PAR HOON.
4. MAI-NAY AP-NAY LAR-KAY KOH SU-BAH SAY NAH-HEE DAY-KHA. TOOM-HARA SHAH-HAR BAH-HOOT HEE BARAH HAL.
5. MOO-JHAY MAHAF KAR-NAH. MOO-JHAY YAH-HAN AYE ZYAH-DA SAH-MAY NA-HEE HOO-AH.
6. K-YAH KAH-HA TOOM-NAY.
7. YAH K-YAH HAL.
8. BHA-EE MAI TOOM-HAREE BAH-AT NAH-HEE SAH-MAJ SAK-TAH. BUS YAH-HAN KIS SA-MAY A-TEE-HAI. K-YAH MAI SA-HEE BUS STOP PAR HOON.
9. MAI TOOM-HAREE BAH-AT NAH-HEE SAH-MAJ SAK-TAH.
10. HAH-N. YEH-THEE-KH HAL. MAI TOOM-HAREE BAH-SHA NAH-HEE SAH-MAJ-TAH. MOO-JHAY MAH-AF KAR-NAH PAR AH-BHEE MOO-JHAY TOOM-HA-RAY DESH AYE KUH-CHAH HEE DIN TOH HU-YAY HAIN. MOO-JHAY TOOM-HA-REE BAH-SHA SEE-KH-NAY KAH AH-BHEE SAH-MAI HEE NAH-HEE MILAH. MAI AHP-NAY LAR-KAY SAY BIH-CHUR GAH-YA HOON. OOS-SAY TOH TOOM-HA-RAY

DESH MAY RAH-TAY CHAI SAH-AL HOH GAH-
YE HAIN. JAH-B DOH MAH-HEE-NAY PAH-LAY
OOS-KEE MAH KAH INTH-KAHL HOO-AH
TOH OOS-NAY MOO-JHAY YA-HAN BOOH-
LAH BHEH-JHA OR MAI AH GAH-HAY. WOH
BAH-RA HON-HAR LAR-KA HAI. MOO-JHAY
MAHAF KAR-NAH KEE MAIH-NAY AH-BHEE
TOOM-HA-REE BAH-SHA NA-HEE SEE-KHEE
PAR MAI SEE-KH LOON-GHA.

11. MOO-JHAY MAH-AF KAR-NAH. MAI TOOM-
HAREE BAH-SHA NA-HEE SAH-MAJ SAK-TA.

12. NA-HEE BHA-YEE TOOM AH-B K-YAH KAH-
ROGAY.

13. NA-HEE NA-HEE BHA-YEE. MAI MAH-AFEE
MAH-NG-TA HOON.

14. NA-HEE.

15. MOO-JHAY OR NAH SAH-TAO. MAIH-NAY
TOOM-HARA K-YAH BIGARAH HAL MOO-
JHAY OR NAH SAH-TAO. MOO-JHAY IN-SEH
BACHAH-LOH.

16. PREM KYAH WOH MAY-RAH LARKAH HAI.
PREM (PRAY-EM) BAY-TAH MOD-JHAY
BACHAH-LOW. MAI FAH-NS GA-YAH HOON.
YEH DOH GOON-DAY MOO-JHAY MAR RA-
HAY HAIN. MAI BA-HOOT GHAH-BARA GAYA
HOON. PRAY-EM.

17. AHB TOOM K-YAH KAH-ROGAY. MOO-JHAY
MAH-AF KAR-DOH BHA-YEE. MAIH-NAY SOH-
CHA TAH KEY WOH MAY-RAH BAY-TAH
PRAY-EM HAL MOO-JHAY TELEPHONE KAR
RAHA MAI-NAY SOH-CHAH THAH-SHA-YAHD
WOH PRAY-EM HOH.

18. PRAY AIM.

19. TOOM PRAY-AIM KAY BA-RAY MAY K-YAH
KAH RA-HAY HO. TOOM-NAY PRAY-AIM KOH
KYAH KEY-YAH. TOOM OOS-KAY BAH-RAY
MAY K-YAH JAN-TAY HO. K-YAH TOOM JAN-
TAY HO WOH KAH-HAN HAI.

20. TOOM K-YAH KAR RA-HAY HO. K-YAH TOOM
    PRAY-AIM K-OH BOO-LAH RA-HAY HO.
21. CREE-PAYAH MOO-JHAY AP-NAY LAR-KAY
    SAY BAH-AT KAR-NAY DOH.
22. CREE-PAYAH MOO-JHAY AHP-NAY LAR-KAY
    SAY BAH-AT KAR-NAY DOH. MAI TOOM-
    HARAY HAH-TH JOR-TAH HOON. MAI TOOM-
    HAY JOH MANGO-GAY DOON-GAH. BUS MOO-
    JHAY OOS-SAY BAH-AT KAR-NAY DOH.
23. PRAY-AIM BHAI-YAH MOO-JHAY AH-KAY LAY
    JA-OH. MOO-JHAY AP-NAY LAR-KAY SAY BAH-
    AT KAR-NAY DOH MOO-JHAY OOS-SAY BAH-
    AT K-YOHN NAH-HEE KAR-NAY DAY-TAY.
24. TOOM-NAY AI-SAW K-YOHN KI-YAH. TOOM-
    NAY MAY-RAY LAR-KAY KOH K-YAH KA-HAH
    HAI.
25. PRAY-AIM, BHAI-YAH PRAY-AIM MOO-JHAY
    AH-KAY LAY JAH-OH K-YAH? MOO-JHAY NAY-
    HEE PA-TAH MAI KAH-HAN HOO-N. MOO-
    JHAY AH-HP-NAY GHA-AR LAY CHAH-LOW
    YA-HAHN DO-OH BAD-MASLI LAR-KAY, JO
    BAH-HOOT KHA-TAR-NAHK HAI – OON-SAY
    HAI NAH-HEE BAH-CHA SAK-TAH AH-PA-NAY
    KOH. TOOM AIK-DAM MOO-JHAY AH-KAY
    LAY JA-OH.
26. PRAY-AIM, PRAY-AIM, YA-HAHN AA-OH. SAH-
    RAK KAH NAH-AM HAI . . . YEH TOOM-NAY K-
    YAH KEY-YAH.
27. TOOM-NAY YEH K-YOHN KEY-YAH. CRI-PA-
    YAH MAY-REE MAH-DAH-D KAH-ROW.
28. PRAY-AIM, PRAY-AIM, MAI AH-PA-NAY LAR-
    KAY KEY AH-WAH-AZ K-YON NAH-HEE SOON
    SAK TAH. PRAY-AIM! TOOM-NAY MAY-RAY
    SAH-AHTH AIH-SAW K-YOHN KEY-YAW. BAY-
    TAH PRAY-AIM, K-YAH TOOM HO?
29. PRAY-AIM, PRAY-AIM, BAY-TAH K-YAH TOOM
    HO – PRAY-AIM PRAY-AIM – MOO-JHAY BAH-
    CHALO PRAY-AIM.

# Line

*For my Father*

'Sleep with dogs, wake with fleas.'
(Webster, or somebody like that)

*Line* was first presented together with *Acrobats* by The New Comedy Theatre at the Theatre de Lys, in New York City, on 15 February 1971. It was directed by James Hammerstein, the production was designed by Neil Peter Jampolis and additional staging was by Grover Dale. The cast, in order of appearance, was as follows:

| | |
|---|---|
| **Fleming** | John Randolph |
| **Stephen** | Richard Dreyfuss |
| **Molly** | Ann Wedgeworth |
| **Dolan** | John Cazale |
| **Arnall** | Barnard Hughes |

*Line* in an earlier, one act version, was presented by Ellen Stewart on 29 November 1967, at Café LaMama ETC, in New York City, with the following cast:

| | |
|---|---|
| **Fleming** | Paul Haller |
| **Stephen** | Israel Horovitz |
| **Molly** | Ann Wedgeworth |
| **Dolan** | John Cazale |
| **Arnall** | Michael Del Medico |

*Directed by* James Hammerstein
*Assistant Director:* Bonnie Frindel

## Characters

**Fleming**
**Stephen**
**Molly**
**Dolan**
**Arnall**

## The Place of the Play

A line.

## The Time of the Play

Now.

## Note
The play is to be performed without an intermission.

If a curtain-raiser is needed, the author suggests his play, *Acrobats*, for that purpose.

*As the audience enters the theatre,* **Fleming** *is standing behind a fat, white strip of adhesive tape that is fixed to the stage floor. The play has begun.*

*He is waiting . . . waiting . . . waiting.*

*The stage is without decoration other than* **Fleming** *and the line. The lighting is of that moment when late night turns to early morning: all pinks and oranges and, finally, steel-gray blue.*

**Fleming** *checks and rechecks his feet in relation to the line. He is clearly first there, in first place.*

*He steps straight back now and again, testing his legs and the straightness of the line that will follow.*

**Fleming** *has carried a large war-surplus duffle with him, full of beer, potato chips, whatever he might need for a long-awaited long wait.*

*Back to the audience, he reaches into the bag and takes something out. He stands, hands penis-high, in a small pantomime of urination. He turns again to the line and reveals that he has peeled a banana. He eats it.*

*His feet are planted solidly at the line now, yet his body breaks the rigidity, revealing his exhaustion. He is waiting . . . waiting . . . waiting.*

*He dips again into the bag and produces a bag of potato chips, a can of beer (flip-top) and a rather nice cloth napkin, which he tucks into his shirt-top. He opens the beer, eats the chips, drinks, belches and does it all again. His feet never move from the mark now.*

*He leans back and sings, softly at first, 'Take me Out to the Ball Game', possibly confusing the lyrics. He drinks, belches and spills potato chips all over the place, then continues singing again to end of song.* **Stephen** *enters quietly. He watches* **Fleming** *carefully.* **Fleming** *senses* **Stephen**'s *presence. He stops singing and, waiting for* **Stephen** *to speak, does nothing. Neither does* **Stephen**.

**Fleming** *gets on with it. Singing carefully now.* **Stephen** *cuts him off with a soft question.*

**Stephen**　Is this a line? (**Fleming** *stares directly into* **Stephen**'s *eyes, but doesn't answer.*) Excuse me, mister. Is this a line? (*After studying* **Stephen**'s *clothing and manner,* **Fleming** *rechecks his feet and turns from* **Stephen**, *facing straight ahead.*) Is this a line, huh?

**Fleming**　(*does a long, false take*)　What's it look like?

**Stephen**　(*walking over, leaning between* **Fleming**'s *legs, he literally caresses the tape*)　Oh, yeah. There it is. It's a line all right. It's a beautiful line, isn't it? I *couldn't* tell from back there. I would have been earlier if I had started out earlier. You wouldn't think anyone would be damn fool enough to get up this early. Or not go to bed. Depending on how you look at it. (**Fleming** *stares at* **Stephen** *incredulously.*) Oh, I didn't mean you were a damn fool. (*Pauses.*) Not yet. Nice line. Just the two of us, huh?

**Fleming**　What's it look like? What's it look like?

**Stephen**　That's all you ever say, huh? 'What's it look like?' – 'What's it look like?' (*Pause.*) Must be nice.

**Fleming**　Huh?

**Stephen**　Being first. Right up front of the line like that. Singing away. Singing your damn fool heart out. I could hear you from back there. Singing your damn fool heart out. You like music? (**Fleming** *turns his back to* **Stephen**, *who now begins to talk with incredible speed.*) I'm a music nut myself. Mozart. He's the one. I've got all his records. Started out on seventy-eight. Moved up on to forty-fives. Then I moved on to thirty-three and a third when I got to be thirteen or so. Now I've got him on hi-fi, stereo and transistorized snap-in cartridges. (*Displays a portable cartridge tape recorder.*) I've got him on everything he's on. (*Pause.*) Must be nice. (*Pauses.*) Want to trade places?

**Fleming**　You yak like that all the time?

**Stephen**　(*peeks over* **Fleming**'s *shoulder at the line*)　That's a good solid line. I've seen some skimpy little lines in my day, but that one's a beauty. (*Whistles a strain from* The Magic Flute.) That's Mozart. Want me to whistle some more? Or we could sing your song. 'Take Me Out to the Ball Game'. I know most of your pop songs from your twenties, your thirties and your forties. I'm bad on your fifties and your sixties. That's when *I* started composing. And, of course, that's when Mozart really started getting in the way. But, have it like you will – just name the tune. 'Course, don't get me wrong. I'd rather be whistling my own songs any day of the week. Any night, for that matter. Or whistle Mozart. *The Magic Flute. Marriage of Figaro.* Go on. Just 'Name that Tune'. I can sing it in Italian, German, French or your Basic English. Hell, if he could knock them out at seven, I should be able to whistle at thirty, right? Christ, I am thirty, too. Not thirty-two. Thirty *also*. Three-o. Thirty. He was thirty-five. Around the age of Christ. What hath God wrought? (*Pauses, arms out and feet pinned together as in crucifixion.*) God hath wrought iron! (*Pauses. Waits to see if* **Fleming** *has crumbled yet. Sees* **Fleming** *is confused, but still on his feet, so* **Stephen** *continues.*) Thirty-five. That's how old he was. He thought he was writing his funeral music all right. He was, too. Isn't that something, to have that kind of premonition? That's what you call your young genius. The only real genius ever to walk on this earth, mister. Wolfgang Amadeus Mozart. W-A-M. (*Yells at* **Fleming**'*s face.*) WAM! WAM! WAM! (**Fleming**, *thunderstruck, turns and overtly snubs* **Stephen**, *who is perched, ready to take first position, if* **Fleming** *falls.* **Fleming** *stays afloat, so* **Stephen** *takes his wallet out of his pocket and studies its contents carefully. He pokes* **Fleming**.) You want to read my wallet?

**Fleming**   Huh?

**Stephen** (*begins to unfold an enormous credit-card case*)   You want to read my wallet? You can read my wallet and I'll read your wallet. You can learn a lot about people from their wallets. Avis cards. Hertz cards. American Express. Air Travel. Bloomingdale's. Saks. Old phone numbers. Bits and scraps. Contraceptives. Locks of hair. Baby pictures.

Calendars. Business cards. And the ladies. Businessladies
have cards. ID cards. Not the ladies, I mean. I mean the
men who own the wallets who you're learning about, right?
(**Fleming** *sings two bars of 'Take Me Out to the Ball Game'.*)
Hey. Don't turn your back on me, huh? Let me read your
wallet. I've read mine before. I read my wallet all the time.
Hey, will you? Here. Take my wallet, then. You don't even
have to let me read yours. (*Forces his wallet into* **Fleming***'s
hands.* **Fleming** *is absolutely astonished.*) That's it. Go on.
Read. (**Fleming** *obeys, wide-eyed.*) There. See that ID card?
That lets you know who I am, right away. See? Stephen.
Steve. Or Stevie. Gives you a choice, even. And where I
work. See that? Now look at the pictures. My kids. That
one's dead. That one's dead. That one's dead. That one's
dead. There are more. Don't stop. More pictures. (*He leaves
the wallet in* **Fleming***'s hand and begins a wide circle around him,
almost forcing* **Fleming** *out of line.*)

**Fleming**   How'd you lose all those kids?

**Stephen**   Lose the kids?

**Fleming**   Dead. All these dead kids? (*Sees that the picture are
lithographs of Mozart.*) Hey! Those are drawings!

**Stephen**   Who said they were kids?

**Fleming** (*waits, staring*)   Oh, boy. Here we go. (*Sings three
bars of 'Take Me Out to the Ball Game', after jamming* **Stephen***'s
wallet back into* **Stephen***'s pocket.* **Stephen** *joins in for one bar.
In unison.* **Fleming** *stops.*)

**Stephen** (*sings another bar, then stops, asks*)   Do you really
think this line is for a ball game? Huh? There's no ball game
around here. I mean, I wouldn't be here if there was a ball
game. Ball games aren't my kind of stuff. I loathe ball
games, myself. You like ball games?

**Fleming** (*at this point, the situation has gone beyond* **Fleming***'s
comprehension, and his confusion surfaces as a rubber duck*)   Who
are you?

**Stephen**   That's why I gave you my wallet. If everybody would just pass their wallets around, sooner or later something would happen, right?

**Fleming**   Yeah.

**Stephen**   Can you imagine if you met the President and he gave you his wallet to read? You'd know everything about him. Or the Mayor. Kings. Ballplayers, even. Read THEIR wallets. Boy, would you know it all soon enough. Scraps of paper that held secrets they forgot were secrets. Meetings they were supposed to make. Locks of hair. Pictures of babies they forgot they had. Names. Addresses. ID cards. Secret money hidden in secret places. You'd know everything, wouldn't you? (*He has* **Fleming** *going now. He increases the speed of his delivery, eyes flickering, hands waving, watching* **Fleming***'s terrified responses.*) You see, friend, all those up-front people are fakes. Fakes. There's never been a real first place . . . never a real leader. Except you know *who*.

**Fleming**   Who?

**Stephen**   War heroes? All frauds. If there had been one really efficient war, we wouldn't be here, would we?

**Fleming**   I'm first. All I know is I'm first.

**Stephen**   First. It's just a word. Twist the letters around, you get tsrif. God backwards. Dog. Split the first three letters off the word therapist, you get two words: the rapist. Spell Hannah backwards, you get Hannah. Spell backwards backwards, you get sdrawkcab. I tell you, show me one of your so-called winners, and let me have one look at his wallet; just one. I'll never have to count the money, either. There's never been a real first before. Never. I know, friend. I know. See that line? Turn it on end, you know what you've got? A number one. But how do you hang on to it? How do you really hold it, so you're not one of those wallet-carrying, secret-compartment fakes like all of them? Answer that question and I'll let you follow me in. You could be second.

**Fleming**  What do you mean 'second'? I'm first. I'm right at the front.

**Stephen**  For the moment.

**Fleming**  Don't get any smart ideas.

**Stephen**  The only conclusions I draw are on men's-room walls. Now if you'd shut up for a while, I'll sing my wallet. (**Stephen** *sings his Hertz card lyric to* Eine Kleine Nachtmusik.) 'This non-transferable Hertz charge card entitles the person named to use Hertz Rent A Car service under the terms of the Hertz Rental Agreement on a credit basis. Where you desire to make immediate payments, the card enables you to rent without deposit. Payment for rentals charged is due within ten days after the billing date. This card is subject to invalidation and modification without notice and is the property of the Hertz system . . .' (**Molly**, *a plump woman, wanders onto the stage. When he sees her, he continues to sing the Hertz lyric, but changes the melody to a tacky love sing. He stops* **Molly** *as she crosses the stage.*) Hey. You looking for a line, lady?

**Molly**  Line?

**Stephen**  That's right. This is a line. You're third. Number three. There used to be just two of us here. Me and Fleming. This is Fleming. Who are you?

**Fleming**  How'd you know my name, huh? How'd you know my name?

**Stephen** (*to* **Fleming**)  I read your wallet. (*To* **Molly**.) You're third. That's not too bad. You won't have to wait long.

**Fleming** (*checks to see if* **Stephen** *has stolen his wallet, then screams*)  You didn't read my wallet! Nobody's read my wallet, except me!'

**Molly** (*joining the line*)  Third? I'm third, huh? How long have you been waiting?

**Stephen**   About nine and a half minutes. Fleming must have been here all night. Were you here all night, Fleming? He looks it, huh?

**Fleming**   How the hell did you know my name? How'd you know?

**Molly**   Third place. How soon do they open?

**Stephen**   You'll probably see a crowd before that. There's always a crowd. The crowd that says, 'Maybe there won't be a crowd, let's go anyway.' That crowd. You'll see that crowd, won't she, Fleming?

**Fleming**   How'd you know my name? How'd you know my name?

**Stephen**   Fleming, don't be a bore! What's your name? Mine's Stephen.

**Molly**   Molly. I'm Molly.

**Stephen**   Hello, Molly. Glad you're third. Fleming, this is Molly.

**Molly**   Hello.

**Fleming**   Hey, kid. Hold our places in line. Come here, ma'am. (*Takes her aside, whispers.*) That kid's crazy. Watch out. He's one of them freaky weirdos. He's been saying crazy things to me.

**Stephen** (*moves into first position*)   I can't guarantee your places. The crowd's going to come sure as hell and I can't guarantee anybody's place. The fact is, Fleming, I'm first now.

**Fleming**   What?

**Stephen**   I'm first. (*Straddles the line.*) Look at me. I'm up first. Up front. Front of the line. (**Molly** *jumps into second position.*)

**Molly**   You could have held our places. Nobody else is here.

**Stephen**   It's just not right. Besides, Fleming wouldn't hold anybody's place. You can tell that just from looking at him. He's never held anybody's place in his life.

**Fleming** (*enraged, but trying to maintain control*)   Kid, I've been standing there all night. All night. Waiting. Waiting in the front of the line. The very front. Now I think you'd better let me get right back up there. (*As* **Fleming** *continues,* **Dolan** *enters and walks toward the line. He carries a canvas-topped artist's portable stool.*) Just step back one place and let me in there. (**Dolan** *quietly steps into line behind* **Molly**. *To* **Dolan**.) I'm up front.

**Dolan** (*sitting*)   Huh?

**Fleming**   I'm first. That kid just took my spot. You're fourth.

**Dolan**   I don't mean to argue, but I count third. You're fourth.

**Fleming**   Skip it? Bull, I'll skip it. (*Walks up to* **Stephen**.) Give me back my place, kid, or I'll knock you out of it. (**Stephen** *drops to the floor in a lotus position.* **Fleming** *stares, again astonished.*) Get up!

**Dolan**   I hate to argue, but get out of the front, mac! The kid was up front and I'm third. The lady's second.

**Molly**   He *was* up front, actually.

**Dolan**   Well, he can go second if you want him to, lady. I'm third. (**Arnall** *enters and walks directly into the line.*)

**Arnall**   Molly?

**Molly**   Arnall. Here I am.

**Arnall**   You think I can't see you? You saved my place?

**Molly** (*to* **Dolan**)   I was saving his place, sir. We had an arrangement.

**Dolan**   Not that I want to run things, but that's too bad. No place was saved. He can go fourth.

**Fleming**   I'm fourth! For Christ's sake what am I saying? I'm *first*.

**Arnall** ( *jumps into fourth position*)   I'm fourth.

**Molly**   I'm second.

**Dolan**   I'm third.

**Stephen** (*after the stampede, to* **Dolan**)   Obviously, I'm first. My name's Stephen. Who are you?

**Dolan** (*shaking* **Stephen**'s *hand*)   Dolan's what they call me. How long you been waiting?

**Stephen**   About twelve and a half minutes.

**Arnall**   Jesus. If I could have found my clean shirts, Molly . . . If I could have found where you hid them . . . I would have been here half an hour ago. I would have been first.

**Fleming**   I've been here all night.

**Arnall** (*considers it*)   How come you're fifth? (*Pause for a 'take' from* **Fleming**.) You're not even in line. Why aren't you first?

**Fleming**   I *am* first. Goddamn it! I *am* first. That crazy kid grabbed my place. How'd you know my name, kid?

**Arnall**   Fleming?

**Fleming**   How the hell do *you* know?

**Arnall** (*pulls* **Fleming**'s *T-shirt neck to his eyes*)   It's written on your undershirt. (**Fleming** *spins around trying to read the label.*)

**Stephen**   I read your undershirt.

**Fleming** (*to* **Dolan**)   Look, I've been here all night. I've been standing right at the front of the line all night. You know that's true. (*To* **Molly**.) You saw me here, lady. You know I was first.

**Molly**   You stepped out of line. (*To* **Arnall**.) He stepped out of line, Arnall.

**Arnall**   Serves you right, then, Fleming. If I could have found my clean shirt, I would have been first. My dumb wife hides my dumb shirts. Isn't that terrific? She hides my shirts. I could have been first by half an hour. But she hid my shirt. You know where I found it? (*Simply.*) I couldn't find it.

**Fleming** (*after rapt attention to* **Arnall**'*s shaggy-shirt story, furiously*)   This is ridiculous. I was first. All night. (*To* **Arnall**.) I just took your wife aside to warn her about that crazy kid. He jumped the line. He jumped in front. That's not fair, is it? I was here all night.

**Dolan**   You're fifth. There's plenty here for five. You'll get your chance.

**Fleming** (*to* **Arnall**)   That's not the point. Goddamn it. There's only one first and I waited up all night. All night in the line all by myself. And he took it away from me. Now that is definitely unfair.

**Arnall** (*completely against* **Fleming**'*s problem*)   I hate to go anywhere at night with the shirt from the day still on. You never know what kind of germs you come in contact with during the day. You never can tell, can you?

**Stephen**   Life's full of dirt.

**Arnall**   Our place is full of dirt. My wife never cleans. If it were up to her, we'd be up to our lips in dirt. Day and night. That's why I'm late. What movie's playing?

**Fleming** (*he's had it!*)   Movie?

**Arnall**   I thought we were going to the movies, Molly?

**Molly**   Arnall, don't cause a scene!

**Stephen**   Your shirt looks terrific, Arnall.

**Arnall**   Looks are deceptive. Hospitals look clean, don't they? But if you ever ran a check for germ count, oh boy, wouldn't you get a score? After all, people come there – to hospitals – because they're ridden with germs. Take an old building full of germ-ridden people, paint it stark white, you got yourself a place that looks clean, but underneath that look, there's just a white hospital – full of germ-ridden people.

**Stephen**   How do you feel about that, Fleming? Do germ-ridden people disturb you too?

**Fleming**   Don't get smart with me, kid. I was waiting here a long time before you, and you know it. (*To* **Dolan**.) He's trying to distract your attention from the fact that he *took* first place . . . he didn't earn it. No, sir. *I* earned it. I waited up for that place. He took it!

**Dolan**   Well, I don't want to be the one who starts any arguments, but he *is* in first place, and he was in first place when I first got here.

**Stephen**   Fair *is* fair, Fleming!

**Fleming** (*yells*)   Don't 'fair' me, kid, or you'll have a fat lip to worry about!

**Dolan**   Now listen to me, Fleming.

**Fleming** (*screams*)   What do *you* want?

**Dolan** (*screams*)   Lower your voice!

**Arnall**   Easy, Dolan, easy.

**Dolan** (*to* **Fleming**)   Look, I don't want to start any trouble, but it seems to me if you want to be first, be first. Move the kid. If you want to be second, be second. Move his old lady. (*And with that,* **Dolan** – *Mister Niceguy* – *nearly strangles* **Arnall**. *He catches himself before* **Arnall** *dies. He brushes* **Arnall***'s jacket and smiles. To* **Arnall**.) And don't you – Goddamn it – 'easy' me. I'm nice and easy all the time. I'm Mister Niceguy. Get it? Mister Niceguy.

**Arnall**   Move *who*?

**Dolan**   Your old lady.

**Fleming**   Your old lady.

**Arnall**   You can't do that.

**Dolan**   And why not?

**Fleming**   And 'why not' is right.

**Arnall** (*archly*)   She's second. She's in line. That's the way things are. She's in second place. She can beat you there.

**Fleming** (*has an original thought*)   Hell, she did! I spent the night in first. Right up there at the white line. Got my sack here with food and drink. I'm prepared. Prepared to be first. Goddamn it! Not second. Not third. Not fifth. I'm prepared for first. But, mind you, if I want to move your old lady and be second, I'll just move your old lady and be second. Just like that. (**Arnall** *steps out of line into* **Fleming**'*s way, as* **Fleming** *pretends to move toward* **Molly**. **Fleming** *quickly jumps into line in* **Arnall**'*s spot.* **Fleming** *is now fourth.*)

**Arnall** (*stunned*)   Hey. Hey, you dirty sonofabitch. Sonofabitch. You took my place. He took my place. What the hell is this? Get out of line, Fleming. Move out, Fleming. You took my place!

**Fleming** (*laughing*)   That's what a woman does to you, what'syourname. That's what a woman does.

**Arnall** (*humiliated*)   Stop laughing, you sonofabitch!

**Fleming** (*a mule giggling*)   That's what a woman does to you.

**Arnall** (*walks up to* **Molly**, *squares off*)   He's right! (*He slaps* **Molly** *on the hand.*)

**Molly** (*amazed and furious*)   Arnall. Arnall. Damn you. How could you? (*She chases him, slapping his head.* **Dolan** *and* **Fleming** *quickly move up one space, laughing.*)

**Dolan** (*a jock's scream of victory*)   I'm second. I'm second.

**Fleming** (*a neat imitation*)   I'm right behind you.

**Arnall** (*giving the proof of the pudding*)    Now look, you bitch.
Now look. We're both out. They moved up. You moved up,
you sons of bitches. You snuck up.

**Dolan**    You stepped out.

**Stephen** (*whispers*)    Out of line, out of luck!

**Dolan** (*picks it up*)    Out of line, out of luck!

**Fleming** (*instinct*)    Out of line, out of luck.

**Arnall**    Out of line, out of luck? That supposed to be
funny, huh? That's supposed to be a joke? Out of line, out
of luck?

**Fleming**    Who said that?

**Arnall**    You said that. 'Out of line, out of luck!'

**Fleming** (*a bit boggled, but giddy*)    Well, then . . . that's right!
That's what a woman does to you, Arnall. You lose your
place.

**Molly**    You made me do that, Arnall. You made me do
that.

**Arnall** (*too heavy for him*)    Shut up, you bitch. You start first
with the shirts, now my place, now your place. Just shut
up . . . I've got to think.

**Stephen** (*sings*)
    Se voul venire nella –
    I'm first.

**Fleming**    Don't be smart, kid. I don't forget easily. You'll
get yours.

**Stephen**    I got mine. I'm first! (*Sings.*)
    Se vuol venire nella mia scuola,
    La capriolo le insegnero.
That's a song my mother taught me. I'll never forget it,
either. (*Sings.*)
    Se vuol venire . . . (*etc.*)

**Fleming**   Forget it.

**Molly** (*sidling up to* **Stephen**)   Your mother?

**Arnall**   Stay away from him, Molly.

**Molly**   Shut your dumb mouth, Arnall. Just shut up. (*To* **Stephen**.) Is she young? (*She puts a foot on* **Fleming**'s *bag. Her leg is Mrs Robinson's.*)

**Stephen** (*a sweaty Benjamin*)   'Metza-Metz.' (*Sings.*)
   Se vuol venire nella mia –

**Molly** (*interrupts*)   You've got a pretty face, you know that?

**Arnall**   Molly! For crying out loud.

**Molly** (*to* **Stephen**)   Don't pay any attention to him. (**Arnall** *walks to the other side of the stage and sits.*)

**Stephen**   I'll pay attention to whom I choose. To *who* I choose? Whatever I choose. You know what I mean.

**Molly**   I was saying that you have a pretty face.

**Stephen**   Yes, you were.

**Molly**   Good bones. Strong bones in your face. Like James Dean.

**Stephen**   James Dean?

**Molly**   The movie star. The one who got killed in his Porsche. That's who you look like. James Dean.

**Fleming**   Who's James Dean? A movie star?

**Dolan**   Killed in his what?

**Stephen**   Is James Dean still dead?

**Molly**   Don't make jokes about James Dean. He was a beautiful boy. And I'm telling you that you remind me of him.

**Stephen**   I wasn't trying to be funny.

**Molly**   I always wanted to make love with James Dean.

**Fleming**    Holy Jesus!

**Dolan**    Shut up. (*He wants to hear.*)

**Stephen**    Why didn't you?

**Molly**    I never met him, silly. He's a movie star. And then he got killed. If I could have met him, I would have made love to him. If I had been Marilyn Monroe, I'd have played with him.

**Fleming**    Monroe? Joltin' Joe's missus?

**Molly**    I could have made him happy. (*Pauses.*) I could make you happy.

**Stephen**    I don't have a Porsche.

**Molly**    It's very warm here, don't you think? Don't you think it's very warm here?

**Stephen** (*unbuttoning his shirt, just a few buttons*)    Yeah. I can't remember a time this hot. It makes you want to take all your clothes off, doesn't it?

**Molly** (*she takes his hand in hers*)    All your clothes.

**Stephen**    Unbearable.

**Molly**    Unbearable.

**Molly** *and* **Stephen**    Torture. (*They kiss, a long deep passionate kiss. Suddenly, they break apart and dance off, in a comically insane minuet.*)

**Stephen** (*sings. Optional: he sings in German, French, Italian or English, although Italian is preferred*)
Should he, for instance, wish to go dancing,
He'll face the music, I'll lead the band, yes.
I'll lead the band.
And then I'll take my cue, without ado,
And slyly, very, very, very, very, very slyly.
Using discretion, I shall uncover his secret plan.
Subtly outwitting, innocent seeming,
Cleverly hitting, planning and scheming,

I'll get the best of the hypocrite yet,
I'll beat him yet!

(*As* **Stephen** *sings.* **Dolan** *and* **Fleming** *talk.* **Arnall** *walks forward quietly to watch* **Molly** *and* **Stephen** *as they dance. All are astonished.*)

**Fleming** (*almost a whisper*)   You've got to hand it to that kid.

**Dolan**   Shh. Her old man's watching.

**Fleming**   It's disgusting.

**Dolan** (*watching the lovers*)   What's disgusting?

**Fleming**   Her old man watching like that. It ain't natural.

**Dolan**   Yeah. It certainly ain't natural.

**Fleming**   Sonofabitch. you've got to hand it to that kid. I never would have guessed.

**Dolan**   I had a woman once in a car.

**Fleming**   What happened? (*By now, their attitudes should reveal that* **Molly** *and* **Stephen** *are copulating by dance.*)

**Dolan**   The usual thing.

**Fleming**   That's all?

**Dolan**   Yeah.

**Fleming**   Oh.

**Dolan**   I've never had a woman in a line.

**Fleming**   Me neither.

**Dolan**   It's funny watching like this, ain't it?

**Fleming**   Yeah.

**Dolan**   I'd rather be doing it.

**Fleming**   Yeah. (*They both continue to stare goggle-eyed.*)

**Dolan**   I'm getting horny.

**Fleming**    Yeah.

**Dolan**    Yeah.

**Fleming**    Yeah. (*The 'yeahs' start to build in a crescendo as the lovers reach their first climax.*)

**Arnall** (*from nowhere*)    Yeah.

**Dolan**    Yeah. Yeah.

**All**    Yeah! Yeah! *Yeah! Yeah!*

**Stephen** (*sings his orgasm*)
    Piano . . . Piano . . . Piano . . . !

(*After they dance,* **Molly** *takes first!* **Stephen** *sings again, exhausted, but 'dances her' out of first place, tired, but not to be undone.*)

**Fleming**    He's doing it again!

**Dolan**    I can't take much more of this!

**Fleming**    What are we going to do?

**Dolan**    You figure it out, pal. I know what I want. (*He jumps forward and grabs* **Molly**. *Sings 'I Want a Girl Just Like the Girl That Married Dear Old Dad'.* **Arnall** *tries to jump into first position. But* **Stephen** *does a terrific baseball slide into first.* **Arnall** *is forced into the slot* **Dolan** *vacated, second.* **Fleming** *is stunned.*)

**Stephen**    I'm still first. I'm still first!

**Arnall** (*to* **Molly**)    Bitch. Bitch. You bitch!

**Stephen** (*to* **Arnall**)    You're second. You were nowhere. You were nowhere.

**Fleming**    What happened?

**Arnall**    He slid into first.

**Fleming**    Yeah. But what happened? (*In the meantime,* **Dolan** *and* **Molly** *are dancing as* **Dolan** *sings. Note: after each 'dance',* **Molly** *calmly attempts to return to first and brush her hair.*

**Dolan** *continues singing happily. Over his song, the dialogue continues.)*

**Fleming** (*finally realizing*)   This is terrible. I forgot to move up.

**Stephen**   You didn't move up. You didn't move in. Fleming, you disappoint me. (*He lies down on the floor, goes to sleep.*)

**Fleming** (*to* **Arnall**)   You just let your old lady do that? I mean, does she do it all the time?

**Arnall**   All the time. All the time.

**Fleming**   That's terrible. That's a terrible thing. You must get embarrassed.

**Arnall**   It doesn't hurt any more. Not after all these years.

**Fleming**   Why don't you throw her out?

**Arnall**   Why? She's predictable.

**Fleming**   Predictable?

**Arnall**   Consistent. I never have any surprises with Molly. She's pure. All bad.

**Fleming**   That's good?

**Arnall**   Surprises hurt. You should know that. Look how hurt you were when you didn't move up. Or 'move in'. You were surprised and hurt, right?

**Fleming**   That's bad.

**Arnall**   Right. My philosophy is quite simple. Never ever leave yourself open for surprises, and you'll never be surprised. Surprise brings pain, pain is bad. No surprise, no pain. No pain, no bad. No bad, all good. (*Proudly.*) I've got it made.

**Dolan**   Da-ah-aahd!

**Arnall** (*after a pause*)   They're finished now. Want to take a whack at it?

**Fleming**   What?

**Arnall**   Go on. Go ahead. Have a bash. Have a go at it. It'll do you good. Go on. I don't mind.

**Fleming**   You sure?

**Arnall**   Positive.

**Fleming**   Do you mind if Dolan holds my place in line?

**Arnall**   Of course not.

**Fleming**   Hey, Dolan.

**Dolan**   What?

**Fleming**   Hold my place in line, will you? I'd like to have a bash.

**Dolan**   Have a what?

**Fleming**   Have a go at it. That's what her old man calls it. Hey, Dolan. Hold my place, will you?

**Dolan** (*slides into* **Fleming**'s *place and falls there*)   Go get it. (**Fleming** *stares at* **Dolan**, **Molly**, **Arnall**, *and the lot again. He grabs* **Molly** *and drags her upstage slightly, he 'counts' a foxtrot beat. He sing his song and they dance.*)

**Fleming**   One two three – one two three – one two three – and – (*Sings 'Take Me Out to the Ball Game'. As he continues his song, the dialogue does not stop.*)

**Dolan**   I like the way you think, Arnold.

**Arnall**   You mean my little philosophy?

**Dolan** (*a bit confused*)   Yeah, I guess you could call it that. Your little philosophy. I like the way you think, Arnold.

**Arnall**   *Arnall.* (*Spells it, then goes on like a house-on-fire.*) A-R-N-A-L-L. My mother wanted to call me Arthur. My father liked Nathan. Thought it was strong. My grandmother liked Lloyd, after Harold Lloyd. So they took the A-R from Arthur, the N-A from Nathan, the L-L from Lloyd, and called me Arnall. What do you want?

**Dolan**   I like the way you think, Arnold. I want to tell you how touched I am. I have a little philosophy myself; I call it the Under*dog* philosophy.

**Arnall**   Under*dog*?

**Dolan**   Did you ever hear of Arnold Palmer? Arnold Palmer is the world's richest golfer. He always looks like he is going to lose, but he almost never loses. He's the world's richest golfer.

**Arnall**   I don't get it.

**Dolan**   Everybody wants to be first, right?

**Arnall**   Right.

**Dolan**   Now you can be obvious about it. Just jump in like the kid and yell and brag about being first. Or about deserving to be first. What I mean is you got to stand back a little. (**Dolan** *has walked* **Arnall** *around in a circle and is about to take second place.*) Maybe in second place for a while. Then when nobody's looking, you kind of sneak into first place. But first you got to build up everybody's confidence that you're really one hell of a nice guy. You smile a lot. You say nice things all the time like, 'Great night for a line,' or, 'Terrific wife you've got there, Arnall, kid.' Then, when everybody likes you . . . you sneak up.

**Arnall**   I still don't get it.

**Dolan** (*now in second place*)   You notice I'm second in line? You notice I was second to make it with your wife. Second in this line to make it . . . right?

**Arnall**   Right.

**Dolan**   There you are.

**Arnall**   Why do you call that Under*dog*?

**Dolan**   The easiest way to kick a dog in the balls is to be underneath him. Let him walk on top of you for a while. Take good aim. And . . .

**Arnall**   I get it. (**Fleming** and **Molly** *waltz into view, and then off.*)

**Dolan**   Good boy. Terrific wife you got there, Arnall. Kid. Great night for a line. (**Arnall** *is crying.*) What's the matter?

**Arnall**   My philosophy is quite simple. Never ever leave yourself open for surprise and you'll never be surprised. Surprise brings pain. Pain is bad. No pain, no bad. No bad all good. I've got it made. (*Weeping now.*) I've got it made.

**Dolan**   You've got to learn to take it easy, Arnall. You're making a wreck of yourself with all that unhappiness. You got to get happy.

**Arnall**   I have a real philosophy, real philosophy. I'm supposed to be gleeful. All the time. I didn't know. I really didn't know. I knew she had friends.

**Dolan**   Certainly she had friends. She's very friendly.

**Arnall**   But I thought they were just friends.

**Dolan** (*checking* **Fleming**)   They'll be done soon.

**Arnall**   I can't stand it. I can't stand it. (*He rushes to* **Fleming** *and* **Molly**. *He taps* **Fleming** *on the shoulder, 'cutting in'.* **Fleming** *nods and moves into line.*)

**Fleming** (*realizing*)   Hey, I didn't finish. I didn't finish. I didn't finish. I didn't finish.

**Dolan**   Hop in line. You can be third.

**Fleming**   But I didn't finish! Didn't you see?

**Dolan**   See? Of course I saw. You were doing it with his old lady. Right in front of his eyes!

**Fleming**   *You* did it in front of his eyes.

**Dolan**   Jesus, don't remind me.

**Fleming**    I didn't finish. For Christ's sake, I'm hornier than ever.

**Stephen**    What took you so long?

**Fleming**    Shut up, kid. Shut up before I finish with *you*.

**Arnall** (*tapping out a bunny-hop beat*)    Molly. It's me, Arnall. Your husband.

**Molly** (*shocked*)    Arnall? What the hell are you doing?

**Arnall** (*dancing the bunny hop*)    I'm doing it. With you. My wife. A surprise, Molly! A Surprise!

**Molly**    You've lost your place in line. You stepped out of line!

**Arnall** (*tapping away*)    I couldn't stand it. Watching all those others doing it with you. It drove me crazy. It made me want you, Molly. I really want you.

**Molly** (*tapping with him*)    Oh, Arnall. You're such a bore.

**Arnall** (*humming 'Tiptoe Through the Tulips' before he speaks*) Please, Molly. Please.

**Molly** (*they're dancing now*)    Well, you're doing it, aren't you?

**Arnall** (*hums 'Tiptoe' and dances a bit*)    I am. Oh. I am. Oh, I like it, Molly. I like it.

**Molly** (*bored sick*)    Hurry up, Arnall. Hurry up.

**Arnall** (*stops*)    Shall I sing?

**Molly** (*angry*)    Just hurry up, Arnall. Just hurry up. (**Arnall** *sings: 'Tiptoe Through the Tulips', picking it up in the middle and continuing to end of song. Exits.*)

**Arnall** (*pauses*)    Now that's the way it should be. A man and his wife. That's a beautiful thing. Great night, huh? (**Stephen**, *helping* **Arnall** *and* **Molly** *gain speed, sings his wallet.*)

**Stephen** (*to 'Tiptoe' tune*)
  Saks card and a Hertz card and an Avis card
  And a Un-ih-Card Card
  Diners Club and a Chemical New York.

**Dolan**   That's a beautiful sight, isn't it?

**Fleming**   It's terrible. *Terrible*. I never finished.

**Dolan**   Just wait, Fleming. Let the husband finish first.
That's decent enough. Then you can finish. You can start
from scratch.

**Molly**   Hurry up, Arnall.

**Fleming**   Yeah, Arnall. Hurry up. (**Arnall**'s *erection and
song begin to 'die' off stage.*)

**Stephen** (*sings a dirge*)
  That's one's dead. That one's dead.
  That's one's dead. That one's dead.

**Dolan**   Sing a happy song, kid. For Christ's sakes. That
part of your wallet depresses the hell out of me.

**Stephen** (*sings again*)
  Henry Brown, insurance man.
  Harry Schwartz, the tailor.
  Alvin Krantz, delivery service.
  My Uncle Max, the sailor.
  Franklin National Saving Bank.
(**Molly** and **Arnall** *bunny hop onto stage with gusto.*)
  Doyle, and Dane and Bernbach

**Dolan**   That's nice. That's got a beat.

**Stephen** (*stops. Speaks*)   He's ready! He's ready!

**Arnall** (*screams*)   Surprise, Molly! Surprise!

**Dolan**   That's a beautiful thing. (**Arnall** *collapses in*
**Molly**'s *arms.*)

**Arnall**   Were you surprised, Molly?

**Molly**    Let me go, Arnall.

**Fleming**    No. Not yet. Not yet. I never finished. (*He grabs* **Molly**.)

**Molly**    Hey.

**Fleming** (*explaining, a whiny child*)    I never finished.

**Molly**    Take the gum out of your mouth.

**Fleming**    Oh.

**Arnall**    What place am I in?

**Dolan**    Third.

**Stephen**    Last.

**Arnall**    I'd rather be third.

**Stephen**    You're in last place.

**Dolan**    Shut up, kid. Don't listen to the kid. You're third. Two from the front. You did very well. I watched you all the way.

**Arnall**    It's been a long time. My legs are all rubbery. I'm very nauseous. I've got to practice up a little, maybe. A little practice and I'd be better.

**Dolan**    You did good.

**Arnall**    I'll practice up some. (**Fleming** *sings 'Take Me Out to the Ball Game'. They dance off.*) Oh, God! Him again.

**Dolan**    Don't watch. You'll feel better. (*Pours beer into* **Arnall***'s mouth.* **Fleming**, *off stage, continues song at a more rapid speed.*) You feeling any better now?

**Arnall** (*screams*)    I want it again.

**Dolan**    You what?

**Arnall**    I want it again. Molly's mine. I want it again. I liked it.

**Dolan**    You'll get sick again, pal. You know it makes you sick.

**Arnall**    I like it. I like it. (**Fleming** *and* **Molly** *dance back on – past* **Arnall**. *They stop in front of* **Dolan**.)

**Dolan**    Fleming. (*No answer.*)    Fleming! (*No answer.*) Fleming. (*He reaches over with his foot and kicks* **Fleming** *a hard one in the behind.* **Fleming** *wheels around, dazzled.*)

**Fleming**    What's the matter?

**Dolan** (*flatly*)    Her old man wants it again.

**Fleming** (*overlapping*)    He had it already.

**Dolan** (*overlapping*)    He wants it again.

**Stephen** (*wise-ass*)    He wants it again.

**Fleming** (*angrily*)    I heard Dolan.

**Dolan** (*flatly*)    He wants it again.

**Arnall** (*cockily*)    I want it again.

**Fleming** (*as though no one knows. To* **Molly**)    Your old man wants it again.

**Molly** (*a pronouncement*)    I want the boy.

**Dolan** (*senses the unjust*)    But your old man wants it.

**Molly** (*a solid pronounce*)    I want the boy.

**Dolan** (*realizes he might move up the Big Space*)    She wants you.

**Stephen** (*exhausted with the understanding of this complicated moment*)    I heard her.

**Molly** (*moving in*)    I want you, boy.

**Stephen** (*holding his eyes*)    I heard you.

**Arnall** (*overlapping*)    She likes them young.

**Fleming** (*overlapping*)    What about me?

**Dolan**    You had two chances.

**Fleming**   I didn't finish.

**Dolan**   You had two chances.

**Fleming**   I was almost finished. Some bastard kicked me!

**Dolan**   Two chances. I only had one. The kid only had one.

**Fleming**   The kid took two.

**Dolan**   Two on one chance. *He's a kid.*

**Arnall**   She likes the young ones. She always likes the young ones.

**Molly**   Come here, boy.

**Stephen** (*pretends to be engrossed in his wallet*)   American Express. Chemical New York. Unicard. My library card! (*He is pulled out by* **Molly**. **Dolan** *jumps up into first position.* **Fleming** *jumps over* **Arnall**.)

**Dolan**   I'm first! I'm first.

**Stephen**   You've made me lose my place.

**Molly**   You have such a wonderful bone structure.

**Arnall**   She always always likes them young. (**Stephen** *knows he's out for now. He laughs. He and* **Molly** *dance off, singing together in harmony.*) I'm last, last, last. *Last dammit!*

**Dolan**   You're third. (*To* **Fleming**.) Tell him he's third.

**Fleming**   You're third.

**Arnall**   I'm last. There are only three of us. One, two, three. Three is me. I'm last.

**Dolan**   Two over there. Those two. The kid and your terrific wife.

**Fleming** (*counting on his fingers*)   That makes five.

**Dolan**   You're two from the front and two from the back. Two from the first and two from last. You're the average.

(**Stephen** *sings lightly now as he and* **Molly** *dance.* **Arnall** *tells his story to the world.*)

**Arnall**    I would like to tell the story of my marriage. I worked hard every night. I knew she had friends, but I never knew they were doing it. (*Pauses.*) That's the story of my marriage. (*There is a shaggy-dog silence.*)

**Dolan**    As first man, I say that Arnall gets a chance to do it again as soon as the kid is finished. (**Stephen** *screams the ending of his song, 'Piano'.*) The kid is finished.

**Fleming**    Have a bash, Arnall.

**Arnall**    I'll lose my place in line. Never mind.

**Dolan**    Stay put, then. Fleming? You want a whack at it? You want a third, uh, try?

**Fleming**    I'm second. It ain't worth it now. You want another one, Dolan? Huh? Why don't you have a go at it? Give it another bash.

**Dolan**    You're pretty obvious, Fleming. Pretty obvious. Did anybody ever tell you how dumb you are? Did anybody ever take the time to tell you just how really dumb and stupid you really are?

**Fleming** (*after a hideously long pause*)    You think I don't know? You think I'm too stupid to know how dumb I am? Brains ain't everything, you know? I ain't exactly at the end of the line. It ain't over yet. (**Stephen** *walks to the opposite side of the line and squares off with* **Dolan**, *eye to eye.* **Stephen** *speaks with simple authority.*)

**Stephen**    The line's facing the wrong way.

**Dolan** (*incredulously*)    What the hell are you talking about, kid?

**Stephen** (*to all, an announcement*)    The line's facing the wrong way. (*To* **Dolan**.) The line's facing the wrong way. I'm first. (**Stephen** *and* **Dolan** *eye each other for a full half-minute with terrifying tension. Nobody moves.* **Stephen** *smiles a* *frozen smile.* **Dolan** *wipes his hands with a handkerchief, checking everyone in line. As* **Dolan** *checks to one side* **Molly** *quickly sneaks around into second place, behind* **Stephen**. **Dolan** *does a take.* **Arnall** *quickly slides around, following* **Molly**. *He's now third in* **Stephen**'s *line.* **Dolan** *does a full take. Then* **Dolan** *turns to* **Fleming** *and signals* **Fleming** *to 'take it easy', to wait, to rest.* **Fleming** *nods agreement. Suddenly, as soon as* **Fleming**'s *settled down,* **Dolan** *races into fourth place in* **Stephen**'s *line.* **Fleming** *sees and races after him, ending up last. When* **Stephen**'s *line is settled, the very instant, in fact, that* **Stephen**'s *line is full,* **Stephen** *steps over the line into the true first position. He smiles. All others freeze, staring at him.* **Molly** *breaks and jumps into second.*)

**Molly**    I'm second! (**Dolan** *bolts into third.*)

**Dolan**    I'm third!

**Fleming** (*leaping into fourth*)    I'm fourth!

**Arnall** (*limping into last*)    I'm last. Bitch-damn-crap! I'm really last now.

**Dolan** (*overlapping*)    Oh, man. That was rotten, kid. Really and truly filthy rotten.

**Fleming** (*overlapping*)    That kid is no good. I told you that kid was no good.

**Arnall** (*overlapping*)    Always the young ones. I'm sick of it. Sick of it. Sick of the young ones getting to be first.

**Dolan** (*screams*)    We'll get him, Arnall.

**Fleming**    Not finished. Not first! We'll get him. (*Screams.*) We're gonna' get you, kid!

**Arnall** (*whining*)    Cuckolded. Cuckolded. I'm a buffoon. (*Screams.*) A buffoon!

**Molly** (*desperately sexual, caressing with her voice*)    You have the face of a president. A movie star. A senator. You have a Kennedy's face. A beautiful face.

**Fleming** (*overlapping*)    Breathe the air now, kid. Breathe it deep! We're gonna' get you!

**Dolan** (*overlapping*)    Third. First to goddamn third!

**Arnall** (*overlapping*)    Last. Really last. This time there's no question.

**Stephen** (*a maniacal scream*)    SHUT UP, IDIOTS!

**Fleming**    Who the hell are you calling 'idiot'?

**Stephen**    All of you. Idiots. Fools. Lemmings. Pigs. Lint.

**Dolan**    Lint?

**Molly**    Lint?

**Arnall**    Lint?

**Fleming**    Lint?

**Stephen**    Lint!

**Fleming**    Oh boy. Oh boy. That's the limit. We're gonna' have your ass, kid.

**Stephen**    It's too late, idiots. I've won. I'm in first and anyone who isn't in first is an idiot. We've got nothing in common, so why talk about it?

**Dolan**    We've all got something in common, kid. And don't you forget it, either.

**Stephen**    What's that, Dolan?

**Dolan**    We've all been at his terrific wife. Whatever she's got, we've got.

**Fleming**    That's true. We're like a club. Whatever she's got, we've got. (*Does a huge 'take' to* **Arnall**.) What's she got?

**Stephen**    They're right, damn you. You let them all have you. Even your husband.

**Arnall** (*hopefully*)    Molly?

**Molly**    Nobody had me.

**Fleming**   Nobody but all of us!

**Molly**   Nobody had me.

**Stephen** (*turns sharply about to* **Molly**)   Everybody had you . . . everybody.

**Molly**   Nobody had me.

**Dolan**   She's crazy, too. (*To* **Arnall**.) You've got a crazy wife, mister.

**Molly**   Nobody had me, get it? Nobody. *I* had all of you. *I* did the doing. Not you. *I* made the choices. You all wanted to be first, what kept you from it, huh? What kept you? (*Pushes* **Stephen** *over the line, out of first place, viciously. He falls to one side, downstage left. Shocked.*) I'm first now. *Me!*

**Stephen** (*wandering, confused*)   You pushed me. She pushed me.

**Molly**   I'm first now!

**Dolan**   She's crazy. You've got a crazy wife, mister. This is a terrible night.

**Stephen**   Don't flatter yourself, Molly. Not for a second. You've screwed your way to first and you'll be screwed right out of first. That's the way it's always been and that's the way it's always going to be. This line's my last, Molly. You really think I'm going to let you come in first.

**Molly**   I am first. I am first. And I'm not moving. I screwed my way to first and now I'm resting. Maybe this is my last line too. Look who's first. Just look who's first. Me. Molly. Just where I knew I'd be from the moment I saw this line.

**Fleming**   You got yourself a real bitch for a wife there, Arnall. A real bitch.

**Arnall**   I know. I know.

**Molly**   I know what you've been thinking all night. Here we are, four big shots. One woman in line. Might as well roll her over, just to kill time. That's what you're always thinking. That's what every line's about, right? And you think in any other place you'd never give me a look . . . but . . . as long as we're all killing time together . . . why not? 'Course, under *normal* conditions, she'd never be good enough for me. Well, I've got a piece of news for you all: under any conditions, none of you is good enough for me. Not a one of you!

**Stephen** (*crosses to her*)   Molly. You're good enough for me.

**Molly**   Go to the back of the line, boy. You didn't satisfy me. You didn't make it. You didn't thrill me. You need experience. You make love like a child.

**Stephen**   What about my beautiful bones?

**Molly**   Go to the back of the line.

**Dolan**   That's telling the wise-ass kid. Go to the back of the line, kid. You heard the lady.

**Molly**   Don't gloat. Don't lick your lips. I could have done better with an ape than with you.

**Fleming**   Terrific, Molly. An ape, Dolan. An ape.

**Molly**   Are you the one with the beer and the gum who's too old and tired to finish?

**Fleming**   What's that supposed to mean?

**Arnall**   Molly? Molly? Is it me?

**Molly**   Don't be a bore, Arnall. You couldn't satisfy a carney.

**Dolan**   You've run out. If none of us satisfied you, who did?

**Molly**   None of you. Simple as that. I am an unsatisfied woman still looking for a man. You all failed.

**Dolan**   I've had better than you, tubby, and I mean some real beauties. And they've screamed for more. Screamed for more!

**Molly**   More money? OK. Sure. I can understand that.

**Fleming**   I've had models.

**Dolan**   Screw your models. I had one in a car once.

**Fleming**   Yeah. You told me.

**Molly**   I'm first. I'm unsatisfied. I've had four men. One three times. One unfinished. And I'm unsatisfied.

**Arnall**   Don't let her get to you. Don't let her get you going. She'll drive you all crazy. Make surprises. Ruin all your philosophies. She'll hide your shirts.

**Molly**   Arnall, you're such a bore.

**Stephen** (*crosses to her. Whispers*)   I've got something to tell you.

**Molly**   To the back of the line, sonny. You lost. You're last . . . move.

**Dolan**   You're out of line completely, kid. She's right. When the crowds come, you'll be left out altogether. (**Stephen** *wanders to right portal.*)

**Molly**   I hope there's a man in the *crowd*. One man.

**Arnall**   You see what I mean? She won't let up now. Now that she's first, she'll just keep pouring it on.

**Dolan**   She's worse than *my* old lady. Much worse. My old lady's a dog, but nothing like yours. Yours is the biggest dog of all. Queen dog. Yeah. She's the biggest dog of all. How'd you get stuck with her, anyway?

**Arnall**   She picked me up at a party. I was at a party. The lights were dim. I felt a hand sneak between my legs. I was only fifteen. It was Molly. She taught me everything I know. I don't know anything either.

**Stephen** (*a proclamation*)    When I make love to a woman, I never shut my eyes. Never. I watch. I watch and I listen to every movement she makes.

**Fleming** (*embarrassed*)    Shut up.

**Dolan** (*wants to hear* **Stephen**'s '*secret*')    You shut up, Fleming.

**Stephen**    I listen to every movement she makes. So that every time I move, I understand her response. One little wiggle to the left, one little wiggle to the right and I get a response I remember. I make notes. I have a whole loose-leaf binder filled with notes and half another filled as well. All kinds of notes. How to wiggle front and back. How short women respond. How tall women respond. How certain ethnic groups respond.

**Molly**    What did you learn from me, little boy?

**Stephen** (*his guise has worked. He knows it. He sets up his next line carefully, ready to strike. He moves into position close to* **Molly**) Never screw an ugly, greedy slob like you. Always to follow my natural desire. Only screw who I want, when I want. If I had followed my natural desire, I never would have screwed you. Not once. Not twice, certainly. Not three times. It was all an incredible waste of my incredibly valuable time. That's what I wanted to tell you.

**Molly** (*explodes*)    You little squirt. You little jerk. (*She charges at him in a rage. He knocks her aside and regains first position . . .* **Molly** *is out of line.*)

**Stephen** (*with a flourish*)    Gentlemen, I am first again.

**Fleming**    You've really got to hand it to that kid. Go on, Dolan. Hand it to the kid.

**Dolan** (*he is standing on* **Stephen**'s *toes*)    Nice work, kid.

**Arnall** (*a small bitch*)    I'm not last. You're last, Molly. I'm ahead of you. You're last.

**Dolan** (*ruefully*)    Nice work, kid.

**Stephen**   Say it again, Dolan.

**Dolan**   Nice work, kid. (*He pushes* **Stephen** *violently off stage.* **Dolan** *takes first.* **Stephen** *falls into the audience.*) Look who's first now, will you?

**Dolan**   I'm first.

**Fleming** (*jumps forward*)  I'm second.

**Arnall** (*jumps forward*)   I'm third.

**Molly**   I'm fourth.

**Stephen** (*starts walking up the aisle*)   I'm out.

**Dolan**   In every crowd, there's a winner. A winner. I waited back there. I hung in. Look at me now.

**Stephen** (*from the back of the theatre*)   You broke the rules, Dolan.

**Dolan**   What rules?

**Stephen** (*from another aisle*)   He pushed me.

**Dolan**   *She* pushed you.

**Stephen** (*screaming*)   She's a woman. That's different.

**Fleming**   That's true, Dolan. It's different when it's a woman. Especially *that* woman.

**Arnall**   You see, Molly's always breaking rules. She breaks everything. Dishes. Cups. Saucers.

**Molly**   Just shut your dumb mouth, Arnall.

**Fleming**   Yeah. Shut up, Arnall. We got to figure this out.

**Dolan**   What's to figure out? I'm up front. Head of the line. I won. That's pretty simple.

**Fleming**   Yeah, but you pushed the kid. We sort of had an unwritten rule here. I mean, none of us did any pushing.

**Dolan**   You want to push me, Fleming?

**Fleming**    Hey, look. Don't start that stuff! I'm a hell of a lot tougher than you, pal. You want to start that stuff and that's the kind of stuff you'll get. You know what I mean?

**Stephen** (*walking back to the stage*)    I'd hate to see you start a fight over me, Fleming. It's probably better that I just stay right out of line. You people can handle things on your own. You don't need me.

**Fleming**    Yeah, I suppose.

**Dolan**    What the hell are you trying to do, kid? You're gonna' just *let* me stay in first? You ain't gonna' trick me out of it?

**Stephen** (*standing, facing the stage*)    You don't trust people. That's your trouble, Dolan. You think everybody's out to get you all the time, don't you?

**Dolan**    I don't think of anybody but NUMBER ONE. I hung in back there in second all that time. I knew what I was doing. I've watched you up there. I knew when to strike. I knew when my iron was hot. I waited it out. I'm first. That's simple, isn't it?

**Stephen** (*leaning on the stage*)    There are ways of getting to first that are acceptable and ways of getting to first that are unacceptable. Women and children excluded, of course.

**Fleming**    That's right.

**Dolan**    What's right?

**Fleming**    The thing he said about women and children. That's always the way about women and children.

**Stephen**    Women and children first.

**Fleming**    Women and children first.

**Stephen**    Dolan's not a women.

**Fleming**    Dolan's not a children.

**Arnall**    Dolan's none of those things.

**Molly**   Dolan's nothing.

**Stephen**   Everybody's something.

**Fleming**   Not Dolan! (**Fleming** *pushes* **Dolan** *violently off stage, and takes first!*) Holy Christ! I'm in first place!

**Arnall**   I'm second.

**Molly** (*jumping up*)   I'm third.

**Dolan** (*crawling back on stage*)   For Christ's sakes. For crying out loud. Fleming pushed me.

**Stephen**   You changed the rules. You pushed first.

**Dolan**   She pushed first.

**Fleming**   Holy Christ! I'm really in first place. I'm first guy. Top dog. (*And he pushes* **Dolan** *off stage again.*)

**Dolan**   He pushed me tight out of first place.

**Molly** (*pushes* **Arnall**)   Be a winner, Arnall. (*She pushes* **Arnall** *so hard, he clobbers* **Fleming** *right out of first place.* **Arnall** *is first now.*)

**Fleming**   Hey. Hey. Hey. (**Dolan** *crawls back onto the stage and* **Fleming** *crashes into him –* **Dolan** *flies off stage again.*)

**Arnall**   I didn't do that. She did that. She pushed me so hard I pushed you. I didn't push you. Honest to God, I didn't push you. Here. Take it back. (**Arnall** *walks right out of first place, trembling. He leads* **Fleming** *by the hand back into first place.* **Molly** *stands frozen. Astonished.* **Dolan** *crawls back on stage and into second.*)

**Fleming**   I'm first again.

**Dolan**   I'm second. Hah! I'm second.

**Arnall** (*slipping, mincing into third, in front of an astonished* **Molly**, *he says simply*)   I'm third.

**Molly**   Arnall, you damn dumb fool. Look what you did. Look what you did, you damn dumb dummy.

**Arnall**    I gave that to you, Fleming. I gave you first. But you've got to protect me!

**Fleming**    From what?

**Arnall**    Her.

**Fleming**    Why?

**Arnall**    Please, Fleming?

**Fleming**    Why?

**Molly**    Damn you, Arnall. Damn you. (*She beats him, as a child swatting a mosquito.*)

**Arnall**    See? See what I mean? I need help, Fleming. Help me, Fleming.

**Fleming** (*walks to* **Molly** *and talks to her, reasonably*)    Now look, ma'am. I don't want to hurt a lady. I've never hurt a lady.

**Arnall**    She's no lady.

**Dolan** (*jumps into first, incredulously*)    I'm first again! (*Everybody freezes, out of line, as* **Dolan** *stands alone.*)

**Fleming**    Now just wait a goddamned minute!

**Dolan**    I'm first, first! (**Fleming** *clobbers* **Dolan**.)

**Arnall**    This is awful. (*Jumps in first.*)

**Molly**    This is your fault, Arnall. (*Pushes* **Arnall** *out.*)

**Stephen** (*from the audience, giggling*)    I'd say it was Dolan's fault.

**Dolan**    Knock it off, kid.

**Stephen**    Hell, I'll knock it off. If you hadn't broken the rules and pushed me, we'd be in a perfectly straight line. This is chaos, friends. Chaos. (**Arnall** *dashes into first place.*)

**Molly** (*attacking* **Dolan**, *she kicks his testicles*)    Move out of there. Move. (*They all end up in a horrible fist fight, ending with*

**Dolan** *hitting* **Molly** *fiercely . . .* **Arnall** *crawls in and bites*
**Molly***'s leg.)*

**Fleming** (*astonished*)    You hit her. You hit her!

**Stephen**    See? See what you have? Chaos. Pure, plain and
simple. Chaos.

**Fleming**    You're goddamned right it is, kid. Goddamned
right. (*He has* **Dolan***'s arm pinned.*) Help the kid back in the
line. Go on.

**Dolan**    Are you crazy?

**Fleming**    I've seen this happen before. Help him back!

**Stephen** (*walking into line, into first*)    Anybody mind my
being first?

**Dolan**    I held back, dammit! I waited! What is this?

**Fleming** (*screams at* **Dolan**)    Don't!

**Dolan** (*frightened*)    OK. OK. (*He suddenly lurches for first.*
**Fleming** *grabs him and beats him with three quick terrifying*
*punches.*) Ughhh. Ahhh. Ughhh.

**Fleming**    I said 'don't' and I mean 'don't'! Everybody
hear me? Huh? Everybody hear me clear.

**Dolan** (*whipped*)    I'm second.

**Fleming**    OK. I'll stay in third. 'Til we get straightened
out. You, Arnall. You get fourth. And you, you fat bitch,
you started this pushing business. You get in fifth.

**Arnall** (*as a three-year-old child*)    I'm not last. You're last,
Molly. I'm ahead of you. You're last.

**Fleming**    Everybody shut up! (*Pauses.*) OK, kid. What do
we do now?

**Stephen**    Shut up and listen. (*He presses the 'on' button on his*
*tape recorder and Mozart's* Eine Kleine Nachtmusik *fills the*
*theatre.*) Can you feel him? Mozart. *Eine Kleine Nachtmusik.*
The Allegro. He was younger than me when he wrote this.

A baby. The Allegro. Then Andante. Then Minuet. Then Rondo.

**Arnall**   Austrian, right? Isn't he Austrian, Stephen?

**Stephen**   That's Mozart, for Christ's sakes! It's Mozart. I'm not first. I'm second. Stop. Please. This is crazy. This is a crazy thing. (*He turns off the recorder.*)

**Fleming**   You're the crazy thing.

**Arnall** (*really spooky*)   You know how he died, Stephen? Singers came in and sang him to death. His *Requiem*, Stephen. They sang while he died.

**Stephen** (*staring at the Mozart he sees ahead of him*)   It's not true. It's not true.

**Arnall**   But I was there, Stephen. I saw it. I heard it.

**Stephen** (*weeping*)   Stop it. Stop it.

**Arnall**   I was there, Stephen. He was writing the percussion up until the last. Boom-boom. Boom-boom. (*He marches singing 'boom-boom'.*)

**Stephen**   I'm losing my mind.

**Molly**   Arnall. You weasel, Arnall.

**Arnall**   Boom-boom. Just shut up, you bitch. Just shut up. Boom-boom.

**Stephen**   No! This isn't happening! I'm first. Look at me. I'm first. I earned this, I know I did!

**Fleming**   Bullshit, you did! We'll get you, kid.

**Dolan**   We'll get you, kid.

**Arnall**   Want me to sing it, Stephen? The *Requiem*? Want me to sing the *Requiem* now? (*He sings as a choirboy: 'La-ab cree-mosa, Ita-es-eela' etc. He continues the* Requiem *and* **Stephen** *seems totally hypnotized. He walks toward* **Stephen** *and then past him. He moves around past* **Dolan** *and* **Fleming***, who stare wide-eyed. He swings around again, softly singing, heading straight for first* *place.*) Boom-boom. Boom-boom. It could be lovely, Stephen. Lovely. I'll sing . . . (*Checks, sees.*) . . . and Dolan . . . boom-boom . . .

**Dolan** (*taking a nod from* **Arnall**)   Boom-boom . . . boom-boom . . .

**Arnall**   . . . and Fleming . . . boom-boom . . .

**Fleming** (*confused, follows with his voice*)   Boom-boom . . . boom-boom . . .

**Arnall**   will do their work . . . BOOM BOOM . . . BOOM BOOM . . . BOOM BOOM . . .

**Dolan** *and* **Fleming**   BOOM BOOM . . . BOOM BOOM . . .

**Arnall**   BOOM BOOM . . . BOOM . . . BOOM . . . BOOM BOOM . . . (**Stephen** *grabs his neck in anguished pain. He screams a most hideous scream and falls forward onto his face. He writhes on the floor, sobbing in agony.* **Arnall** *walks quietly into first place.*)

**Fleming** (*after a huge pause*)   That's terrible. I'll never sing with you again, Arnall.

**Dolan**   Holy Jesus Christ! Will you look at that? (**Stephen** *is silently staring from the floor. He sees* **Arnall**. *He stands slowly, almost berserk now. He lunges at* **Arnall**, *grabbing his throat.*)

**Stephen**   You little twirp. You little plucked chicken. You step back, Arnall. You're playing with fire, Arnall. Fire. You move now or I'm going to strangle you, Arnall. You'll be dead, Arnall.

**Arnall**   Please, Stephen. Please. I only want Molly. I don't want first. Only Molly. Please, Stephen. Please? (*But* **Stephen**'*s too far gone. He squeezes* **Arnall**'*s throat.*)

**Stephen**   You move or I'll kill you, Arnall. Do you believe me? (**Arnall** *and* **Stephen** *stare at each other. A long hold.*)

**Arnall** (*defeated*)   Yes.

**Stephen**   Back of the line, Arnall.

**Fleming**   Yeah, Arnall. Back of the line. I can't see what the kid is saying when you're standing there. You're blocking me from the kid.

**Dolan**   That ain't right, Arnall. Move back, Arnall.

**Fleming**   Move back, Arnall.

**Molly** (*fiercely*)   You heard them! Move! (**Arnall** *walks slowly to the end of the line. Broken. Defeated.*)

**Fleming** (*breaking the horrific silence of* **Arnall**'*s total humiliation*) What's next, kid?

**Stephen**   The end. I beat all of you, not with luck, but with genius. There's only one person to beat, and you can't see him in this line. I can see him in this line. (*He is now screaming at the place in front of him.*) I'll beat you. I'll die youngest, the best. And after I'm gone you'll see I can take it with me! (*He turns on the recorder to an unbearable volume and slides the machine across the stage. It lands, blaring and staring up at a startled* **Arnall**. *Slowly, carefully,* **Stephen** *picks up the line – that white piece of tape that is first place itself – and eats it, as a berserk strand of spaghetti.* **Arnall** *picks up the tape recorder and smashes the 'off' button: killing it, as though he were swatting an insect.*)

**Arnall** (*in the now-deafening silence, carefully*)   You are crazy! You are an insane, horrible child. (*He draws a deep, deep breath.*)

**Stephen** (*he's swallowed the tape by now*)   How dare you, you cuckolded little nothing! You let your wife – your fat horrible wife – screw on the street while you do nothing more than watch. She screws and you watch. And tomorrow you'll crawl in bed beside her with your chubby clean-but-sweaty little body begging for a whore's kisses!

**Molly**   You animal! You animal! Hit him, Arnall! Hit him!

**Arnall**   We're much older than you are, son. You could show some respect.

**Stephen** (*the final insult follows*)   Maybe I hate you most, Arnall. Just maybe. (*Like a bullet.*) You're a loser, Arnall.

**Fleming**   It's OK, Arnall, you can hit him. Boom Boom. Boom Boom.

**Stephen**   I won! I did it! I did it. I did it. I won. I won. (*Chasing them all.*) Come on, Arnall. It's OK now. Hit me. Scratch my eyes out. Kill me.

**Arnall**   Me?

**Stephen**   You. Anybody. Come on. Let's get on with it.

**Dolan**   We're gonna get you, kid.

**Stephen**   Do it, Dolan. Do it.

**Fleming**   Go on, Arnall. Get him. Boom Boom

**Molly**   Hit him, Arnall. Boom Boom. (*She gets the recorder and gives it to* **Arnall**.)

**Arnall**   Me?

**Dolan**   Kill him, Arnall. Boom Boom.

**Arnall**   Me?

**Dolan** *and* **Fleming**   Kill him, Arnall. Boom Boom.

**Stephen** (*laughs maniacally*)   I can take it with me. I finally won! (**Stephen** *kneels, head up, eyes closed – waiting to be killed.* **Dolan**, **Fleming** *and* **Molly** *chant 'Boom Boom' over and over, urging* **Arnall** *to kill* **Stephen**.)

**Arnall**   You son of a bitch. You son of a bitch! (*He takes tape recorder and raises it to kill* **Stephen**. *He stops, as* **Molly** *shrieks.*)

*They all stop and jump back one step.*

**Stephen** (*opens his eyes, stands, amazed*)   What's wrong? Why are you stopping? Somebody's got to kill me.

**Arnall**   Us?

**Fleming**   Kill him?

**Molly**   Kill him?

**Stephen**   You've got to kill me. I've got to die first. Please . . . please . . . please . . . please . . . (**Dolan** *walks into first position, but of course the line is gone.* **Dolan** *is astonished.*)

**Dolan** (*a whine*)   Where's the line?

**Fleming**   The line! Where is it?

**Arnall**   The line!

**Molly**   Arnall! The line's gone.

**Arnall**   Where'd it go?

**Stephen** (*burps a little, smiles*)   I ate it.

**Fleming**   What?

**Stephen**   I ate it. (*He groans.*)

**Molly**   He ate it. He ate it?

**Fleming**   He ate it. He ate it?

**Dolan**   He ate it?

**Arnall**   He *ate* it?

**Stephen**   I ate it.

**Molly**   See? I'm right. He *is* crazy. He's really crazy.

**Fleming**   I told you that, lady. I told you that the second you walked up. He's really crazy.

**Stephen**   What is this? I'm supposed to die! (*He's stunned, as it appears that he isn't going to die after all.*)

**Molly**   He wanted us to beat him so he'd die so there'd be a dead kid in first. And we were supposed to just watch.

**Arnall**   How could we watch a thing like that?

**Fleming**    Why not? We've been watching everything else.

**Molly**    Oh, my God! What if I'm pregnant?

**Arnall**    Pregnant? Molly. A son? A son, Molly?

**Fleming** (*thrilled, laughs a relieved laugh*)    I never finished.

**Molly**    He finished. The way it counts.

**Fleming** (*pointing to* **Stephen**)    You see, Arnall? They never really forget the first one.

**Arnall**    What?

**Dolan**    Jesus! What a wife you've got there. What a rotten night! (*To* **Stephen**.) Give us back the line, kid. They're going to open soon and we need a line.

**Molly**    They'll open and we won't have a line. (*Steps behind* **Stephen**.) And I'm only second.

**Arnall**    I'm right beside you.

**Fleming**    Me too.

**Dolan**    For crying out loud! We're all second!

**Fleming**    This looks very phoney. Give us back our line, Steve.

**Molly**    Please, Stevie. Please.

**Arnall**    Give it back, Stephen.

**Dolan**    Cough it up, Stephen. Steve, Stevie. Cough it up. (**Stephen** *begins to gag and choke. The line begins to appear.*)

**Fleming**    Hey. The line.

**Dolan**    There it is!

**Molly**    The line.

**Arnall**    He *did* eat it. (**Dolan** *grabs the line from* **Stephen**'s *mouth and runs across stage.*)

**Dolan**    He took it with him. (**Stephen** *rises, dazzled.*
**Dolan** *runs downstage.* **Fleming** *runs to* **Stephen**.)

**Stephen**    I didn't take it with me. I didn't go anywhere.
Damn it all. I'm not dead. (*He begins to go through a series of
contortions as a woman in labor.*)

**Dolan** (*standing victoriously, his own line on the floor*)    I'm first. I
had to wait for my chance, but I'm first. Had to wait. Wait.
Hang back. But I'm first. (**Stephen** *gags again and a second
piece of tape appears: another line.* **Fleming** *grabs the line and stares
at it as a moron might, then follows* **Dolan***'s example, setting his line,
downstage right.*)

**Fleming**    I'm first! Finally, I'm first! I should be first. I was
the first one here. Fair's fair. (**Stephen** *retches as he stands up.*
**Molly** *steps forward and kisses* **Stephen** *full on the lips. She comes
away with a piece of line as her reward, between her teeth.* **Stephen**
*is now a dispenser. He walks mechanically, emitting sounds like a
berserk Coca-Cola machine.*)

**Molly** (*setting her line down: her first*)    He gave me first. He
made me first. He gave me first place. (**Fleming**, **Molly** *and*
**Dolan** *now stare, dreamy-eyed with victory. All of them will continue
repeating their victory speeches until* **Arnall***'s final line, which he will
repeat alone in the silence.* **Arnall** *slaps* **Stephen** *on the back and a
line falls into his hands.*)

**Arnall** (*after placing his line upstage right*)    Molly. Darling. I'm
first. I didn't want to be first. I never wanted first. But I'm
first. And I like it, Molly! First is good.

**Stephen** *still walks as a machine, puking up a final scrap of line.
He grabs it and just as he places it on the floor downstage centre, he sees
the others in their victory. He understands and casually throws his line
away. As he turns to leave, the lights switch off.*

## Note on Songs

The songs mentioned by title in *Line* are protected by copyright and may not be used in performance without the written permission of the copyright owners. Groups wishing to use these songs in production should direct their requests as follows:

For permission to perform the song 'Tiptoe Through the Tulips', contact Warner/Chappell Music, 9000 Sunset Boulevard, Los Angeles, CA 90069.

For permission to use the compositions 'I Want a Girl' (just like the girl that married dear old dad), and 'Take Me Out to the Ball Game', music by Albert Von Tilzer, words by Jack Norworth, published by Broadway Music Corporation–Jerry Vogel Music Co. Inc., contact the Harry Fox Agency Inc., 205 East 42nd Street, New York, NY 10017.

# The Widow's Blind Date

For Anke, Barbara, Catherine, Chris, Diane, Dossy, Gill, Heidi, Jill, Kim, Marietta, Mary-Beth, Patricia, Al, Bob, Biff, Bush, Charles, Christian, David, Ebbe, Frank, Frank, Götz, Grey, Hawk, Jacques, John, Olivier, Paul, Peter, Philippe, Pop, Sheldon, Tom and Uncle Max

*The Widow's Blind Date* was produced in New York by
David Bulasky, Barbara Darwell and Peter von Mayrhauser
at Circle in the Square (Downtown) on 7 November 1989. It
was directed by Israel Horovitz, the set design was by
Edward T. Gianfrancesco, the lighting design was by Craig
Evans and the costume design was by Janet Irving. The cast
was as follows:

| | |
|---|---|
| **Archie Crisp** | Paul O'Brien |
| **George Ferguson** | Tom Bloom |
| **Margy Burke** | Christine Estabrook |

*The Widow's Blind Date* was first presented as a staged
reading by the New York Playwrights Lab under the
auspices of the Actors Studio, featuring Jill Eikenberry,
Robert Field and Ebbe Roe Smith, directed by Sheldon
Larry. The play received its world premiere at the Los
Angeles Theatre Center, featuring Frank McCarthy,
Charlie Parks and Patricia Wettig, directed by Bill Bushnell.

## Characters

**Archie 'Billy-Goat' Crisp**, *30s: solid, thick, butts in; a goat*
**George 'Kermie' Ferguson**, *30s: twitches, sudden dangerous moves; a weasel*
**Margy Burke**, *30s: lean, worried, swoops; a goshawk*

## Time

Late afternoon, Saturday, October, the present

## Setting

Baling-press room, wastepaper company, Wakefield, Massachusetts.

## Note on Accent/Pronunciation

North Shore 'Pahk Yo'r Cah in Hah'vid Yahd'
Massachusetts accents are essential to the playing of this text. 'Margy' is pronounced with a hard 'G' – 'Mahh-*gh*ee; 'sure' is pronounced 'shoo-ah' etc.

# Act One

*5 p.m., Saturday afternoon, late fall, yellow light, slight chill in the air.*

*A tinny-speakered radio plays 'easy-listenin'' tunes.*

*Interior of baling-press room. Large, high-ceilinged space with skylights and hanging, caged-in bare bulbs as light source.*

*Eight bales of newspaper stretch across the front edge of the stage, separating the audience from the stage. The bales will be removed in the opening minutes of the play by the actors, who, in a sense, 'set the stage' . . . start the play.*

*A huge baling press is set upstage center of room: the main object. Stage left of the baler is a dune-like mound of loose newspapers from which armfuls of newspapers are carried to the press, into which they are loaded. Opposite side of the baler, upstage, a small mountain of newspaper bundles, tied with twine; stacked. A smaller mound of bundled newspaper is in evidence downstage right of baler. Loading doors are placed mid-stage right. 800 lb bales of newspaper are in evidence all around perimeter of stage. Each bale is 4 feet wide by 3 feet thick by 4 feet high.*

*It is possible that a large hook and chain is suspended from the ceiling, on a track. Also, a roller track may be constructed in front of the baler to be used for propelling completed bales from baler to bale stack.*

*A sharp-toothed hand truck is in evidence, also used for transporting bales from place to place in shop; and for loading doors onto truck for shipment to mills. Note: If the stage is large enough, it is suggested that a gasoline- or electricity-powered 'Towmotor' [forklift] be included among the scenery/props. Also, an enormous floor scale should be insinuated into the scenic plan, upstage right wall, so that completed bales can be shuttled by hand truck (or driven by Towmotor) across the scale, and weighed.*

*Upstage, there is a locker – probably housing the radio.* **Archie**'s *'dress-up' clothes (suit, shirt, tie, good shoes, etc.) are in evidence, inside locker, as are* **George**'s *jacket and scarf. There is an old easy chair,* *probably a vintage leatherette 'Barca-lounger', set downstage of the locker.*

*The baling press should be large and ominous. A version of an old-fashioned wooden baler is wanted [c.1940], with removable walls, a weighted, permanent base, and adjustable top. Such a baler functions as follows: the press walls form an empty 'box', which is filled with over-issue newspapers or magazines. The top of the baler is fitted in place, steel oblongs lock into side grooves more distant from top, causing top to squash over-issues of magazines into a bale. When the proper size is achieved, men negotiate the tying of the bale with long black wire. When bale is tied, the steel oblongs are carefully removed from the baler's side teeth and all sides and top are removed, causing the bale to stand alone. A roller track is stored under the baler, slides out and is slotted into position at the baler's front door for bale removal. A hand truck is brought to the end of the roller track, and the bale is removed. The baler's front door and sides are replaced, the press is refilled, the process is repeated.*

*The lights come up on switch on* **Archie Crisp** *and* **George Ferguson**. **Archie** *is in the midst of performing a story for* **George**, *who is enthralled. As* **Archie** *tells his story, he moves the bales upstage, clearing the audience's view of the front edge of the stage.*

**Archie**   So, this jamoca thinks he can take me real fast, throws a left, and I roll under and come up from down like a fuckin' toad, George . . . and I throw my two arms out wicked straight and yell 'Whooooo-eeee!' . . . and he looks left and right . . . and I butt this jamoca with the top of my head, and he is out! O.U.T.! (*He continues to move the remainder of the eight bales, upstage, lining them up, neatly, like soldiers, ready to be tagged, weighed and loaded on to an imagined truck, presumably outside the loading doors, off stage.* **George** *sweeps, cleans. Note:* **Archie***'s work must be substantial, authoritative: the boss's work.* **George***'s labor, by contrast, is menial, unimportant: the helper's work. They both swig beer from cans as they work and chat.*)

**George**   So, what do I do next?

**Archie** Sweep up under there, OK? And then separate the over-issues from the loose shit in the pit, like I showed you before.

**George** How many bales we got now?

**Archie** Counting this, five, plus the two corrugated . . . seven . . . so's we need one more after this. Then we still got to sort 'em and run 'em over the scale and weigh 'em before we load. (*Pause.*) I might hav'ta go away and come back.

**George** We loadin' tonight?

**Archie** Use your head, will ya'? You can't leave a load out there, all night. It's an open truck. The night air gets into these bales, they'll weigh twice as much in the morning.

**George** I don't mind stickin', now, for the sortin' and weighin' part . . . I mean, I ain't got too much goin' in the plans-for-tonight department . . .

**Archie** Oh, yuh, well, I got kind of a supper thing I got ta do . . . I'm on for supper with Margy . . .

**George** Margy? Swede's sistah, Margy? (*He runs to radio, shuts it off.*)

**Archie** Oh, yuh, yuh. I bumped into her down Mal's Jewel Craft a while back. She called me up . . . to have supper with her.

**George** She called you up?

**Archie** Oh, yuh, well, yuh, she did, yuh . . .

**George** Jees! Still the aggressive one, Margy, huh?

**Archie** Oh, well, yuh, I guess . . .

**George** I read in the paper she was comin' ta town. Swede's finally dyin', huh?

**Archie** She said that, yuh. Bad shape, yuh.

**George** She's up and done som'pin' famous, I guess, huh? You read it in the *Item*?

**Archie**   Me? Now. Never touch a paper after I leave here. I get my fill, sorta, I guess . . . line line of work 'n' all . . .

**George** (*laughing*)   I even clipped the article . . . to show you. I can't goddamn believe it, Arch! It's unbelievable! You got supper going with Swede's sistah?

**Archie**   Hey, listen huh, ya know? Sure . . . Sure! Swede Palumbo's sistah Margy. She finds me . . . attractive.

**George**   Oh, yuh? Maybe she can find you a *job*! (*Laughs.*) Where're you pickin' her up? 33 Elm?

**Archie**   Uh uh. She's pickin' *me* up, here, six sharp.

**George**   *Here?*

**Archie**   Yuh, here. Somethin' the matter with here?

**George**   It's a junk shop, for Christ's sakes . . . (*Laughs.*) Boy, you really got 'em hoppin' for you, Arch . . . I gotta hand it to ya . . . Pickin' him up at his goddamn junk shop . . . What a guy . . . (*Laughs.*) Hey, maybe you could send her over ta' my place, later, huh? For old times' sake . . .

**Archie** (*twists* **George**'s *arm, forcing him to the ground*)   Take it back! Take it back! Ya' *derr*!

**George**   Lemme up, ya' jerk!

**Archie**   Take it back, take it back!

**George**   *Archie . . . God damn it . . . GOD DAMN IT, Archie!*

**Archie**   You take it back?

**George**   OK, yuh, OK, yuh, I take it back. (*Pause.*) Now lemme up, huh?

**Archie**   You're free. (*Releasing* **George**.) Let's finish this bale, OK?

**George** (*stands, rubs arms*)   Top of your head, huh?

**Archie**   I split his jaw.

**George**   Any bleeding?

**Archie**   Why? You thirsty, or som'pin'? (*There is a pause in the chat. The men work, wordlessly.* **George** *restarts the conversation.*)

**George**   Blind-Peter-Holier-Than-Fucking-Thou-Palumbo . . . Never liked the peckah . . .

**Archie**   Which one of us did?

**George**   You gonna try to get anything off her?

**Archie**   Who?

**George**   Swede's sistah.

**Archie**   Margy? Nothin' ta get. She's flatter'n a pancake . . . two raisins on a breadboard.

**George**   Carpenter's Delight: flat as a board and easy to screw!

**Archie**   *Pirate's* Delight . . .

**George**   What's that?

**Archie**   Sunken chest! (*They share a laugh.*)

**George**   Margy ain't so bad, actually.

**Archie** (*grabs* **George** *from behind, tickles him*)   You were lookin'? You were peekin'? You were snoopin' in between the buttons when she stretches? You were watchin' her take off her coat . . . on the arms-behind-the-back part . . . when the two of them were shoved right out there . . . on view for all? That what you were doin', George?

**George**   Who? *Me?*

**Archie**   Just us balin' here, right? I mean, I ain't seen nobody else pressin' these bales, right? Just you and me . . .

**George**   Yuh, I've thought about it now and again. But I haven't seen her in twenty years, Arch.

**Archie**   How come you never moved on her?

**George**   On Swede's sistah?

**Archie**   You sufferin' from a sho't memory problem, or what?

**George**   I never moved on Swede's sistah on account of she was married. Also counta Swede. Also on account of I haven't actually seen her since high school.

**Archie**   She ain't been married in years and years!

**George**   Even worse. Widows give me the creeps, ya know. I look at her and her kids, and alls I can think about is what's-his-name dyin' an all . . . What's his name.

**Archie**   You know . . . what's-his-name.

**George**   What's his name?

**Archie**   What's his name? . . . Uh, uh, uh, *don't tell me*! Uh, uh, uh . . . (*Suddenly.*) I got it! Cootie!

**George**   Cootie Webber?

**Archie**   Wasn't that him?

**George**   Are you nuts? Cootie Webber never married Swede's sistah. Sides . . . ain't Cootie Webber still alive?

**Archie**   You crazy? Cootie Webber got hit by lightning . . . head of the lake.

**George**   You out of your mind? Cootie Webber ate bad clams.

**Archie**   You off your gourd? (*Turns and faces* **George**.) A woman's got a right to take off her coat, same as a man, when she comes in. The world's changed, in case ya' haven't noticed! You got no right to be starin' at her like she's public property, any more, 'cause she ain't. You get me? *Get me?*

**George** (*after a long pause*)   You're really gone on her, huh?

**Archie**   I like her.

**George**  It doesn't give you the willies . . . that she's got one husband in the grave . . . and kids? That doesn't give you the willies, Arch?

**Archie**  Death is a part of life, the way I see it.

**George**  No doubt about it.

**Archie**  A widow's got a right to go out with me . . . same as a non-widow.

**George**  I can see that.

**Archie**  I like her.

**George**  I never stared.

**Archie**  I never said you did.

**George**  I mean, I noticed she was good-lookin' and all . . .

**Archie**  Kinda flat-chested, though . . .

**George**  It's a gland, that's all. For feeding babies. I mean, how excited can a person get over a gland, right? You know what I mean? You follow me?

**Archie**  I like 'em, myself.

**George**  Margy's, or in general?

**Archie**  In general, I like 'em to be more ample than Margy's . . . I like them in general . . . to be more ample than . . . what Margy has to offer.

**George**  I was thinkin': If Swede heard us going on about his sistah this way, we'd be goners, right.

**Archie**  What are you? Nuts or something?

**George**  He's got a temper, Swede . . .

**Archie**  The man's dyin', George. What have you got goin' upstairs? Mashed potatoes? 'Cause there sure ain't no gray matter up there!

**George**   Alls I'm sayin' here is 'ya never know!' . . . Dyin' or not, Swede Palumbo wouldn't've shed a tear if the school bus run us down . . . and that's a fact . . . (*Smiles.*) Course, it's *you* he really hates, ain't it?

**Archie**   What's this?

**George**   Senior Class Beach Party . . . what was Swede yellin', poor blind son of a bitch? 'I'm gonna kill you, Billy-Goat Crisp! I'm gonna kill you dead! Billy-Goat's gonna die!' Ain't that right?

**Archie**   What am I hearin' here?

**George**   Still makes me laugh ta think about it . . .

**Archie**   If you spill one word about this in front of Margy, I'll kill you, George.

**George**   What, are you kidding? You don't think it's gonna come up?

**Archie**   I'll be the judge of what stays down and what comes up. You get me? (**George** *giggles.*) I don't hear an answer here, George. (**George** *laughs.*) I wanna hear an answer, you! (**George** *tries to stop his laugh, but a fresh laugh explodes from him.* **Archie** *is enraged.*) I'm gonna' butt your jaw with the top of my head . . .

**George**   C'mon, Arch, it just stands ta reason . . .

**Archie**   Nothin' stands ta reason, you get me? You open your mouth one time on that subject, and you won't be standin' to piss, let alone standin' to reason! You follow me, George? Huh?

**George**   OK, OK!

**Archie**   I'll hav'ta kill ya', otherwise . . .

**George**   I just said 'OK', OK?

**Archie** (*after a pause*)   OK.

**George** (*an involuntary giggle*)    Heee . . . (*Shows palm to* **Archie**.) Just a laugh.

**Archie**    And keep your eyes to yourself, you hear me?

**George**    Honest to Christ, Arch, I never once looked. Cross my heart.

**Archie**    Cross your ass, George! I don't like what I'm hearing from you, George, ya know that? There must be ten thousand different women around, ya know, if you add up Wakefield, Reading, Stoneham, Melrose and Woburn. You got no right to be movin' in where I'm having supper tonight.

**George**    God strike me dead if I'm movin' in, Arch.

**Archie**    You better mean what you say.

**George**    I mean what I say. God strike me dead, and that's a fact. (*Pause.*) Don't you worry. (*Smiles.*) I wouldn't add in Woburn women, if I were you, though.

**Archie** (*smiles*)    True enough.

**George**    Woburn women are dogs.

**Archie**    The worst.

**George**    Pigs.

**Archie**    The lowest.

**George**    I wouldn't touch 'em on a bet.

**Archie**    Rot your hand.

**George**    Remember Ax Landry?

**Archie**    The skinny one?

**George**    Went with Rufus What's it's Woburn cousin . . .

**Archie**    The fat one with the wigs?

**George**    Remember?

**Archie** (*hoots with laughter*)    Who could forget?

**George**   Ax. Dumb fuck.

**Archie**   Wicked dumb.

**George**   His sistah, Dixie Cups . . . she had a mouth like a toilet, huh?

**Archie**   Wicked awful.

**George**   She says to me one night, up by the bandstand, lookin' out at Lake Quannapowitt . . . summer . . . peaceful . . . sittin' on the grass . . . me with my arm around her . . . thinkin', peaceful . . . she says to me . . . (*Changes his posture, now in imitation of Dixie Cups Landry.*) 'A lot of people wonder why I wear cotton underpants.'

**Archie**   What?

**George**   I swear ta Christ, Arch! Out'ta nowhere this broad is tellin' me a lot of people wonder why she wears cotton underpants.

**Archie**   What?

**George**   I swear ta Christ, Arch! Outta nowhere this broad is tellin' me a lot of people wonder why she wears cotton underpants.

**Archie**   You're makin' this up.

**George**   On my mother's grave . . .

**Archie**   Ax Laundry's sister? (**George** *nods affirmatively.*) I'll be dipped . . . (*Looks up.*) What happened after?

**George**   After she said that? (*Smiles.*) Well . . . (*Pauses.*) The good part. I says, 'How come?' And she says, 'How come a lot people wonder? Or how come I wear them?' (*Pauses, confidentially.*) 'How come you wear 'em?' I ask . . . quietlike . . . serious. (*Pauses.*) 'Ask me nicely,' she says. So I do. 'How come you wear cotton underpants, Mary Ellen?' I ask. She looks up, pokerface . . . (*Imitates her*) 'So *it* can breathe,' she says. 'So *it* can breathe.' (*Pauses, laughing, mock* *disgust.*) Imagine, huh? Straight out, no shame, thinks this is funny. Ax Landry: his sister.

**Archie**    Dumb fuck. (*Standing, shaking leg.*) C'mon, George, let's shake a leg. Grab the roller, will ya'? (*They slot roller into front of baler to facilitate unloading of bale.*)

**George** (*moves to the baler; works*)    I, personally, would never take out a Woburn girl, even if she was the Pope's niece.

**Archie**    There isn't a one of them that washes herself properly.

**George**    They never learned properly . . .

**Archie**    It's all in the bringing up.

**George**    You said a mouthful.

**Archie**    The manners. The washing and the scrubbing . . .

**George**    The don't talk back to your parents . . .

**Archie**    The mind your manners . . .

**George**    The go to bed early and get up early.

**Archie**    The you mind your tongue around your mother and your sistahs . . .

**George**    The honor thy father . . .

**Archie**    The honor thy father . . . (*Pauses.*) I do agree with you there, George. The honor thy father's the thing. (*Pauses; lost in memory. Then, quietly.*) Jesus . . . I never figured when I was twelve and doin' this, that twenty/twenty-five years later I'd still be here, you know . . . doing this.

**George**    You could be doin' worse.

**Archie**    Oh, yuh? What! (*Laughs. He rolls hand truck to base of roller truck.*) Let's shake a leg here, huh? (*He shakes his leg, doing the 'shake a leg' joke a second time. He goes behind baler to shove bale forward and out of baler.*)

**George** (*calls out to* **Archie**)   You always had the sense of humor, Arch. Even when you weren't funny . . . (*He 'shoulders' bale; waits for* **Archie**'s *help.*)

**Archie** (*runs to* **George**. *Together, they guide bale down roller track to hand truck. As they unload the bale, they chatter*) Careful . . .

**George**   Careful . . .

**Archie**   Got it?

**George**   Yuh, yuh . . . let her go . . . Careful!

**Archie**   Careful!

**George**   Right. I got her! (**Archie** *rolls hand truck to line-up of bales; hurls bale forward and off hand truck, into stock. Then* **Archie** *gets two beers from locker.*)

**Archie**   Bury the roller. (**George** *replaces roler under baler, out of the way.*) Seven down, one to go . . . After this one, we got the over-issue bale, then we just got ta make the crap clean-up bale, George. Nothin' loose can be left in sight lyin' around. My Uncle Max goes apeshit if it ain't tidy when he gets in here, mornin's . . . So's anything here that isn't part of the building and don't have the strength to run away, up and in the baler! Like this . . . and *this* . . . *Oopp* . . . (**Archie** *moves to* **George**, *pretending he's going to throw him up and into the baler.* **George** *rolls backwards into baler, giggling nervously.* **Archie** *has carried two beers with him. He shakes* **George**'s *can.*) Little reward for you, George.

**George**   Yo, thanks, Arch. Little wet for the whistle . . . (*He flips can open; it explodes spraying* **George** *with beer.* **George** *is delighted.*) Heyyy!

**Archie**   Early show for you, kiddo! Lower the gate, Georgie. (**George** *lowers gate. They drink beer a while, tired, but pleased to be one another.*)

**George**   Where's this load goin'?

**Archie**   Fitchburg. Felulah's Mill.

**George**    Wicked lot'ta drivin', huh?

**Archie**    Oh, yuh, wicked. My uncle's outta here by four in the mornin' . . . He hits Fitchburg by six or seven, gets unloaded by maybe eight, back here by ten, maybe ten-thirty. It's no fuckin' life for humans, I can tell ya that.

**George**    I never liked Fitchburg.

**Archie**    Fitchburg never liked you, George.

**George**    Bunch of boozers.

**Archie**    The worst.

**George**    Can't be trusted.

**Archie**    All cons and ex-cons.

**George**    They'd steal yo'r eyeteeth.

**Archie**    Fillings and all.

**George**    That's the truth.

**Archie**    When's the last time we seen each other, George? Before the funeral? Three years ago?

**George**    Nearly, at the reunion.

**Archie**    At the Fifteenth?

**George**    Yup.

**Archie**    Shit, time flies.

**George**    So, ah, where're ya takin' the widow for supper? Hazelwood?

**Archie**    That's for me to know and you to find out!

**George**    Whoa!

**Archie**    I'd love ta bullshit with you all night, but I've got to get this over-issue bale done and get out of here . . . OK?

**George** *sips his beer, slowly, happily. He sits back in the reclining chair, reclining . . . certainly not working)*  I'm enjoyin' this workin' with ya, Arch. I kid you not! This is enjoyable . . .

**Archie**   Oh, yuh? Well, get to work! (*They load paper into the baler a while.*) Well, ya know, George, sometimes, it's life's tragedies that bring people closer than life's joys . . .

**George**   Well said, Arch . . .

**Archie**   I ain't finished.

**George**   Sorry.

**Archie**   Sometimes, George, it's the tragedy more than the joys of life that brings two guys like you and me back into close contact.

**George**   Yup, you were sayin' that . . .

**Archie**   I mean, we've had our differences over the years, haven't we?

**George**   Oh, sure . . . Many differences, Arch . . . (*They pass each other carrying bundles to baler. Neither seems to take notice of what the other is saying.*)

**Archie**   I mean, I've really *hated* you, George . . . and with due cause . . . but when guys like us share the tragedy that we just have . . .

**George**   Oh, *I* see! You mean losin' Spike the Loon as we did . . .

**Archie**   I never like hearin' people say 'losin'' when they mean somebody died. It always seemed dumb ta me. Like when Pa died, and people'd say, 'Jees, Archie, you lost your Pa . . .' and I'd think ta myself: Do they mean I lost him like in Filene's Bargain Basement kinda thing?

**George**   Yuh, I guess. Just sayin' d-e-a-t-h out loud is kinda morbid, though . . .

**Archie**   You got ta be able ta take the bad with the very bad . . . that's life . . .

**George**    I s'pose. There's the morbid with the very morbid . . .

**Archie**    Right. The way Spike the Loon died was very morbid . . .

**George**    Gives me the willies . . .

**Archie**    Spike the Loon worked for me and my Uncle Max, right here in this shop, ever since he flunked out ta Salem State . . .

**George**    No great brain there . . .

**Archie**    Why? Yo got the cancer cure figured out?

**George**    I was just sayin' Spike the Loon wasn't any genius . . .

**Archie**    He was a friend.

**George**    I thought you couldn't stand him?

**Archie**    That's only recent years . . .

**George**    Oh . . .

**Archie**    See, George, you got ta live each day like it was your last . . .

**George**    I dunno . . .

**Archie**    I know. That is an ancient Oriental philosophy. I heard it on WBZ, Sunday night . . . call-in show . . .

**George**    Japs called in?

**Archie** (*glares at* **George**, *angrily*)    Jesus, you can be one aggravating son of a bitch, George. What I'm tryin' ta do here is ta give you a compliment, but you're makin' it damn near impossible . . .

**George**    Sorry, Arch . . .

**Archie** (*'toasts' him with beer can raised*)    Look, I woulda be'n in real trouble gettin' this load out for my uncle for tomorrow, what with Spike the Loon dead and all . . . but

. . . who's here ta help, no questions asked? Not a stranger, but a former best buddy, 'cause that is life. Georgie K. Ferguson, townie and friend from his toes to his limp pecker to the top of his Boston Bruins stocking cap, right? . . . This former best buddy looks across to Archie Crisp at the funeral of their mutual lifelong friend and co-worker, Spike the Loon, and asks if there is anything he can do ta help out at the shop. And I says 'yes' and here he is . . . helpin' . . . Now that is worth more ta me than any rich bitch from Wakefield's Park section or Stoneham's Spot Pond district, and that is the God's-honest!

**George** (*sips and tips his beer*)   I'm drinkin' ta that, Archie.

**Archie**   Hop in, George. (**George** *hops into the baler.*)

**George**   I personally ain't be'n that close ta death before . . . I said the 'D' word. (*Crosses himself.*) 'Course there was a time I did stay too long under water . . .

**Archie**   Takin' a swim in the lake?

**George**   Takin' a bath, in the tub . . . (*Pauses.*) I was little, (*Pauses.*) Trying to beat my brother's record. (*Pauses.*) We were quite competitive . . . with one another. (*Pauses.*) Takin' a bath. (*Pauses.*) That was about as close as I've come to it, I suppose I watched my dog die . . . Vergil . . . my cocker . . . I watched him die. That was something to see . . . four hours it took . . . Four hours and twenty-two minutes . . . (*Pauses.*) He died by the clock . . . in the pantry . . . (*Pauses.*) I watched *that* . . . (*Pauses.*) God damn. God damn . . .

**Archie**   I remember Vergil. Nice. Nice . . .

**George**   Hit by a '51 Studebaker. Squashed.

**Archie**   I remember . . .

**George**   '51 Studies looked the same front and back . . . You couldn't tell whether they were coming or going. Vergil probably got confused.

**Archie**   No doubt.

**George**    God damn.

**Archie**    Nice little mutt.

**George**    They went bankrupt, too, those cars. They don't make 'em any more. Gone! Off the face of the fucking earth!

**Archie**    Not much of an idea, even then.

**George**    It would've be'n one thing, ya know, if he'd died right off the bat. But four hours and twenty-two minutes of painful excruciation? And for *what*, I ask you? For goddamn *what*? Studebaker cars go totally fucking bankrupt and that is *it*, right? I mean, Vergil is gone and so is the entire *brand*! This is beyond fucking ironic and tragic! This is definitely Robert Frost-your-balls/seek out and find Studebaker himself and *run him down*! Am I right on this?

**Archie**    The good with the bat, George. Only natural. But you've got ta move on from it. You can't dwell on it. It's all a part of life. Part of life. (**Margy Palumbo** *enters at the loading platform, behind the baler, far upstage, looking about nervously, confused.*)

**Margy** (*softly*)    Archie Crisp?

**George** (*stays in the baler, looks, taunts* **Archie** *in grade-school way*)    Hey, Archie, *somebody's* here! (*Sees* **Margy**.) Hey, Arch, look who's here . . .

**Archie**    I see her! I see her! (*He runs grabs a towel; wipes ink smears and dirt from his skin. He pulls his suit jacket on over sleeveless undershirt. He is in a panic, trying to look presentable. He grabs his watch from locker shelf.*) Christ, it's five-pah'st-six! We pissed away an hour! (*He calls out to* **Margy**.) Just a minute!

**George** (*hides in baler, peering out at* **Margy**)    Jesus, Arch, she got *old*!

**Archie** (*upstage*)    Shhh. C'mon, huh, George . . . Shut it, huh. She can hear and all . . . (*Calls out to* **Margy**.) Hey, Margy, down here . . . (*Worried; to* **George**.) Mind your language, OK?

**George**    Sure, Arch, sure . . . no sweat . . . *no fuckin' sweat!*
(**Margy** *enters baling-press area; stands facing* **Archie** *and*
**George**. *She wears a full black skirt, long black coat-sweater, full
peasant-cut blouse, overbelted. She wears driving [eye]glasses, which
she will soon remove. She carries a purse. Her car keys are still clutched
in her hand.*)

**Archie**    Hey, Marg.

**Margy**    Hello, Archie.

**Archie**    How's it goin'? Long time, huh? How long since
we saw each other – before Mal's the other day?

**Margy**    Fifteen years, maybe, huh?

**Archie**    Not that long. I saw you in Santuro's, buyin' subs
. . . maybe ten/twelve years ago, after you, uh, lost your
husband . . . You came back up here for the funeral and all.
You remember seein' me?

**Margy**    Did we talk?

**Archie**    To each other? No . . . You remember George
Ferguson?

**Margy** (*sees* **George**; *freezes. She stares blankly for a moment;
doesn't seem to recognize* **George**)    No, I'm sorry, I don't. Nice
to meet you.

**George**    We went to school together.

**Margy**    We did?

**George**    Sure. All twelve years. Georgie Ferguson? Gould
Street? Up near the Stoneham line?

**Margy** (*smiles at* **George**, *blankly*)    No. Sorry. (*To* **Archie**.)
Nice to see you again, Archie. Nice to see you.

**Archie**    Nice yourself, Marg. (*There is a short silence, which*
**George** *will break.*)

**George** (*still in baler*)    There was a squirt-gun fight in second grade and you got hit in the face and you cried and told Mrs Linder . . . you remember?

**Margy**    I . . . I think so.

**George**    That was me. I squirted you.

**Margy**    On purpose?

**George**    Accident.

**Margy**    I remember.

**George**    George Ferguson. Second row, third seat in from the left . . . nearly in the middle . . .

**Margy**    Yes, I think so . . . Georgie Ferguson . . . I think so . . . (*She smiles at* **George**.)

**George**    Great ta see ya again, Margie. How's it goin'? (*There is another short silence.*) How's Swede doin'?

**Archie**    Hey, George! C'mon, huh?

**Margy**    Swede's dying. They don't think he'll make it through the night, tonight. He's dying . . . That's why I'm here, right now . . .

**George**    In town?

**Margy**    Hmmm?

**George**    Why you're here in Wakefield, or why you're here at Archie's Uncle Max's junk shop?

**Archie**    Don't mind him . . .

**Margy**    I've been over at Melrose-Wakefield Hospital since eight, this morning . . . (*Pauses.*) They've got him on a respirator . . . (*Pauses.*) I told the doctor I'd get back there by eight-thirty or so. He's sleeping now . . .

**George**    Swede?

**Margy**    Mmm. Swede.

**Archie**   Well, now . . . that's a tragedy . . . (**Margy** *and* **George** *both look at* **Archie** *waiting for his move.*) Well . . . his age, huh? Death: That's the worst . . . (*He looks at his shoes, silently.*)

**George** (*confidently; smiling*)   I remember Swede when he could see . . . (*There is another short silence.*)

**Archie** (*stares* **George** *down. Sits by* **Margy** *on bale*)   So, Margy . . . how're the kids doin'?

**Margy**   Fine.

**Archie**   How many you got now?

**Margy**   Same as ever.

**Archie**   Five?

**Margy**   Two. (*Pauses.*) Rosie and Raymond.

**Archie**   Little Cootie?

**Margy**   I beg your pardon? . . .

**Archie**   Your son?

**Margy** (*smiles quizzically*)   I don't understand.

**George** (*moves a bale downstage center and sits*)   Your boy. Your son. Archie thinks you were married to Cootie Webber . . .

**Archie**   Wasn't that him?

**Margy**   My husband?

**Archie**   Yuh.

**Margy**   Who is Cootie Webber?

**Archie**   He wasn't your ex?

**Margy**   Edgar Burke . . .

**Archie**   . . . Your husband?

**Margy**   Passed away twelve years ago . . .

**Archie**    Sorry to hear that.

**Margy**    The children were still babies . . . Raymond was only three months old; Rosie was two and a half . . .

**George**    You didn't waste much time, did you?

**Margy**    Hmmm?

**George**    Havin' the kiddoes: You didn't waste your time.

**Archie**    What are you sayin', George?

**George**    I was just telling Margy here, that I could see she didn't waste any of her valuable time . . . waiting to get right down to have the little ones. She got right down to it . . . (*To* **Margy**.) Didn't cha?

**Margy**    We waited two years.

**George**    How old are you now?

**Margy**    Nearly thirty-seven . . . soon.

**George** (*walks around space while calculating*)    Twelve years since he died . . . add two for the kid is fourteen . . . plus nine months for the being pregnant and all . . . that's fifteen . . . plus the two you waited . . . is seventeen . . . that makes you about twenty when you hooked up with him . . .

**Archie**    You didn't go to college?

**George**    I thought you were in the college course?

**Archie**    You didn't get accepted?

**George**    You change your plans or what?

**Margy**    I went to college.

**George**    For just a year?

**Archie**    Junior college or a regular full college?

**Margy**    Boston State . . .

**George**    Boston Teachers?

**Margy**   Well . . . yes.

**Archie**   You a teacher?

**Margy**   No . . .

**Archie**   You had to quit teaching when you were having your baby, huh?

**Margy**   No, I finished. We waited . . .

**George**   Oh. Right.

**Archie**   Right.

**George**   I couldn't figure how you could've done both, ya know what I mean. Teachers can't have babies . . .

**Margy**   Now they can . . .

**George**   Uh uh.

**Margy**   They can. The rule changed. They changed the rule.

**Archie**   Is that a fact?

**Margy**   It is.

**Archie**   I wouldn't want my teacher to be having her own children . . .

**George**   Me, neither . . . (*Sits on bale.*)

**Archie**   They've got no need . . . (**Margy** *looks at* **Archie***; quizzically.*) They've got all us kids, anyway: you, me, George . . .

**George**   Swede, Cootie, Delbert . . . (*Pauses.*) What did you say his name was? (**Margy** *looks at* **George***, blankly.*) Your husband's.

**Margy**   Edgar's?

**George**   Yuh.

**Margy**   Edgar's name?

**George**    Yuh.

**Margy**    You want to know what Edgar's *name* was?

**George**    Yuh.

**Margy**    Edgar's name was Edgar.

**George** (*annoyed; a childish tone*)    His *lah'st* name!

**Margy**    Oh. I see. You mean Edgar's *sur*name. Your question was unclear. (*Pauses.*) Burke.

**Archie**    Related to Doctor Burke?

**Margy**    Oh, yes, Doctor Burke . . . top of Prospect Street . . . Nope, uh uh. Edgar came from different Burkes.

**Archie**    Greenwood?

**Margy**    Uh uh. Edgar's family's from Woodville District . . .

**George**    Oh, yuh? *Burke?*

**Margy**    Why do you *doubt* me, George? The name was Burke.

**George**    What did the father do?

**Margy**    Edgar's? Oh, well, he worked . . . head of the lake.

**George**    Filling station?

**Margy**    Uh, no . . .

**George**    Lakeside Furniture?

**Margy**    Cemetery.

**Archie**    Oh, yuh? Doin' what?

**Margy**    Well, uh, lawn care.

**Archie**    Oh, yuh? Lawn care, huh?

**George**    You mean graves and all?

**Margy**   Well, yuh, that, too . . .

**George**   Lawn care and digging kind of thing?

**Margy**   I guess.

**Archie**   Oh, yuh?

**George**   Willies: That's what this gives me. I swear to Christ!

**Margy**   Hmmm?

**Archie**   What are you driving these days, Marg?

**Margy**   Me?

**Archie**   A Chrysler LeBaron?

**Margy**   No.

**George**   A Pontiac Monte Carlo?

**Margy**   No . . .

**George**   Maybe one of those Jap jobs! A Toyota? A Nissan?

**Archie**   Mitsubishi?

**George**   Suburu!

**Archie**   Mazda!

**George**   Isuzu!

**Margy**   My husband's father's car . . . That's what I'm driving: my husband's father's car.

**Archie**   No kidding?

**Margy**   Ancient.

**George**   Model-T sort of thing?

**Archie**   Something classic?

**Margy**   '51 Studebaker . . . two door . . . (*Smile.*) Powder blue . . . (*Pauses; smiles again.*) You can't tell the front from the back . . . (*Pauses.*) I can't, anyway . . . I'm always opening the trunk to check the oil. That sort of thing. Wicked funny . . . odd . . . unique, though, if you like that sort of thing . . .

**George**    Do you?

**Margy**    Hmmm?

**George**    Like that sort of thing?

**Margy**    The Studie? Sure. I love it. Makes me feel . . . nice. (*She giggles.*) I'm always opening the trunk to check the oil . . .

**Archie**    Was he kinda skinny?

**Margy**    The antecedent to the pronoun 'he' is not precisely clear, Archie. Do you mean my father-in-law? Was my father-in-law skinny?

**Archie**    Well, no. Your *husban'* . . . Is your husbin' skinny?

**Margy**    Is my husband skinny? My husband has been dead and in his grave for twelve years, Archie! Don't you find the question 'Is he skinny?' rather *grim*?!

**Archie**    I didn't mean 'is', I meant 'was' . . .

**Margy**    Oh, was . . .

**Archie**    . . . In high school . . .

**Margy**    Was my husband skinny in high school. (*Pauses.*) Oh, I see . . . (*Considers this.*) I suppose. He was more tall than skinny.

**George**    He play ball?

**Archie**    Naw, I woulda known him . . .

**George**    Basketball, I mean . . .

**Archie**    I woulda known him, George. I knew everybody.

**George**    Was he definitely our year, Marg?

**Margy**    Definitely.

**George**   I'll hav'ta look it up . . . In the yearbook.

**Archie**   How come you never came to any of our reunions?

**Margy**   Our what?

**Archie**   Our reunions.

**George**   Our reunions.

**Margy**   Oh, well . . . I just didn't.

**George**   Didn't want to.

**Margy**   Yes. I didn't want to.

**Archie**   How come? They were pretty rich . . .

**Margy**   I'll just bet they were!

**George**   They were good . . .

**Archie**   They were fun . . .

**George**   Good to see the old gang sort of thing . . . (*Gets up to play with* **Archie** *at centre.*)

**Archie**   Makes you laugh.

**George**   Shadow Flint, with his weird hats . . .

**Archie**   'Longest Hair? Fred who's'its . . . (*He moves toward* **George**.)

**George**   'Longest Distance Traveled?' . . . Arthur, the Jew . . .

**Archie**   'Most Kids?' . . . Remember who?

**George**   Maureen . . .

**Archie**   And Whopp'ah . . . Every reunion . . .

**George**   Started right away . . .

**Archie**   Spike the Loon used ta always say Whopp'ah nailed Maureen first time while they were still in their caps and gowns . . .

**George**  'Most Kids' by a mile . . . Every reunion . . .

**Archie**  Wicked devout Catholics . . .

**George**  Makes you laugh.

**Archie** (*laughing*)    You missed a couple of great ones, Marg . . . The Fifth . . .

**George**  The Tenth was better . . .

**Archie**  The Tenth was good, too . . . The Fifteenth was great! . . . (*Laughs.*) The Twentieth comin' up soon, too . . .

**Margy**  Maybe I'll peek in . . .

**Archie**  You got ta see it ta believe it . . .

**George**  Unbelievable . . .

**Archie**  Everybody lookin' awful . . .

**George**  Beer bellies . . .

**Archie**  Bald . . .

**George**  Some dead, even . . . (**Archie** *stares at* **George**; *a pause.*) Sorry, Marg, huh?

**Archie**  He didn't mean anything. Did you, Georgie?

**Margy**  It's OK.

**George**  I'm really sorry . . .

**Margy**  It's *OK* . . . (*Pauses.*) *Ree*ally . . . (*Pauses.*) I'll need a date.

**Archie**  For the Twentieth? (*She smiles.*) Should be no sweat for you, Marg . . . (*He smiles.*) Good-lookin' girl . . .

**George**  Got her own car and all . . .

**Archie**  No sweat at all. Not at all . . .

**George**  I wouldn't mind takin' ya myself, Marg . . .

**Margy** (*darkly*)    Oh, OK, George. It's a date . . .

**George**    Hey! Well! Great!

**Archie**    That s'posed ta be funny?

**George**    Naw . . . just kidding. Arch . . .

**Archie**    I don't find that kind of kiddin' too ho-ho-that's-rich funny, George . . .

**George**    Meant no harm, Arch . . .

**Archie**    *Not funny now, not funny then* . . .

**George**    C'mon, Arch . . .

**Archie** (*goes to* **George** *to confront him*)    What is it? In your blood? Or *what*? You out of control or som'pin'? Or *what*?

**George**    You startin' in again, Arnold?

**Archie** (*to* **Margy**)    I go back a ways with this one, Marg . . . (*Pauses.*) We got a history. (*Pauses.*) All the ways back to West Ward School . . . I shoulda known then, I swear ta Christ! (*Pauses.*) A history. George Ferguson messing with Archie Crisp's girls . . . Can't find none of his own. He's got to move in on his buddy like . . . you follow me, Marg? (*Pauses. Looks at* **Margy**, *at bales.*) I mean, don't be flattered none if this one makes a move on you, 'cause it's not that he's likin' you any . . . (*Pauses.*) The fact is, he made some wicked awful remarks just before you came in through the doors, didn't ya, Georgie?

**George**    *C'mon,* Arch!

**Archie**    *Bullllshit,* buddy! *Bullllshit!*

**George** (*to* **Margy**)    Here we go.

**Archie**    First grade. I'm seeing Esther what's'it. Walking her home from school every day. What do you think I find out? This one here: he's sending her notes. Notes. He's slipping them to her behind my back . . . Six to eight of 'em fell out ta her reader . . . *Dick and Jane* and six to eight goddamned love letters from old George K. Ferguson . . . (*Pauses; then angrily.*) God damn it, Georgie. *God damn it!*

**George**    This was a resolved matter. This was an incident that was put to bed.

**Archie** (*at* **George**)    I'm wakin' it up, George. I'm callin' it right down for breakfast . . .

**Margy** (*calls out*)    Excuse meee! (**Archie** *and* **George** *turn to her; their altercation postponed.*) Listen, you guys . . . you two should be alone. You two seem . . . busy. I should . . . well . . . *go.*

**Archie**    What's this? (**Margy** *goes to locker, gets her coat, pocketbook; moves toward door, pausing only to say her goodbye.* **Archie** *stands stunned.*)

**Margy**    It was lovely to see you both, again, really, but I do think enough in one lifetime is actually *enough* . . . so, I'll just be moseying along . . . (**Archie** *rushes to loading doors, stands and blocks* **Margy**'s *exit. He talks to her, plaintively, sincerely.*)

**Archie**    Oh, God, please, don't go, Margy. Please. Stay . . . (*To* **George**.) I'll kill you, George. (*Leans against door, blocking* **Margy**'s *intended exit. He forces her forward, downstage*) Please stay, Marg. Please don't go. I was so happy to be seein' you like this . . . to be goin' out with you and all. Please . . . don't go. He's not my friend, Marg. Georgie K. Ferguson is no friend of Archie Crisp's. Honest ta God. I'm not like that at all. Don't you worry none. (*To* **George**.) I'll kill you, George. I swear to God, I'll kill you! (*To* **Margy**.) Please stay with me. Don't go. *Please?*

**Margy**    I don't think so, Archie, really . . . I mean, well, *why?*

**Archie**    Because it's *us!* Because we haven't talked . . . we haven't, I dunno', *be'n together yet!* Jesus, Margy, I think about you all the time. I mean, gawd! I've be'n *waitin' and waitin' and waitin'* for tonight, and here it is, and, oh, God, please . . . don't go. Stay. you got nothin' to worry about here . . . with us . . . (*Flashes a look at* **George**.) It's OK. I swear to you. Please? Stay?

**Margy** (*looks at* **Archie**. *Pauses. Looks at* **George**. *Pauses. Speaks to* **Archie**, *softly*)   OK, Archie. I'll stay. I'll do that for you . . .

**Archie**   That's good. That's great. (*To* **George**.) She's staying. (*To* **Margy**.) That's really *so incredibly great*! (**Margy** *hands* **Archie** *her coat. He is puzzled for a moment, but then realizes that the coat is to be replaced on the hanger/hook. He does this. Turns, smiles at* **Margy**, *awkwardly*. **Archie** *is delighted*. **Margy** *looks about the room, silently. She looks at* **George**; *smiles. She looks at* **Archie**; *smiles; speaks*.)

**Margy**   What's his 'K' for?

**Archie**   Huh?

**Margy**   His 'K' . . . you mentioned a 'K'. I have a vague memory of an extremely nasty little guy with a 'K' in the middle. What's it for? (**George** *moans*.)

**Archie** (*giggles*)   Tell her.

**George**   C'mon, huh, Arch?

**Archie**   You tell her, or I'll tell her. You got a choice.

**George**   Kermit.

**Margy**   No kidding?

**Archie** (*to* **George**, *teasing*)   Kermie, Kermie . . .

**George**   C'mon, Archie.

**Archie**   Kermie, Kermie, Kermie . . .

**George**   God damn it, Archie, c'mon . . .

**Archie**   Kermie, Kermie, Kermie, Kermie . . .

**George** (*throws a punch, while* **Archie** *sidesteps, laughing*)   I said COME OFF IT, ARCHIE! (*Work at baler*.)

**Archie** (*laughing, moves across the room away from* **George** *to* **Margy**)   I love a laugh.

**Margy** (*a sudden memory*)    Esther *Larkin*: that was the name of your first girlfriend. She lived on the corner of Prospect and Elm. Pigtails.

**Archie**    Yup. That's her.

**Margy**    Edgar went with Esther Larkin.

**Archie**    Who's Edgar?

**George**    Her *husband*. (*Throws paper into baler.*)

**Archie**    Oh. (*Smiles.*) Too much alcohol. Rots the brain.

**George**    You can say *that* again!

**Archie**    They call this one 'Chief Hollow Leg' . . . counta there's no end in sight for the precious brew . . .

**George**    Me? That's a laugh! This one, Marg: he's invested his life savings in Tap-a-Keg . . . (*Laughs.*)

**Archie**    She don't know what you're talkin' about.

**George** (*to* **Margy**)    Tap-a-Keg's out on Route One. You've never been?

**Margy**    Yes, George, I must confess: in the matter of Tap-a-Keg, I have never been.

**George**    We could shoot down there one night, together, Marg. In your powder-blue Studie.

**Archie**    You makin' another move here?

**George**    What da ya mean?

**Archie**    What do you mean 'What da ya mean?' (*Imitates* **George**.) We can just shoot down there together, Marg . . . in yo'r powder-blue Studie-doo . . . (*Imitation ceases.*) *Bullllllshit*, buddy! *Bullllshit!* That is a definite move you're makin' on my supper date and I don't like what I'm seein' at *all! Not at all!*

**George**    This one's seein' moves that aren't bein' made.

**Archie** (*pulls rank*)   Why don't you knock off, George? I can finish up here . . .

**George** (*hurt; defensively*)   I'll knock off, but you won't get your bales wired or weighed or loaded on no truck for no uncle by no ha'pahst four in the mornin', and that's a definite *fact* . . . less you're figurin' Margy here's gonna do some of your work for you.

**Margy**   I wouldn't mind.

**Archie** (*laughs*)   Woman your size wouldn't get much pressed, Marg.

**George** (*laughing as well*)   This baler wants beef . . . like me and Arch . . .

**Archie**   Bales weigh eight hundred pounds . . . some of 'em . . .

**George**   Minimum . . .

**Archie**   Takes weight and muscle . . .

**George**   Beef . . .

**Archie**   Be'n doin' this for years . . .

**George**   Archie's got a skill.

**Archie**   This is *man's* work.

**George**   Man's work.

**Margy**   I wouldn't mind helping.

**Archie**   Doin' what?

**Margy**   Why not?

**George**   Why not, Arch?

**Archie**   OK, no reason. Work beats just watching, huh?

**Margy**   Working certainly does beat just watching, Archie.

**George** (*checking out* **Margy**'s *breasts*)    Take your coat-sweater off, Marg . . . (*He reaches for her coat-sweater, staring.* **Archie** *glares at* **George**, *staring him down.* **Margy** *smiles at each of them; slips out of her coat. To* **Archie**; *a child's defense.*) I didn't mean anything there . . . (**Margy** *hangs her sweater on a coat-hook, upstage of the baler. She turns and faces* **George** *and* **Archie**. *She stares at them, directly. She will now tell a story that is patently sexual.* **George** *and* **Archie** *will leer at her, somewhat dumbfounded, not only by what she says, but by her direct staring, and her direct smiling. By the end of her story,* **Margy** *will be in control of the men.*)

**Archie**    Here are some gloves. Grab a bundle, toss it on up to Kermit, and you're on the clock. (**Margy** *goes into position; begins.*)

**Margy**    We used to have a four-on-the-floor stick shift. Old black DeSoto. Edgar said I'd never be able to press the stick down. It took a lot of weight and muscle. Beef. (*Pauses.*) I did it. I took the stick in my hand and I kind of stood over it. All my might . . . I pushed . . . it gave . . . the gears meshed . . . We jerked forward. Burned rubber. (*Pauses.*) First to fourth in fifteen seconds and that's no bull. We blasted off. Rubber all over the road. (*Pauses.*) Women can drive, when they want to. You'd be surprised. (*Moves to* **Archie**, *turns, beside him; faces baler.*) So? How does this thing work? (**Archie** *and* **George** *are dumbstruck.* **Archie** *breaks the silence.*)

**Archie**    I take a sizable bundle in my hand and load in from the front for a while . . . Then I pull myself up on to the lip and throw down from the top till she's ready . . . Then I start my down-strokes . . . pressing the shaft-head there by jiggling this wheel . . . squashing her down, notch by notch, which forces the shaft-head lower and lower. Once things get goin' good, I use long, smooth strokes, till she comes into shape. When the belly of the bale's as flat as she's ever gonna be, I wire her up, tie her off, and I'm on to the next one.

**Margy** (*after a pause; smiles*)   That is . . . impressive, Archie. I am . . . impressed. (**Archie** *moves next to* **Margy**, *talks to her with some degree of confidence.*)

**Archie**   In what grade did Edgar go with Esther?

**Margy**   Edgar and Esther? Go with? Oh, well . . . ninth grade.

**Archie**   I sure am a blank on your husband, Marg.

**Margy**   Edgar wasn't very loud . . . not back then. Not recently, either, I suppose . . .

**George**   Couldn't'a be'n . . . (**Margy** *turns, looks at* **George**.) Loud. Couldn't'a be'n. I would'a heard of him, if he'd'a made a noise.

**Archie** (*to* **George**)   What's the matter with you?

**George**   What do you mean?

**Archie**   What do you *mean*, 'What do you mean?' (*He moves near bales.* **Margy** *counters to look at baler. Angrily.*) This girl is talking about a deceased husband, George. What you've got here is a sympathetic moment and you're talkin' really low class . . . *no* class! (*Pauses.*) Sometimes, I'm truly embarrassed to have be'n your friend . . . (*To* **Margy**.) George Ferguson and I were formerly close friends, Marg . . . Not for years. (*Pauses; to* **George**.) When you're a kid you take what's in the neighborhood. You don't think about it: you take it. You were in the neighborhood, so I'd figured we were friends and hung out with you. I mean, don't flatter yourself none, George. Now that I see you and I'm not a kid . . . well . . . I'm hardly comin' on to you like a friend, right? *You're* the one's runnin' over here to *me* to help . . . not the reverse.

**George**   Just what the hell're you sayin', Arch? You wouldn't help me if the chips were down? . . .

**Archie** (*quickly*)   If the chips were down for you, George, I wouldn't be runnin' to you out of friendship. I'd run to you, alright, but it would be out of pity . . . out of feelin' sorry for

you, yes, but certainly never . . . not ever . . . out of
friendship. (*Pauses.*) You understand that? You follow? (*To*
**Margy**.) They see sugar where there's salt: that kind of
thing.

**Margy** (*cuts **Archie** off*)   Aren't you getting hungry,
Archie?

**George** (*whoops as might a large bird*)   Whooooaa-a, Archie!
Your supper date's gettin' anxious here. Ohoooo-aaahhh
oooooo!

**Archie**   What are you? Soft in the head?

**George**   You getting a little hollow in the stomach,
Margy?

**Archie**   You're getting hollow in the head, George!

**George**   Munch, munch, hey, Marg?

**Archie**   What are you? Talking dirty now?

**George**   This one can't take a joke at all, Marg.

**Archie**   I'll bust your squash!

**George** (*laughing, as he shadowboxes with **Archie***)   . . . Got
no sense of humor, Archie! You got none!

**Archie**   This'll put a smile on your face! (*He tries to butt*
**George** *with the top of his head; misses and falls forward against*
*bale.* **George** *laughs.*) What are you laughing at? (*He tries to*
*butt* **George** *once again. This time,* **George** *sidesteps* **Archie**,
*who races past* **George** *and falls on to the dune-like mound of loose*
*newspaper, upstage.* **George** *whoops with laughter.*) What's so
goddam funny? (**Archie** *stands, goes to baler and slaps its side;*
*then he goes to a bale and kicks it.*) God damn. God damn. God
damn! (*He goes to* **Margy**, *looks at her.* **Margy** *laughs.*) What
are *you* laughing at?

**Margy**   You. Butting your head in the air like a goat . . .

**George** (*thrilled*)   A goat, Arch, a goat! She remembers! A
goat!

**Archie** (*to* **George**)   I'll kill you!

**Margy**   You always did that, Arch, even when we were in first grade. you butted your head in the air and made little goat-like noises . . . (**George** *giggles, happily.*)

**Archie** (*to* **Margy**)   I don't like this . . . (*He goes to* **George** *and slaps him, with a fierce backhand.*)

**George**   Hey, c'mon, Archie, huh?

**Archie** (*to* **Margy**)   Every time you make a smart remark that runs me down, I'm gonna hurt your friend here. You get me? You follow me?

**George**   No more smart remarks, Marg.

**Margy**   To which smart remark, precisely, do you refer, Archie?

**Archie**   OK . . . (*Slaps* **George**.) *That* one . . . 'precisely' . . .

**George**   *Hey, dammit!*

**Archie** (*holds* **George** *in a hammerlock*)   I got feelin's here, ya' know . . .

**Margy**   OK, Archie. No more smart remarks.

**Archie**   OK, good. (*Lets loose of* **George**.) You're free.

**George** (*sulking; humiliated; he throws paper into the baler. He gets a bundle, loads it into baler as well*)   Let's get some work done. I've got a heavy date tonight and I don't wanna be late.

**Archie** (*laughs*)   You got a heavy what?

**George**   Let's get some work done, OK?

**Archie**   No, no . . . C'mon, Georgie . . . I wanna hear that again: You've got a heavy *what?*

**George** (*quietly*)   I said 'date' . . .

**Archie**   Date? Is that dried fruit? Like a fig?

**George**   Yuh, dried fruit. Like a fig.

**Archie** (*to* **Margy**)   You hear that? George has got to get out ta here count a big fig.

**George**   Yuh. Right. You got it, Arch. I've got to get out ta here count a big fig, so let's get ta packin', OK? (*Turns to* **Archie**, *squares off.*) That OK with you, Arch, if we finish here?

**Archie** (*giggles*)   I thought up a good one! You listening, George? Here it comes. Stay out ta the sun, George, 'cause if you stay in the sun too long, you yourself will be . . . a *dried fruit*. (*He whoops and cackles.*)

**George**   Wicked funny.

**Archie**   *You get it?* (*Chuckling and rasping.*) You get it, George? A dried fruit! *You get it?*

**George**   No, I didn't get it. I'm a Mongolian idiot, so I missed the point. (*Turns away; then in a sudden back.*) A *course*, I got it, ya goddamn goat! What da ya think I am? Thick in the head? You coulda pulled that one on a wood fence, the fence woulda got it. (*Turns away; then in a sudden back.*) *God damn it, Archie! God damn it!* (*Then ever so softly; his feelings are hurt.*) God damn it, Archie. God damn it . . .

**Archie**   What was it you called me? (*Pauses.*) Came in between the 'Mongolian idiot' and the 'wood fence' . . . You remember?

**George**   Uh, uh, I don't.

**Archie**   Starts with a 'G' . . .

**George**   C'mon, Archie . . .

**Archie**   That really pisses me off, ya know that? . . .

**George**   Don't be dumb, Arch . . .

**Archie**   Makes me see red . . .

**George**   Just 'cause I called you Goat?

**Archie**   What am I hearing here?

**George**   Everybody calls you Goat . . .

**Archie**   I'll break your back!

**George**   Goat's as much your name as Archie is . . .

**Archie**   I'll rip your pecker off!

**George**   *Goat is your name, God damn it!*

**Archie**   Oooooo! Ooooo-*ooooo*! (**Archie** *is now choking* **George**.)

**George**   Tell him, Margy! Tell him! Tell him! *Tell him!*

**Margy**   It is, Goat.

**Archie**   I don't like this.

**Margy**   Everybody knows you as Goat . . .

**Archie** (*lets loose of* **George***'s throat*)   I don't like this at all . . .

**Margy**   You've been Goat from the first grade on . . . Arnold . . .

**Archie**   I never liked Arnold, neither . . .

**George**   For God's sakes, uh, Archie . . . Arnold is your God-given name! You were christened Arnold . . . not Goat or Archie . . .

**Archie**   I've always liked Archie . . .

**George**   I can understand that . . . Archie.

**Archie**   I'd rather not be called the other. OK?

**George**   Sure. Sure thing . . . Arch. (*Worries.*) Is Arch OK? Or do you want the whole thing: Arch*ie*?

**Archie**   Arch is fine. Arch is fine. (*Silence.*)

**Margy**   Edgar hated his name. That's why he picked 'Moose' . . .

**George** (*comes the dawn*)    Moose! Moose, for God's sakes, *Moose!*

**Archie** (*the same dawn*)    Moose! Moose Burke! Goddamn. Moose goddamn Burke! Old stiff antlers Moose Burke! How come you didn't say Moose right off the bat? Jez-us, Margy!

**George**    Moose Burke! Hot damn! Moose goddamn Burke! Hot goddamn *damn!*

**Archie**    I remember Moose Burke when he was four . . . No! Three! Little Moosie Burke! (*Cackles.*) Moosie Burke! Little Stiff-Antler Moosie!

**George**    I remember Moose when he could run the hundred in ten-two . . .

**Margy**    That wasn't Edgar . . .

**Archie**    That wasn't Moose? . . .

**George**    What, are you kiddin' me?

**Margy**    That wasn't him at all . . .

**Archie**    No . . . That was Artie What's'it . . . the Jew. He won Longest-Distance-Traveled two three times . . . Skinny . . .

**George**    Artie? Yuh. I think so (*Pauses.*) So who the fuck is Moose? (*Embarrassed.*) Pardon me, Marg, huh? My mouth, huh?

**Archie**    Out ta control . . . like a freight train, huh? Say you're sorry to the lady, huh, George.

**Margy**    I don't mind, really. Really, I don't mind . . .

**Archie**    Let's *hear* it, toilet!

**George**    I said I'm sorry, Arch . . . (**Archie** *glares at* **George**.) OK, OK. I'm sorry, Marg . . . I am.

**Margy**    There's no need.

**Archie**   There's need.

**Margy**   There's no need. None.

**Archie**   You mean that, or are you just bein' nice?

**Margy**   I said there was no need. (*Suddenly angry; snaps at them.*) I said there was no need. Didn't you hear me?

**Archie** (*after an embarrassed moment*)   OK, OK. (*To* **George**.) Take it back, George.

**George**   Huh?

**Archie**   No need. The lady says no need. Take it back.

**George**   You mean the apology? (**Archie** *nods;* **George** *stares.*) You mean I should take back the apology? (**Archie** *nods again.*) This is dumb. (**Archie** *glares.*) You mean like, 'I'm not sorry'? . . . (*He giggles.*) This is truly dumb . . . (*Pauses, straight-faced.*) I am not sorry at all, Marge . . . (*Giggles.*) I said what I said . . . (*Pauses; thinks.*) What'd I say? Oh, yuh. Oh, yuh. I'm not sorry I asked who the fuck Moose was . . . (*He laughs, looks at glaring* **Archie**, *who looks at smiling* **Margy** *and shrugs to* **George**, *who shrugs back to* **Archie** *and giggles.*)

**Margy** (*looks at watch*)   We should think about supper, hmm?

**George**   Me?

**Archie**   Not him.

**George**   Not me: Archie, Marg . . .

**Archie**   Not him: I'm the one you called for supper, not George.

**Margy**   I didn't know George would be with us. George is one of the old gang, right, Archie? We're all in this together, right? All-for-one-one-for-all kinda' thing, right?

**George**   Now, that is real nice of you, Marg.

**Archie**   I don't like this.

**George**    I couldn't accept. (*To* **Archie**.) I didn't accept.

**Archie**    He already has a date. You heard him . . .

**George**    True. True. I do. I do.

**Margy**    With whom?

**George**    Who?

**Margy**    With whom?

**Archie**    With a fig.

**Margy**    With whom, Georgie? Somebody we know? Somebody who might have been a cheerleader? A twirler? A top speller? A class clown? A most-likely-to-succeed? With whom, Georgie, whom? (*Pauses; moves to* **George**.) I am really quite curious, George. Really amazingly so. Strikingly so. I should even say *remarkably* so. (*Pauses; waits a moment, staring at the astonished* **George Ferguson***; then, with a strong, studied Boston accent, she again speaks.*) I'm wicked awful anxious for yo'r answer, George! Let's hear it!

**George** (*stunned*)    What . . . what are you . . . askin'?

**Margy**    Who's your date, George? Who's the lucky . . . piece of fruit?

**George**    I . . . I don't have any, Margy.

**Margy**    Any what, George? The antecedent to your pronoun is somehow quite obscure. Any date? Any fruit? Any what, George, hmmm?

**George**    Any date. I got no date.

**Margy**    A good-looking fellow like you? No date? What is this world coming to? (*Pauses.*) There's a Chinese take-out on Route 28, George, down by the miniature golf. You have money?

**George**    Well, yuh . . . for what?

**Margy**    Moo Shoo Pork and three pancakes . . .

**Archie**   What's going on here?

**Margy**   George is going out for food . . . for the three of us.

**George**   I'm not that hungry . . .

**Archie**   You and I are going out alone, Margy. That's a deal.

**Margy**   George is going out, Archie. Right now. You and I are staying here . . . alone.

**George**   What are you? Planning som'pim' while I'm gone, Margy?

**Margy**   In what sense, George?

**George**   With Archie?

**Margy**   Am I planning som'pin'? With Archie? While you're gone, George? (*Pauses.*) Such as what?

**George**   Oh, I dunno . . . hanky-panky . . .

**Margy**   Am I planning hanky-panky with Archie while you're gone, George? Just maybe I am. (**Margy** *walks, wordlessly, around* **Archie**. *She now stands behind* **Archie**, *who looks at* **Margy** *as though she's just agreed to 'hanky-panky' . . . and then some.*)

**Archie**   Write down our orders, George.

**George**   I don't like this.

**Archie** (*takes pencil and paper*)   You write 'em out, Margy, so's George can just give 'em over to the Chinaman . . . OK?

**Margy** (*thickly accented pronunciation here*)   Sure. (*She takes pad and pencil.*) My husband, Edgar, was an absolute fiend for the Oriental . . . especially Moo Shoo Pork. He loved to roll his own . . .

**George**   How come you like Archie, Margy? How come you picked him, say, over me?

**Archie**   What's this I'm hearing?

**George**   I'm just curious, Arch! No sweat! No sweat here at all, huh? No *suh*!

**Margy**   Picked Archie, George? How come? You mean over all the guys in our little gang?

**George**   Well, over, say, *me*, yuh.

**Margy**   Picked Archie over you, ohhh . . . Well, for one thing, George, I forgot you, altogether. Nothing personal in it, mind you, but you'd just melted into the faceless pack . . . you were specifically forgotten, George. In fact, to this very moment, the best I can do is come up with a very porky, very mean little guy with a middle 'K' like yours, but that couldn't've been you, right? (*Smiles, shrugs.*) As for 'picking' Archie, we bumped into each other at Mal's. I smiled, he smiled. I called him for dinner, he accepted. And that is the long and short of it, George. I am getting quite hungry. I would hate to return to my poor brother's deathbed, unfed. It's a tough enough vigil, as it is. Don't you agree? (*Suddenly angry.*) Don't . . . you . . . agree?

**George** (*after a confused pause*)   Yeh, well, I lost a lot a weight right after senior year. Yuh . . . I did.

**Margy** (*gets her sweater, starts upstage*)   Listen, you guys, I'll go off for dinner, OK? You keep working . . . you stay put. I'll go.

**Archie**   Like hell you will! (*To* **George**.) Like hell she will . . . huh?

**George**   I'll do it.

**Archie**   Right. (*He shoves* **George** *toward door.*)

**Margy**   Nonsense . . . I wouldn't want to split you two up . . .

**George**   No, I'll do it . . . (**Archie** *throws* **George**'s *jacket at him.*)

**Archie**   Go, George!

**George**   I said I would . . . (*Starts to loading door.*) I don't know where. (*To* **Margy**.) Where?

**Margy**   Chinese take-out. Route 28, Stoneham. Is it still there? (*Writes out order.*)

**Archie**   Yup. Chinese place, near the miniature golf . . .

**Margy**   Here, George. Hand this note to the Chinese man at the counter, and, for God's sakes, tip him fifteen per cent! Go now, go, go . . . shoo . . . scat . . .

**Archie**   You heard her!

**George** (*starts to loading door, stops*)   I really hate this . . . (*Starts again to loading doors; stops again.*) A nice girl like you, Margy. Swede'd be pissed . . .

**Archie**   Will you get movin'? We're famished here! We want some grub, huh? You're keepin' us from it. George! That ain't nice or polite!

**George**   That's just bullshit! You're just tryin' ta get alone with Margy . . .

**Archie**   I'll kill you, George. I swear ta God I will!

**Margy**   Go, George . . . (*Smiles.*) It's alright . . . (*Pauses.*) Really.

**George** (*moves to door; stops*)   I'm gonna make this real fast. Don't you worry . . . (*Goes to door, stops, returns to locker, finds coat, slips it on, returns to door, stops, returns to* **Archie**, *makes universal 'I've got no money' signal [rubs thumb and forefinger together].* **Archie** *smiles, gives* **George** *$20 bill,* **George** *takes money. Exits.* **Archie** *looks at* **Margy** *and smiles. He moves to the loading doors, closes them.*)

**Archie**   Well, huh, well, look at us, huh, Marg . . . just the two of us, huh? All alone here . . . you and me. Wellllll . . . (*Smiles. There is a short silence.*) How's it goin'?

**Margy**    It's going quite well, Archie. Quite well. I'm so glad to be back . . . to have seen you again . . . and George . . . in the flesh . . . (*Smiles, pauses. There is a short silence.*) We've got our work cut out for us, don't we, Arch?

**Archie** (*motions to baler*)    This? (**Margy** *laughs.*) You mean baling? (**Margy** *stares at* **Archie**, *who shifts his weight nervously from foot to foot.*) Uh, Marg, if we're gonna . . . you know . . . we'd, uh, better, uh, well, uh, you know, right?

**Margy**    I beg your pardon?

**Archie**    Uh, well, there isn't a lot of time, Marg . . .

**Margy**    For what purpose? (**Archie** *walks to her, wordlessly, embarrassedly. He puckers up his lips and waits to be kissed; his lips and face on the open air between them.* **Margy** *stares at him a moment; smiles.*) Oh, I see: kissing?

**Archie**    Do you . . . wanna?

**Margy**    Oh, well, no, Archie, I don't wanna . . . really. I think you and I have done enough kissing for one lifetime, don't you, Archie, really?

**Archie**    I, uh, I can understand 'n all . . . really, sure. Yuh, well, I do, yuh, I do understand. (*Pauses*) I'm a *lunk*, right? A real lunk . . .

**Margy**    No, Archie . . . That's hardly the reason . . .

**Archie**    That's the reason. It's true, too. I'm a lunk . . . a local . . . a lummox, too. I understand, I do, yuh, I do understand. You went away and you got yourself *terrific* . . . really . . . ya did, Marg: You look just *great*! Here I am: Archie Crisp. I mean, Christ! What've I got to offer a woman's traveled halfway round the world, probably? Maybe even all the way . . .

**Margy**    All the way. Yuh. Twice.

**Archie**    Ya see? Twice. Jees, Marg, don't let it worry ya none, really. You don't wanna make love with old Archie Crisp, he's gonna understand, really. Call me crazy, Marg, but I really do understand. Really, I know that. I do, uh, well, I do kinda hav'ta ask a favor of you, though, Marg, if ya don't mind . . .

**Margy**    What's the favor, Archie?

**Archie**    I agree to your stipulation of no lovemakin' and handsoff and all, but Marg? . . . This is really important to me . . . (*He pauses; looks down and then to her directly.*) Don't tell George, OK? (**Margy** *turns from* **Archie**, *smiles. She pauses a moment. Her smile is gone. She faces* **Archie** *again.*)

**Margy**    I was seventeen, Archie. Seventeen . . . (**Archie** *averts his eyes; faces front, bows his head.*)

*The curtain falls.*

# Act Two

*Later, same night.*

*Lights up. If Act One light source was daylight through shop's windows and skylights, Act Two's lighting is from overhead electrical fixtures: caged work lights.*

**George** *sits on chair, stage right, drinking beer, watching* **Margy** *paying rapt attention to* **Archie**, *who performs a story for her, enthusiastically.*

**George** *watches, jealous of* **Archie**'s *attention to* **Margy** *and, at the same time, jealous of* **Margy**'s *attention to* **Archie**.

*Remains of* **George**'s *and* **Archie**'s *eaten Chinese take-out meals visible. Many crushed beer cans (dead soldiers) near* **George**'s *feet.*

**Archie**   When I was a little guy, I used to work here every Saturday. I got two bucks, which was a big deal then . . . wicked big. (*Smiles.*) Used ta be maybe seven, eight winos used ta work here weekends . . . for my Uncle Max . . . before Spike the Loon worked with us . . . I was just a kid. (*Pauses; lost in a memory.*) 'Lum' is what we called the big one. His name was Alfred, I think . . . Some people called him Allie. Most of us called him 'Lumbago' on accounta he had it. For short, we called him 'Lum'. Dumbest, meanest son of a bitch ten towns around, and that's a fact. (*Pauses.*) My particular specialty was to climb into the baler, counta I was a kid and little and all, and push the papers tight into the corners. A good bale has sharp edges. The only thing was, getting inside the press spooked me. Gave me the willies . . . (*Pauses.*) Lum always used to threaten me when I was in here. He used ta say he'd pull the top over me when I was inside. Then he'd say they'd press me in with all the over-issues and sell me in the bale and I'd get driven up to Fitchburg, to Felulah's Mill, and I'd get dumped into the acid bath with the over-issues and come out ta the wet press up there, rolled into fine paper for stationery . . . (*Pauses.*) The miserable son of a bitch! Tellin' that to a kid, huh? He grabbed me in a headlock one Saturday, right here on this spot. Lum. No warning at all. He just grabbed me. I figured I was a dead kid, ya know. I mean, I was eleven and he was forty. The odds weren't exactly on *me*, ya know what I mean? But, I took a major shot and I whipped him around backwards. (*He looks at* **George**, *who averts his eyes.*) I ran myself forward as fast as I could, whipping him around backwards . . . and he flew! He *flew*! He hit the front of the baler so hard, it was like his face exploded. It looked ta me like his head was half opened up. He landed on the stack, and just lay there, blood oozing out of him, staining the papers. (*Pauses.*) I figured I'd killed him. (*Pauses.*) Winos grumblin', lookin' this way and that . . . They started fadin' out ta the shop . . . the winos. (*Pauses.*) I was scared shit. Just me alone and the body: Lum. (*Pauses.*) I figured the cops would give me the electric chair . . . or worse; hangin' . . . (*Pauses.*) I was scared shit. (*Pauses.*) I figured the only way was to get rid of the body, hide him. The winos wouldn't talk. Nobody'd miss him, anyway, right? (*Pauses.*) I started coverin' him up with newspaper, but his blood kept staining through. So, I started draggin' him over to the baler . . . to throw him in. I was only eleven, Marg. Can you get the picture? (*He moves to baler to better illustrate his story.* **George** *will soon move in closer to* **Margy**, *and this time,* **Archie** *will register jealousy. Without a break in storytelling,* **Archie** *will shove* **George** *aside and complete his story.*) Me, eleven, draggin' this forty-year-old drunken corpse by the arm to the press here . . . (*Pause.*) This very very one . . . (*Slaps baler, pauses, smiles.*) You'll never guess what happened, Marg. You'll never in a million years guess . . . (*Laughs.*) Gave me bad dreams for about eighteen years . . . (*Pauses.*) Lum got up. I swear to God. He opens his eyes . . . blinks a bunch a' times . . . and then . . . then . . . (*He laughs.*) Lum gets up, as though from the dead. The cut wasn't all that deep, just bleedin' wicked. He must'a been out as much from the wine as from the hitting the baler. Blood dripping all down him . . . He comes at me. (*Pauses.*) I figured he was gonna kill me, Margy. Get even. He didn't. He shook his head a couple of times . . .

moves to his chino Eisenhower jacket, and he goes away. No pay. No finishin' the day. No attempt whatsoever to do damage to me. (*Pauses.*) That was a big day in the life of this little Arnold 'Billy-Goat' Crisp. I can tell you that. (*Pauses.*) Gaining respect is what life is all about.

**George** (*from the chair*)    Lum ever come back?

**Archie**    Huh?

**George**    Lum ever come back here? To work? To talk to you? Whatever?

**Archie**    What the hell kind of question is that?

**George**    It's a question. It's a question. (*He stands, tosses food container and beer can into trash, walks around back of baler, arrives between* **Margy** *and* **Archie**.)

**Archie**    You mean, did Lum ever come back here to *get* me? Is that what you mean?

**George**    I didn't mean that exactly. I meant, maybe, to work again, to just *be* . . . around here and all. Did you ever have to look him in the eye? Face to face . . . Did he ever . . . well. Yuh . . . I suppose . . . try to get you.

**Archie**    Once, yuh, he did once . . .

**George**    When?

**Archie**    I'm done talkin' on this subject. (*He slams down his packet of newspaper on to the floor instead of into the baler, and storms off away from* **George** *and* **Margy**. *He exits through loading doors, slamming door as he goes.*)

**Margy**    What was that about, George?

**George**    He's still jealous?

**Margy**    Of what?

**George**    Not what: *who.*

**Margy**    Of who? (*Corrects herself.*) Of *whom* . . . (*Smiles.*) Sorry, George, but I've never been comfortable treating an objective pronoun like a nominative pronoun. I'm sure you understand my meticulousness. I do hope you forgive me . . .

**George**   Why do you pretend like you're not a schoolteacher? Everybody knows that you are.

**Margy**   But I'm not.

**George**   But you are. It's a fact. Everybody knows . . .

**Margy**   I work for a college, but I don't actually teach . . .

**George**   New York University?

**Margy**   Well, yes. How did you know that?

**George**   Lucky guess. What do you do if you don't teach?

**Margy**   What do I do? (*Smiles.*) I criticize.

**George**   Really.

**Margy**   Really.

**George**   What?

**Margy**   What do I criticize? What other people write.

**George**   You mean like 'good' or 'bad' sort of a thing?

**Margy**   Approximately that, yuh . . .

**George**   Don't people get *annoyed*?

**Margy**   The people I criticize? Uh, well, sometimes, yes . . .

**George**   You get *paid* for that?

**Margy**   I do. Yes.

**George**   Must be nice.

**Margy**   Being paid to criticize? Nice? This is *exhausting*! (*Smiles.*) What do you do?

**George**   For money?

**Margy**    Yuh. For money.

**George**    I, uh, well, usual thing.

**Margy**    Really?

**George**    Yuh, well . . . yuh.

**Margy**    What, uh, uh, what would that be, George: 'the usual thing'?

**George**    I'm, uh, on the Town . . . (*He looks about nervously to see if* **Archie** *has heard him.*)

**Margy**    On the Town?

**George** (*quietly*)    Yuh, well . . . yuh. I've be'n doin' it straight through . . . since high school and all: on the Town. (*Pauses.*) It's a steady thing, ya know. Not too exciting, maybe. I mean, not som'pin' like what yo're use'ta, for example, but, it's who I am and what I do . . . as far as money goes kinda thing . . .

**Margy**    You're 'on the Town' for money? There was a musical comedy by that name . . . You're not telling me you sing and dance, *professionally*, are you, George?

**George**    I'm on the Town crew. Cleanin', sweepin', shovellin' sort a thing. Whatever's needed, kind . . . I had longevity on the Gultch crew . . . ya remember? Guinea Gultch?

**Margy**    Oh. Right. Italians . . . Water Street . . . Guinea Gultch . . . I'd forgotten that . . .

**George**    I was top dog on the Gultch crew for ten years. Seniority, that sorta thing. (*Suddenly.*) They laid me off. Just before last Christmas. Goddamn town was near broke. They laid me off, and Porker Watson – 'member him? – and Stoney Webster: the rotten three of us. Merry Christmas, huh? The whole goddamn town was very nearly bankrupt. (*Pauses.*) I don't care. I don't. I mean, who wants ta spend their life cleaning up Guinea Gultch, right? It's great when yo're a high school kid, pullin' down maybe sixty-five a week. Hey, that's big bucks, right? But when yo're thirty-seven, goin' on thirty-eight, Marg, and they're still payin' ya the minimum wage, huh?

**Margy**    You haven't worked since last Christmas?

**George**    A year ago last Christmas. No. Nothin'. Things are slim around these parts, Marg. It ain't the good old days, huh? (*Smiles.*) Hell, I ain't kickin' none . . . Give me a chance ta think. All them years, sitting on trucks with six seven eight other guys: no time to think: always laughin' and kiddin' around . . . drinkin' beers 'n all . . . acting like juveniles, really. It was a wicked awful waste a my time. I'm glad . . . (*Quietly.*) Buncha' blow'ahs. (*Pauses; then to* **Margy**, *smiles.*) In the days when you and I were . . . ya' know . . . intimately friends kinda' . . . well . . . ya'know . . . money was easy . . . I mean, what did it take, huh? A couple'a bucks for this or that? Pizzas, dancin', maybe a tank of gas? *Shit!* Easy as fallin' off a log!

**Margy**    When, George?

**George**    When what?

**Margy**    When did I know you?

**George**    All our lives.

**Margy**    Intimately. When intimately? When exactly were we 'intimate friends kinda'?

**George**    You've got to be kidding, Marg.

**Margy**    I'm not, Georgie, I'm not. I don't mean to hurt your feelings, but I remember your name and that is, as they say, just about *it*.

**George**    H.M. Warren School, second grade, Georgie Ferguson. Look at me.

**Margy**    Georgie Ferguson? Georgie Ferguson? Georgie Kermit Ferguson . . . Kermie . . . Kermie . . . Kermit . . . Georgie Kermie . . . G.K . . . (*She looks up, hopelessly.*) A blank. I am shocked and amazed to announce a blank. (*She smiles.*)

You made no impression on me at all, George. Not any.
None.

**George**    Georgie Ferguson. Look at me.

**Margy** (*angrily*)    *I'm . . . looking . . . at . . . you!* (*A short silence;*
**Archie***'s voice breaks into the void, from way off stage.*)

**Archie**    He walked you home and sent you notes.

**Margy** (*she looks about, amazed.* **Archie** *cannot be seen. She
smiles at* **George**)    Sorry, but I believe my silver fillings are
picking up police calls. (**Archie** *enters, hops up on back edge of
baler; repeats his announcement, flatly.*)

**Archie**    He walked you home and sent you notes.

**George** (*yells up to* **Archie**, *above*)    Don't start in, Archie.
That was a long time ago.

**Margy** (*also up to* **Archie**, *above*)    Me or Esther?

**Archie** (*yells down*)    You!

**George**    You, too. (*He pretends to be ashamed.*) I kinda' had a
knack with the girls, I guess . . .

**Margy**    George, is the implication here that you and I
used to . . . *go together?* (**George** *nods.*) We *went* together?
(**George** *nods again.*) Like a couple? Like let's double with
George and Margy, Saturday night, huh? (*Pauses.*) A couple?
George and Margy, Margy and George? That kinda' thing?
(**George** *nods.*) My God, I don't remember them at all.

**George**    I bought you a ball-point . . . Mrs Card's store.

**Margy**    No kidding?

**George**    No kidding.

**Margy**    I use a fountain pen now, George. The world has
changed. Didn't you hear?

**George**    You let me look down your blouse.

**Margy**   Down my blouse? In second grade? (**George** *nods*.) In second grade you looked down my *blouse* . . . at my second-grade breasts? (**George** *nods again*.) The world hasn't changed much in *some* sectors, has it, Georgie? (**George** *shrugs*.)

**Archie** (*roars*)   If this ain't the most goddamn *disgusting display of smut* I ever heard! (*He moves to* **Margy**; *pointing his finger in the accusatory. He is attempting to control his anger, which is a considerable effort.*) I got feelin's, ya know! I got 'em!

**Margy**   I beg your pardon?

**Archie**   I was hiding back there the whole time . . . listening in. I heard every goddamn thing the both'a'ya's said! Didn't you know that?

**Margy**   I had suspicions, yes.

**Archie**   You know that?

**Margy**   I did, yes.

**Archie**   A man doesn't hide unless he wants someone to come looking for him, right?

**Margy**   I am simply amazed to hear your . . . incisiveness, your trenchance, Archie. I agree. I definitely agree. I am . . . in agreement.

**Archie** (*a hostile imitation*)   Well, I am simply amazed to hear you agree, dearie.

**George**   Cool yourself down, Arch . . . c'mon . . .

**Archie**   I'll cool yo'r ass!

**George**   Come on, Archie!

**Archie**   You were lookin' down her blouse?

**George**   *Every*body was!

**Archie**   Bullshit!

**George**    *Bullshit* to *you*! Everybody was, and you know it *full well!*

**Margy**    Could I chime in here?

**Archie**    Stay out ta this!

**Margy**    But it's my blouse!

**George**    You listen to me, Billy-Goat Crisp, you got no right bringing up no dead issues, some twenty-five/thirty years after the fact, ya know what I mean? *Do ya? (Angrily.) God damn it!*

**Archie**    Look at him, why don't ya? Ashamed, right? Isn't he ashamed? Isn't that the look of ashamed that's written all over the son of a bitch?

**George**    *Up yours, I'm 'ashamed'! . . .* that'll be some cold day in hell when you catch Kermie Ferguson 'ashamed' . . . and that's the God's-honest!

**Archie**    As for you, sistah, you got no shame! No shame! It's one thing for me to be coppin' a look: We were boyfriend and girlfriend and that is a fact. But for this Kermie Ferguson son-of-a-bitchin' bastard? No shame. Nooo . . . shame . . .

**Margy**    Could we just hold here a minute?

**Archie**    You start out dirty, you end up dirty. That's a fact.

**Margy**    Could you close it down, please, Archie?

**Archie**    Showin' your tits around in second grade and look at you now. Look at you now. Some filthy mouth, huh? And where did it start? H.M. Warren School, by the snow fence, second recess. That's where. And I'll tell you another thing . . . (**Margy** *slaps* **Archie***'s face. There is a stunned silence.* **George** *giggles a high-pitched giggle, covering his mouth; feminine, childlike.*)

**Margy**   Put a belt on that indecorous and milk-curdling giggle of yours, George. I find it far too girlish for our particular circumstance . . .

**George**   *What?*

**Margy**   Better. (*To* **Archie**.) First off, the matter of my mammary glands . . . my breasts . . . my *tits* . . . my *boobs* . . . my *jugs* . . . my *knockers* . . . my *set* . . . my *funny valentines* . . . (*Smiles.*) my perfect little orbs . . . (*Pauses.*) They seem to be causing you some grief, my breasts. They've been quite something for me, too, over the years. I can't say I find them quite as . . . exciting as you two do . . . lucky for me. Imagine if I were caught up in the irrestistibility of my own breasts? Trying to brush my teeth, for example. I would fumble with tube and brush, unable to keep my hands from my fabulous *poitrine*. My teeth would green and decay: rot . . . Dressing: it would never happen. I'd just keep ripping my shirt away for another look . . . another peek . . . the cop of another feel. First, a bad cold, the pneumonia, then pleurisy . . . dread disease after dread disease . . . ending, no doubt, in death . . . (*Pauses.*) What a pity she had breasts, poor thing. They did her in. (*Pauses.*) Thinking it over, Archie and George, I will gladly give my breasts over to you, for whatever purpose you choose. George, you would wear them on the odd days; Archie, on the evens. And I'll be free to get back to work . . . to get back to sleep at night . . . to end the constant and unrelenting fondling. (*Pauses.*) I want you to have my breasts, guys. I really do. You do seem to envy them . . . (*She begins to unbutton her blouse – two buttons only – threatening to show her breasts to the men.*)

**Archie**   What are you doin'?

**George**   What's a matter with you?

**Margy**   You should look them over before you agree. It's a commitment, having breasts like these two beauties. You should have a look . . . in case you want to divvy them up, for example. I'm told they're not quite symmetrical. You might find one to be somewhat more exciting than the other . . .

**George**    Close your shirt . . . (*He looks away; as does* **Archie**.) Close it.

**Archie**    You heard him.

**Margy**    You sure?

**Archie**    Close it up.

**George**    You sure are weird, Margy . . .

**Margy**    You think so? Every time I've been in the right circumstances for comparison . . . you know . . . ladies' locker rooms . . . faculty physicals for group insurance . . . and other orgy-like nude gatherings of mine, the weaker sex . . . I've, well, compared. (*Smiles at* **George**.) I never found mine to be weird, George. Small, yes, but never weird.

**George**    I didn't mean your chest. I meant your attitude.

**Margy**    Oh. My attitude. I see. Well, I'll just have to watch my mental step, won't I? (*Smiles.*) I do certainly beg your pardon, George. I do certainly. (*Fingers on blouse.*) Last chance, guys.

**George**    Button it up, Marg! You're makin'a fool of yourself!

**Margy**    Archie? Peeks?

**Archie**    Button it up!

**Margy** (*buttoning her blouse*)    Thirty years of laser-beam stares and innuendoes until finally I relinquish my greedy hold on the adored knockers and *my God*! *My God!* (*Imitates* **George**.) 'Button it up, Marg. You're makin' a fool of yourself.' (*Completes buttoning.*) There is much I would like to make of myself in the few spots of time left to make anything at all, George, but a fool, I must admit, is not on my list. (*Smiles.*) We've settled the breast question, yes? (*No reply. She asks again.*) George? (*No reply.*) Archie? (*No reply. She speaks with* *thick Boston accent again.*) I don't hear an answer . . . I 'shoo-ah' am wicked awful anxious to hear yo'r answer. Hmmm? (**George** *and* **Archie** *turn away.*) Now, then . . . the matter of Archie's saying, 'You and I were boyfriend and girlfriend,' meaning, I suppose, you/Archie and I/Margy Palumbo. Is that a fact?

**Archie**    What are you: cute or som'pin'.

**Margy**    Me? Cute? Never!

**Archie**    We were! Boyfriend and girlfriend.

**Margy**    B.F. and G.F.?

**Archie**    Yuh.

**Margy**    Before tonight?

**Archie**    You oughta' have your memory checked.

**Margy**    *I* ought'a?

**George**    Archie's still smartin' 'cause you two were . . . ya' know . . . sweethearts, you might say, and I split you up.

**Archie**    Bullshit, buddy! *Bullshit!* You didn't split nothin' but the supper bill for your last date . . .

**George**    What's that s'pose ta mean? You callin' me *cheap?*

**Archie**    Cheap? You: cheap? That's a laugh! You ain't just cheap. Callin' you 'just cheap' would be like calling the Pope 'just Catholic' . . . You are more than cheap, pally-pal: You are cheap*est* . . .

**Margy**    I don't think you mean 'cheap*est*', Archie. I think you mean 'cheap*err*'. When comparing two cheapskates, one is cheap and the other is cheap*er*. Only when comparison is made among three or more cheapskates does one find the cheap*est*. It's a small point, I know, but . . . *c'est la guerre de la langue Anglaise!*

**Archie** (*to* **Margy**)    I think we've both had enough smart remarks from you, Margy Palumbo. (*To* **George**.) Right?

**George**    Right! enough insults . . .

**Archie**    Highfalutin' airs . . .

**George**    Hoity-toity airs . . .

**Archie**    College-girl bullshit . . .

**George**    You're really tryin' ta start trouble here . . .

**Archie**    Between me and George . . .

**George**    Me and Archie . . .

**Archie**    Split us up . . .

**George**    Yuh. That's it.

**Margy**    Bullll*shit*, buddy!

**Archie**    This is what you went to college for? To talk filthy?

**George**    Swede would be ashamed . . .

**Archie**    *She* should be ashamed! It's disgusting. Honest to God . . . disgusting!

**George**    Great fucking guy, Swede, huh?

**Archie**    And I'm gonna tell you something: I never liked Swede. I never liked *any* handicapped kids too much, frankly. I've got enough problems of my own. You, leadin' him around like you were some sort'a *saint*! . . . All the kids pamperin' the two of yous . . . pretending he was normal and all . . . makin' him Class President and crap like that. 'Peter Palumbo for President, 'Cause He'll Get the Job Done.' I never heard such crap, really! (*To* **George**.) Where the hell do you come off sayin' you like him? Huh? You never liked Swede Palumbo. You hated him! Where the Christ do you get off makin' statements like that?

**George**    Just makin' conversation. Passin' the day. Makin' civil talk. It's only right . . .

**Archie** (*imitates* **George**)   'Only right . . .' (*To* **Margy**.)
You shoulda heard what he was sayin' before you came in
here. He 'likes' Swede . . . hah? What crap. You *remember*
what Kermie Ferguson did to Swede? Do ya?

**George**   C'mon, Arch, huh?

**Archie**   Bullshit, buddy. Bullshit! You don't go shovin'
him inta line . . . shovin' him hard and then come up with 'I
liiike Sweedie-deedie!' Bullllllshit . . . (*There is a sharp intake of
breath from* **George** *and* **Margy***: shocked.*)

**George**   I can't fuckin' believe you just said what you just
fuckin' said! I've be'n watchin' my tongue the whole night!
Honest ta Christ! (*Laughs.*) Makes me *laugh*. (*Roars.*) Makes
me fuckin' laugh! Call me crazy, Margy, but this just makes
me laugh!

**Margy**   Call you crazy? Nawww. I'd never call you crazy,
George. If you're crazy then what am I? Then what is
Archie? (*Pauses, very upset.*) If I were large enough . . .
physically . . . I would probably beat you. I would probably
try to kill you. If I were large enough . . . physically . . . I
would probably try to kill you and I would probably
succeed. (*Pauses.*) But I would never call you crazy, George.
(*Pauses. Attacks* **George***, punches him in a rage. They move onto
dune-like mound of papers.*) If you aren't the most odious son of
a bitch I ever laid eyes on . . . (*She weeps a moment; punches her
fist into her own thigh, twice, in self-disgust.*) Stop crying! Stop
crying! (*She continues to weep. There is a pause.* **Margy***'s attitude
will change here. She has lost ground. The men will be, for the moment,
stronger; more confident than they have been of late.* **George** *is the
first to speak.*)

**George**   Look at her. Cryin' . . . Weepin' . . . Sheddin'
tears . . . Poor kid . . .

**Archie**   God damn. I've hurt her feelings. I feel awful . . .
(*To* **Margy**.) Shush, huh. C'mon now, Marg. I'm feelin' just
terrible that I made you cry. Come on, huh?

**George**   Guys like us, Marg, we don't mean half the things we say. We're just talkin', ya know? Tryin' ta be cool, calm and collected, ya' know? (*Moves close to her. She continues to weep.*)

**Archie**   All kiddin' around straight ta hell, Marg, you want a shoulder ta lean on, kinda, you know you've got mine . . . Georgie's, too. I mean, we're, well . . . your pals.

**George**   Not just boys on the prowl . . .

**Archie**   Nothin' like that . . .

**George**   We're shootin' straight with you know . . .

**Archie**   I always liked you, Marg. And that's a fact.

**George**   He did. I can vouch for that. I remember.

**Archie**   You liked her, too.

**George**   I did. I did. That's a fact. I did.

**Archie**   Why are you crying?

**George**   She's unhappy.

**Archie**   What's makin' you unhappy? What, specifically, Margy?

**George**   Us, definitely. What we said . . .

**Archie**   About what? (**George** *shrugs.*) About what? (**Archie** *moves close to* **Margy**.) About what, Margy, about what? I said something about what? (**Margy** *continues to weep.*)

**George**   I think it was probably me. (*To* **Margy**.) Was it, Marg? Was it something I said? God damn, I'm really sorry . . . I hate when a woman cries . . . (**Margy** *sneezes into a handkerchief. She moves away from the men, but they follow after her, crowding her, forcing her, finally, against the baler. She will stay there a moment, regain composure, her crying will cease. Her strength will return.*)

**Archie**   Most annoying fuckin' thing in the world!

**George**   Drives me crazy . . .

**Archie**   Drives me nuts . . .

**George**   Makes me wanna take right the fuck off!

**Archie**   Get out ta the house! Drive away . . .

**George**   *Move* away!

**Archie**   Make a fist . . . (*Pauses.*) Hit . . . (*Hits his own chest.*) Hit . . . (*Again.*) Make a fist and hit . . . (**Margy** *moves to* **Archie**, *places her hand on his cheek. There is a short silence.* **Archie** *stops raving, settles into her touch, instantly and absolutely calmed.* **George** *is wide-eyed, staring, left out.*)

**George**   Hey, Marg . . . Arch? . . . cut the kiddin' around, huh? (*The touch continues.*) Come on, you guys . . . (*A false laugh wanted here.*)

**Archie** (*short of breath; quietly*)   Ever since second grade, Margy . . . You were the only one. Honest to God . . . (**Margy** *turns from* **Archie**; *faces* **George**, *moves to him. He is frightened. She places her hand on* **George**'s *cheek. She groans, pained to feel* **George**'s *cheek. He giggles, pulls back from her touch. He places his hand on her cheek.* **Margy** *doesn't resist. She moans, pained, somewhat slumped into* **George**'s *hand.*) What gives?

**George**   A touch! Just a touch! We were friends, too, ya' know!

**Archie**   Let loose, George . . .

**George**   Come on, Arch . . .

**Archie**   Drop your hand.

**George**   Jesus, Arch . . . you got some kind of sharing problem, or what?

**Archie**   Drop it, Georgie Ferguson, or I'll mop this place up with you.

**George** (*steps back from* **Margy**)   OK? OK?

**Archie** (*quietly. His feelings have been somehow hurt*)    God damn, Georgie . . . (*Pauses, turns away.*) God damn . . . (**Archie** *is weeping. He turns his face away from* **George**, *who stares incredulously at him for a moment, realizes, laughs.*)

**George**    Look at that, Marg! Look at Archie! Whooo-eee! *OOOO!* The both of yous: *criers!* If that ain't the goddamn'dest thing I ever saw! *Whoooo-eee!* (*He giggles hysterically.* **Margy** *goes to console* **Archie**.)

**Margy**    Archie? . . . Archie, look at me . . . Arch?

**Archie**    Goddamn town'll bury ya . . . You got out, Margy . . . you and the Moose . . . Why'd you come back? Kinda dumb thing to do, Marg, don't you think? (*Pauses.*) I heard you were comin' back. Spike the Loon showed me the *Item.*

**George** (*starts looking through the papers in his wallet*)    I'm gonna get that . . .

**Archie**    'Spike,' I says. 'No way. No way is Margy Palumbo comin' back to this armpit. No way. She's an educated woman.'

**George**    I'll show ya . . . Look at this! I kept the clipping from the *Item.* Margaret Burke, *née* Palumbo . . . this is you . . . Palumbo, and Burke is Moose.

**Archie** (*grabs paper*)    Gimme that. (*Looks at clipping. To* **Margy**.) This is you, yes?

**Margy**    That is me.

**George**    What's the picture in the *Item* for, Margy? Arch? It makes no sense. I read it but it makes no sense.

**Archie** (*throws clipping into baler. Completely new attitude*)    Let's get this bale finished, huh?

**George**    Hey! Picture in the paper for what? What did you do?

**Archie**    Come on, George! You're not gettin' paid to talk! (**Archie** *is energetically loading the baler. He tosses a bundle of* *newspapers to* **George**. **George** *grunts under the weight of the bundle.*)

**George**   Hey!

**Archie**   I'm balin' paper. If you and this famous woman want to help . . . If you don't want to help, that's fine too. It's what I'm paid to do.

**George**   What'd she do, Arch? What'd she get her picture in the paper for? Explain it to me!

**Archie** (*angrily*)   Will you kindly get the bundle to the baler?

**George**   I don't like this. (*Pauses.*) I'd like to point out to you, Archie, that this Margy Palumbo is tryin' . . . and succeedin' . . . in making goddamn fools . . . idiots . . . out ta the rotten two of us.

**Margy**   Archie, I'm not doing that.

**George**   You think Archie Crisp is just some jerk you can fuck over, huh? Fuck him over for a laugh and then scoot, right out and spend the next fifteen/twenty years tellin' your highfalutin' friends about this local, see? . . . This *local* . . . this townie asshole, Archie Crisp . . . and how he came on to her. Still likin' her and all, after all those years since the second grade. (*Imitates* **Margy** *talking to a cultured friend.*) This Archie Crisp, you see, is what you'd call a really steady boyfriend . . . How steady? Second grade right up till age thirty-five/forty . . . How's *that* for steady, huh? Those locals stick like glue, huh? Not much goin' in those locals' lives, huh? . . . Couple of farmers, 'cepting they got no *farms!* (*He bales furiously.*) She's insulting us, Archie! That's it – she's putting us down!

**Archie**   Shut it up, George, huh? Huh? Huhhh? You got the brains of a cruller. (*Tosses a bundle into the baler.*) Leave me out of this. I'm just doing my work.

**George**   You're her supper date, right? I mean she called you, not me? . . . I'm just being friendly and all . . . not

comin' on or causin' trouble or nothin' . . . just bein'
friendly and all . . . for old times' sake . . . (*Pauses.*) And for
the sake of our old buddy, Swede . . . who's kicking off . . .
(**Archie** *looks at* **George**.) . . . out of memory for the Moose
. . . and her former junior high steady, our own Spike the
Loon . . . dearly departed . . . and accounta' she's got kids,
Raymond, et cetera, and her bein' unhappy and all . . .
mentally fuckin' *depressed!* (**George** *is moving toward* **Margy**
*now.*) We behaved respectably with you on account of all
those things, Margy, and what I hear is you can't stop
laughin' at us and insultin' us and playing it smart . . .
playin' it smart . . . (*He lifts bundle up over her head, menacingly.*)
I've got muscle now, Margy. That's one change from the
old days, right? Me, roly-poly and all . . . That's one change
you might a noticed, huh? George Ferguson ain't roly-poly
now! Opposite: George Ferguson is a well-developed man.
. . . He's strong . . . He can lift . . . He's got muscle . . . Uh
huh. (*He throws bundle at* **Archie**.) You workin' or you
watchin', huh? If you want a bale wired and out and ready
for your fat uncle at four o'clock, you got ta move on it,
same as me . . . (*To* **Margy**.) I personally never held with
the idea that women are weak and along for a free ride. (*He
throws a bundle to her.*) Up and into the baler. MOVE!
(**Margy** *catches bundle and throws it at the baler's front door,
screaming primal scream.*) I do not like the attitude you've got
right now! I think your pronouns are fucked up, too! I can't
follow your ante-fuckin'-cedents!

**Archie**    Cool down, George. You're hot . . .

**George**    *I'm hot . . . I'm hot.* Why not, huh? How'm I gonna
stay cool with Miss Margy Palumbo blowin' down my ear
like she does, huh? (*Turns to* **Margy**, *then to* **Archie**.) This
pisses me off. This just pisses me off. (*Grabs two bundles, throws
them into the baler.*) *This just pisses me off!* (*To* **Margy**.) What
you're after here is trouble between me and Archie. That's
the way I've got it pegged. You get your kicks out ta causin'
us to be fightin' and crap with each other. That's the way I
got it pegged . . . (*To* **Archie**.) And I got a good eye. I got a

good eye. (*To* **Margy**.) I don't like the way you call me and
Archie here dumb or stupid for not gettin' our pictures in
the *Item* the way you do . . . (*Displays newspaper photo.*) What's
this anyway, huh? Does this mean that if anything . . . you
know . . . happened to you, that a lot of people would come
snoopin' around on accounta' you're famous, so's they
noticed you were missing kinda' thing?

**Margy**   My children . . . Raymond and Rosie . . . they'd
miss me . . . They'd 'come snoopin'' . . .

**George**   I don't like you using your sex on us the way you
do . . . to split us up . . . me and my best friend, Archie . . .

**Archie**   C'mon, already, George . . .

**George**   Your fame and your power . . .

**Archie**   You're talkin' stupid . . .

**George**   Your eyelids, blinkin' up and down like you
didn't know they were . . . (*Reaches for* **Margy**'s *breasts.*) I
don't like the way you use these on us, neither . . .

**Margy** (*breaking away*)   Please, don't, George.

**Archie**   Keep back . . . 'less you wanna die young, pal . . .

**George**   It's a little late for either of us 'dying young', ain't
it, Goat? Dyin' young at our age ain't no more . . . No more
. . . (*He slips around behind* **Margy** *and fondles her breasts, from
behind her.*) I don't like the way you've been usin' these on
us . . .

**Margy**   George!

**Archie**   Keep back from her, George, 'less you wanna find
your nose on your knee in the mornin'! You get me?

**George**   What's there to get, Arch, huh? What's there
you're saying that's not to get? (**George** *holds* **Margy** *in front
of him, gripping her tightly. She is his shield, his hostage.*) You
wanna come at me, Arch, come on . . . (*Yells.*) COME ON!
(**George** *flips* **Margy** *to one side; squares off with* **Archie**.) *Now*

come at me! (**Archie** *turns downstage, away from* **George** *and*
**Margy**. *He seems paralyzed by his terror now, frozen. His eyes are*
*wide open, but unfocused: blind.* **George** *is amazed and frightened*
*by* **Archie**'s *state. He snaps his fingers in front of* **Archie**'s *empty*
*eyes.*) What is *with* you? You see this, Marg? This one's all
bark. All bark! Not me. Not me! I got no bark at all, right?
No college-boy bullshit, I'm just dumb little Kermie
Ferguson from over Gould Street . . . (*Pauses.*) Who gives a
shit, huh? Who gives a shit? (*Pauses.*) 'member how we used
ta kiss, Marg? The way you used to *tongue* me. Let's show
Arch, huh? (*He kisses her.* **Margy** *responds stiffly. She stands*
*straight.* **George** *breaks away, finds can of beer, swigs; spits in*
*pretended disgust from the touch of* **Margy**'s *lips.*) You've turned
into kinda' a dead fish, Marg . . . (*To* **Archie**.) She's kinda
turned into a dead fish . . . (*Smiles.*) Not like the old days,
huh? You remember how hot she was in the old days, Arch?
(*To* **Margy**.) You remember how hot you were, Bunny?

**Archie**   C'mon, will ya, George!

**George** (*to* **Margy**)   You ain't in no hoity-toity *Worcester*,
or no *Springfield*, or no *Nooo Yawk*, or no *London, England*, or
no *Paris, France* . . . You're in none of those highfalutin',
hoity-toity, swell places, now, Bunny Palumbo! You're
home. *Home!* And when you're home, sistah, you are what
you are. (*Pauses, angrily.*) *What you are!* (*Pauses.*) Gang-banged
at Fisherman's Beach and this one comes up smilin' and
beggin' for more . . . beggin' for more!

**Archie**   George, for the love of Christ . . . I . . . (*He takes a*
*step toward* **George**, *pulls* **George**'s *arm.* **George** *pulls away,*
*violently.* **George** *moves to a bale and kicks and punches it several*
*times.* **Margy** *leans against baler and watches.*)

**George**   No touches! No touches! No touches! (*He punches*
*bale; turns and faces* **Margy**.) Gang-banged! Gang-banged!
The whole goddamned Senior Class party and this one is
still smilin' and beggin' for more . . . (*In a rage; throaty,*
*whispered yell.*) Bunny Palumbo, Blind Swede's sistah . . .
Bunny, Bunny, hop, hop, hop, huh? Right, right? (*Full voice.*)

Fucks like a what? Answer me! fucks like a *what*? ANSWER ME!

**Archie** (*from the baler*)   Leave her be, George! There's no need ta bring any of this back up!

**George**   It's up, it's up! It's already up. (*Moves to* **Archie** *in a rage.*) I'll be the one to say what comes up and what doesn't come up! I'll be the one! You get me? *You . . . get . . . me?*

**Archie** (*almost begging, on the ground*)   I don't see the point, that's all. I just don't see the point . . .

**George**   Because this girl forgets who she is, that's why. This girl thinks she can come back to town and be new . . . and she can't . . . she can't. That ain't the way things are. This girl ain't no Princess Margaret . . . this is plain Margy . . . Bunny Palumbo . . . Blind Swede's no-titted sistah . . . our stuck-up Salutatorian. That's who this girl is! This girl is Bunny, the one who got herself gang-banged, Senior Class beach party, Fisherman's Beach, up Lynn way . . . (*Smiles. He sings.*)
    LYNN, LYNN:
    THE CITY OF SIN;
    YOU'LL NEVER GET OUT,
    BUT, YOU'LL ALWAYS GET IN. (*Moves to* **Margy**.)
    LYNN, LYNN:
    THE CITY OF SIN;
    YOU'LL NEVER GET OUT,
    BUT, YOU'LL ALWAYS GET IN
(*Laughs.*) Man, oh man! This is a girl with a *badddd reputation*, ain't that right? . . . Fisherman's Beach, Bunny-Marg . . . up Lynn way . . . You remember who went first? You remember? (*Stares at* **Margy**.) Do you remember? (*No reply.*) I don't hear an answer . . . (*No reply.*) I don't hear an answer . . . (*No reply.*) I would like an answer! Do you remember who went first? *Do you remember? Do . . . you . . . remember?*
**Margy** (*primal scream*)   *You!*
**George** (*triumphant*)   *Right! Me! Kermie! First!* (*Glares at her again.*) Remember who went second? Do you remember?

**Margy** (*weeping*)   No.

**George**   Think, Bunny, think . . . (*Pauses.*) *Think!* (*Looks at* **Archie**.) What's wanted here is the memory and name of the man who went second . . . number two . . . sloppy seconds . . . *sloppy seconds* . . . (*Laughs. Looks at* **Margy**.) Who could that man be? Who, Bunny, who? Try to remember . . . try . . . Who? Who? I don't hear an answer . . . Who? Who? Who was number two? (*Sing-song; a cheerleader's rhythm.*) Who? Who? Who was number two? Who? Who? Who was number two? Who? Who? Who was number two? (**George** *swats overhead light; it bounces, crazily.*)

**Archie** (*moans*)   Me.

**George**   Another country heard from.

**Archie**   Me. I was number two. It was me. Don't you remember. Bunny? . . . (*Softly.*) Marg? Margy? Don't you remember? (*Pauses.*) It was me, Archie, Billy-Goat Crisp . . . (*Pauses.*) I was talkin' to you all the way . . . all the way. I went all the way . . . talkin' to you . . . Whisperin' in your ear . . . Tellin' you 'I love you, Marg'. (*Pauses.*) I did. (*Bows his head.*) I do.

**George** (*laughs*)   This is terrific! Whooooo-eeeee! (*Pauses; softly, simply.*) This is terrific! (*He walks about in two large circles, forming a figure eight. He is quite pleased with himself. He turns to* **Margy** *suddenly.*) Three! Number Three!

**Archie**   God damn you!

**George**   Three, Bunny, three!

**Archie**   Don't do this, George.

**George**   Number three, number three. Who d'ya see? Number three . . . Number, number three . . . Who d'ya see? Number three . . . (*Giggling.*) I don't hear an answer, Bunny-baby . . .

**Margy** (*simply, softly*)   Peter . . . (*Pauses.*) Swede . . . my brother . . .

**George**   You got it, Bunny! You got it! (*Laughs; walks in figure eight again.*) This is terrific, huh, Arch? Isn't this terrific?

**Archie**   Yuh. You got it, George. Terrific. (*He looks at* **Margy**. *Their eyes meet.*) Why did ya have ta call me?

Couldn't you have stayed away? (*Pauses.*) Jesus, Margy . . . (*Looks away, extremely upset.*) Jesus.

**George**    Number four, Margy?

**Margy** (*softly*)    Cootie Webber . . .

**George**    Are you kidding me? Or what? Cootie Webber? Number four? Nothin' like that . . . Spike the Loon was number four. Porker Watson was number five and Stoney Webster was number six. (*Pauses.*) Cootie Webber was number seven. (*Smiles.*) Me and Spike the Loon went over the line-up, couldn'ta be'more'n three weeks ago . . . I led off, Archie was sloppy seconds. Swede was numero trez, and Spike the Loon was the definite clean-up . . . (*Pauses.*) Cootie Webber was number seven. (*Pauses.*) Cootie Webber was the Moose's best friend, Marg, you remember? Asshole buddies, first grade right up ta Graduation, all twelve years. I myself personally always knew Moose Burke was a complete shithead, but who woulda' guessed he woulda' gone for the town pump, huh? (*To* **Archie**.) Married her. Jee-*zus*! Goddamn married her! What a shithead, huh? (**Archie** *is extremely upset.* **George** *sees him and stops cold, staring.*) If that ain't the most disgusting thing I've ever seen! Billy-Goat Crisp, crying like a girl. (*Whistles.*) God damn . . . (*Pauses: new attitude.*) God damn . . . (**George** *walks in a figure eight now. His bottom lip trembles as he fights back the tears.*) What I can't believe here is that you let this one do it to us over and over again . . . (*To* **Margy**.) He couldn't stand it that I went first. Ya know what I mean? (*Circling her now.*) He pestered me for years. I don't know what for. I mean, ya can't take a true fact and change it . . . just to do away with somebody's jealousy, right? (*Pauses.*) I went first and he went second. Kermie was number one and Billy-Goat took what was left . . . (*Pauses.*) I foxed him, Marg. (*To* **Archie**, *who is still weeping.*) Didn't I fox you? (*To* **Margy**.) He was s'pose to go first. It was all his idea . . . at Fisherman's Beach . . . the love-makin' . . . with you, Marg. That was all Archie's idea . . . You can read all the books you want and speak all the languages goin', Marg, but you ain't *never* . . . *never* . . . you ain't never gonna live that one down. (*Pauses.*) Ain't that a

fact? Ain't it? (*Pauses.*) Sure . . . (*To **Archie**.*) Ain't that a
fact, Arch? She ain't never livin' that one down, right? (*To*
**Margy**.) See? Talking about it doesn't bother me at all,
sistah!

**Margy** (*quietly, at first*)    I'm hardly your sistah, George. In
respect to my dear family, I must say, the implication is just
hideous.

**George**    I don't like your mouth.

**Margy** (*sudden rage. She spits her words. Wakefield accent. She is
the teenaged 'toughie' she once was*)    THEN WHY'D YOU GO
AND STICK YOUR TONGUE IN IT? (*She dances her rage
about.*) C'mon, ya blow'ah! C'mon, ya blow'ah! You wanna
hit a girrlll? Huh? Huh? Huh? C'mon. C'mon, c'mon . . .
Ya look wicked stooopid, George. (*She takes the stage. Her
accent has suddenly returned to normal; as does her manner. Her rage is
her own.*) I was seventeen, George, seventeen. Do you know
how old seventeen is, George? Not very. *Not goddamn very!* Do
you have any idea what it was you stuck into my seventeen-
year-old MIND, George? Do you? *Do you?* (*Pauses.*) Why'd
they pick me? Was I too provocative? Was it the way I
smiled? Did I look available? Did I look like an easy lay?
(*Pauses.*) What was it, George? What was it about me that
you hated . . . so deeply . . . so completely . . . so absolutely
. . . that made you want to *make love*, hmmm? Years,
goddamn *years* of walking around like a zombie, wondering
was I really, deep down, underneath it all, *lookin' for it?* I
remember, ya know, George. I really do. I was kinda staring
off by myself, pitch black out, no moon at all . . . and
alls'a'sudden somebody turns me around and kisses me. I
pull back from him, tryin' ta laugh it off, I say, 'No, thanks,
really . . .' And he's giggling this kinda' high-pitched girlish
giggle. (*She imitates **George**'s giggle, then, suddenly moves to
**George**, faces him, eyeball to eyeball.*) Weren't you giggling,
Kermie, huh? And you hit me. You took your hand and you
hit me. I square off with him . . . with this Kermie Ferguson
blow'ah, 'cause I ain't a'scared of nobody. *No . . . fucking . . .
body!* (*She is now atop mound of newspapers: the sand dune. She will
punch bale to underscore her anger.*) Seventeen years old, five foot

four inches tall . . . and you hit me. And I whack you back and you (*Punches bale.*) hit me and you (*Punches bale.*) hit me and I fall backwards and you hit (*Punches bale.*) me and then you and your kind did what you did. You line up . . . *LINE UP* . . . and you did what you did!

**George**   You loved it.

**Margy** (*crosses to steps in front of baler; squares off with* **George**. *In a rage: Wakefield accent*)   I DID NOT LOVE IT! I HATED IT! I HATED IT! (*Crying as she screams, the Massachusetts accent thickens, dominates her speech.*) You know what I was doing, you jerks? You know what I was doin' while you was doin' it to me? Huh? Huh? HUH? (*Laughs.*) I was thinkin' that I was getting run over . . . by a bus . . . by the *Hudson* bus. That's what I was doin', I swear ta Christ! That's how much I *loved* it! (*Dancing in her raging state, she imitates.*) 'Oooooooo, Arch!' . . . 'Studie-doo' . . . I liked Swede . . . 'Yo, Margyyyy! Open 'em up! spread 'em out! Here comes *love*!'

**George**   Is this what you came back here for, ya' bitch? Ta get even with us?

**Margy**   You bet your ass I'm gonna get even! Yuh, George, yesireebob! I'm gonna get even. I am! Wicked awful even! I'm gonna get sooo even with you, George, I can taste it! Taste . . . it! (**Margy** *turns her back.* **George** *giggles nervously, looks down.* **Archie** *calls out to* **Margy**, *quietly.*)

**Archie**   The only reason I got inta line, Margy, was 'cause I didn't think you'd have me any other way . . . I was never good enough, Margy . . . never smart enough . . . never sophisticated like you were . . . That's why, Marg. Ever since the second grade I've carried a torch for ya . . . som'pin' wicked . . .

**George**   'Ever since the second grade . . .' Jesus!

**Archie**   Nobody planned it, Margy. It just happened! Honest ta God! I mean, well, boys are always talkin' about wantin' ta do it with this one or that one . . . and *everybody* was always sayin' they'd love ta do it with *you*, 'cause you were, well, beautiful. But nobody really *meant* it: jumpin' you. It's just when George, here, well, *started*, everybody . . . wanted to, too. Everybody liked you . . .

**Margy**    You '*liked*' me, Arch?

**Archie**    I did. A lot.

**Margy**    And that's how you showed me you 'liked' me?

**Archie**    I was tricked out of first, I was. Otherwise, Margy, the first words you woulda heard whispered in your ear woulda been 'I love you' . . . because I did and I do. I do still. Marg . . . som'pin' wicked . . .

**Margy** (*after a long pause; calmly*)    'I love you' would not have helped. Do you have any idea what my dreams were like for the first, say, three and a half years after our Senior Class celebration? (*Pauses.*) You think I really missed our reunions, Arch? Really? I had one a night – in my dreams – for three and a half years. That's a shitload of getting-together, don't you agree? (*Sternly.*) Don't you agree? (*No reply. She screams at them.*) *Don't you agree?* (*She stands her ground now, staring directly at* **Archie** *and at* **George**. **Archie** *bows his head;* **George** *giggles. She swallows a sob; pauses. She speaks to* **Archie**, *quietly, excluding* **George** *at first.*) I had no plan to get even, Archie: none. I took this trip home because my brother Peter took what they call in the medical game 'a turn for the worst'. He's extremely weak, extremely frail, extremely close to the end. The doctors told me Peter wouldn't be able to talk to me. But as soon as I sat next to him, he talked. He has a strong memory of our beach party. He wept, and he begged my forgiveness. I gave Peter my forgiveness and it made him feel 'wickid good'. It made me feel 'wickid good', too. Call me crazy, but I kinda' figured you guys'd be begging my forgiveness, too. But, the truth is, after having this little First Reunion, fellas, I would like to kill both of you. I would very much like to watch both of you suffer and die: be dead. (**Archie** *moans;* **George** *giggles.*) It looks like Getting-Even is just the kinda' guy I am.

**Archie**   I, uh, I, uh, 'm sorry, Marg. I really am. I never thought what was done was a good thing. I never thought that. I am . . . uh . . . well . . . ashamed. I wish it never happened. I wish there was a way of takin' it back, 'cause I would. I'm awful sorry, Marg, I am. But I gotta tell ya som'pin': What they did was *dirty*, Marg. What I did was *making love*, and that's the truth. I've never loved another woman besides you, Marg. Not even one. I'm beggin' ya' to believe me and forgive me.

**George** (*in disgust*)   He loves Bunny Palumbo, this Billy-Goat does.

**Margy** (*glares at* **George**, *momentarily; then to* **Archie**)   I believe you, Archie . . . and I forgive you, Archie, I do. (**Margy** *cradles* **Archie**'s *head, watching* **George** *as she does. She prods* **George** *into action.*) Do you see this, George? I've just forgiven Archie.

**George**   I don't like this . . . You're just forgivin' him: not me, too? (*Pauses.*) Stay back from him, Bunny. (*Steps toward them.*) You hear me?

**Margy**   You're not splitting us up, George. I choose my date for the Twentieth, Archie: you. I do . . .

**Archie**   Really?

**George** (*genuinely upset, runs at* **Archie** *and kicks him between the legs, from behind.* **George** *now faces* **Margy**)   You think you can just hop back inta town and be another person from what you are? You are who you are, Bunny, hop, hop, huh? Huh? (*He unhitches belt.*) What I want here is what you gave my friend about an hour ago. What's wanted here is more lovemakin' . . .

**Margy** (*hits* **George**)   Put it out of your mind, George . . .

**George**   It's already *in* my mind! (*He moves to* **Margy**, *who slaps his face, again, violently. He reels backward.*)

**Margy**   Don't you raise your hand toward me . . . ever . . . *ever!* Not a hand . . . not an eye . . . not a word . . . (*She slaps*

*his face.*) From you . . . nothing is wanted, George Ferguson
. . . (*She slaps his face.*) Nothing!

**George** ( *feeling his cheek. He is next to* **Archie** *now, who is
standing, head bowed*)    You hit me? Great! Now, I'm hitting
this one . . . (**George** *backhands* **Archie**, *who screams in pain.*)

**Margy**    God damn you! (*She slaps* **George**.)

**George** (**George** *backhands* **Archie** *again*)    I don't even like
you *talkin'* to me, Marg!

**Margy**    What have they done to you, George? What have
they done to to you to make you so incredibly dumb? (*She
hits* **George**. **George** *backhands* **Archie**.) Have they beaten
you? Have you been tortured? (*She hits* **George** *again.*
**George** *backhands* **Archie** *again.*) I'd like you to stop now,
George. Put your hand at your side . . . George? Did you
hear me? I don't want you to raise your hand to Archie
again. Put your hand down, George. (**George** *smiles. He
suddenly, without breaking his stare at* **Margy**, *hits* **Archie** *with
the back of his hand, dealing a terrible blow.*) George! (*She swings at*
**George**, *who shoves her aside.* **Margy** *falls on her back on the
mound of old newspapers. It looks as though* **George** *will rape her.*)

**George**    Nothin' changes, Margy . . . (*He pulls her up to her
feet, her back to audience.*) Nothin' changes. Not around here.
Nothin' . . . (*He rips her blouse open. She is bare-breasted. Her
naked shoulders glisten against the filth of the old newspapers, and
against the filth of* **George***'s leering, hateful stare.*) I knew it! I
*fuckin' knew it*! (*To* **Archie**.) No underwear on top! . . . You
see this, Arch? (*Yells.*) Do . . . you . . . see . . . this? (*To*
**Margy**.) No shame. No shame, you. No shame . . . (**Archie**
*pulls himself up from the ground and moves towards* **George**, *stands
square with him.*) Hey, Arch, c'mon, huh? . . . You look
wicked awful pissed . . . (**Archie** *grabs* **George**. *The two large
men wrestle.* **George** *gains an advantage, shoving* **Archie** *atop a
low bale.* **George** *runs to baler, finds tool box and grabs a hammer.
He bashes head of hammer against front of baler, as* **Archie** *advances
toward him: a warning.* **Archie** *moves in.* **George** *swings hammer
at* **Archie***'s head.* **Archie** *ducks under, lifting* **George** *high over*

*his head. The hammer crashes down on the baler's steel steps.* **Archie** *rolls* **George** *onto floor, twisting* **George**'s *arm, forcing* **George** *to drop hammer to cement floor.* **Archie** *throws* **George** *across stage into bale of corregated cardboard, face first.* **George** *rolls onto mound of old newspapers.* **George** *rises up on his knees, confused.* **Archie** *butts* **George** *with the top of his head.* **George** *falls over backwards, stunned, hurt badly.*)

**Archie** (*to* **Margy**, *with a madman's rational voice*)   What we do is buy up old paper, bale it, and truck the bales up to the mills and sell them . . . up Fitchburg . . . Ayer . . . Shirley. (*He goes to* **George** *and kicks him in the stomach. He then chases* **George** *behind the baler and kicks* **George** *with a terrible blow.* **George** *then flies back into the audience's view, upstage right, into stack of bales. He returns to* **Margy**, *downstage, continuing his explanation of his quandary around his life's labor. He is terrible upset.*) They buy our paper and they process it, see? And they make it into paper. Use ta bother me that I was workin' so hard takin' paper to people who were makin' paper . . . I mean, it never seemed like too much of a life bringin' paper alls the way up ta Fitchburg, just so's they could make more paper. I mean, what's the world gonna do with so much paper, anyhow? (*Suddenly, silent,* **George** *pulls himself up and circles behind baler on catlike toes. He clears his blurred vision, focuses on* **Archie**. *He then runs straight at* **Archie**, *grabbing* **Archie** *in a headlock.* **Margy** *screams out.*)

**Margy**   *Archie!*

**George** (*desperately*)   Billy-Goat gonna die . . .

**Archie**   *Leggo . . . my . . . head! Leggo!* (*He relives his prophetic story of Lum by running* **George** *backwards, upstage, then flipping* **George** *into baler, face first.* **George**'s *face 'explodes', blood suddenly erupting, staining front door of baler.* **George** *falls away, upstage, face down on mound of old newspapers.* **Margy** *bows her head, leaning against a bale, facing the men.* **Archie** *runs in panic, ratlike, in quick little figure eights, from* **George** *to* **Margy** *and then to the loading door, all the way upstage. When he reaches the loading doors, he stops and calls to* **Margy**. **George**'s *blood is*

*visible on front of baler, like Oriental brush-painting.*) George . . . all
bloody, Margy . . . We're in trouble . . . Margy . . . run . . .
run, Margy, run, run, Margy, run, run, run . . . (**Margy** *goes
silently to* **George***, looks at him. She then looks at blood on baler
door. She touches blood, pulling her hand down through stain, enlarging
stain.* **Margy** *goes to locker; collects her jacket, scarf, sweater, purse.*
**Archie** *runs around back of baler, downstage, calls across to*
**Margy***, begs her to leave.*) Please, Margy run, run . . . run,
Margy, please, run, please? . . . (**Margy** *moves a few steps
toward* **Archie***, stops when she makes eye contact with* **Archie***;
speaks.*)

**Margy** (*simply, clearly*)    I'll be back, Archie. It's a long list.
(*She moves directly to loading doors, exits, slamming door behind her.*
**Archie** *is stunned, unmovingly. He runs in ratlike half-circle to
loading doors, as if to prove to himself that* **Margy** *is really gone. He
again moves to the fallen* **George***.*)

**Archie**    Kermie? Kermie? C'mon, Kermie, we got ta run.
Kermie? It's Billy-Goat, Kermie? (*Rolls* **George** *over; sees that*
**George** *is dead. Groans.*) Oh, Jesus! Archie Crisp just killed
Georgie Ferguson and there's gonna be wicked awful hell-
ta-pay . . . (*Returns to* **George***.*) C'mon, Kermie, huh? We
gotta run! Kermie! C'mon, Kermie . . . Don't be dead,
Kermie, don't be dead! (**Archie** *lifts* **George***'s arm and tries
to coax* **George** *back into life. He drags* **George** *by the feet to front
of baler.*) This ain't funny, Kermie, ya dumb blow'ah . . .
C'mon, huh? This here's wicked awful scary, Kerm!
Kermie! Don't be dead, Kermie . . . (**Archie** *covers* **George**
*with old newspapers.*) Oh, Jesus! Kermie? Don't be dead,
Kermie . . . Don't be dead, Kermie . . . Don't be dead,
Kermie . . . DON'T BE DEAD! (**Archie** *stands, back to baler,
the mound that is* **George***'s newspaper-covered dead body at*
**Archie***'s feet.* **Archie***'s breathing is loud, labored, rhythmical.*
**Archie** *stares straight out into auditorium. His eyes are dead, hollow.
It is the stare of a blind man. He breathes deeply, four audible breaths.
All lights fade out, but for single work light overhead.* **Archie***'s
breathing stops. There is a moment of absolute silence.*)

*Sudden blackout.*

# Park Your Car in Harvard Yard

*For Gillian*

*Park Your Car in Harvard Yard* opened on Broadway, New York, at the Music Box Theatre on 7 November 1991. It was presented by Robert Whitehead, Roger L. Stevens, Kathy Levin and American National Theatre and Academy. The play was directed by Zoe Caldwell and designed by Ben Edwards. The cast was as follows:

**Jacob Brackish**  Jason Robards
**Kathleen Hogan**  Judith Ivey

Earlier versions of the play were produced in 1983 at the Los Angeles Theatre Center, directed by Bill Bushnell, and at the Manhattan Theatre Club in 1984 where the cast was as follows:

**Jacob Brackish**  Burgess Meredith
**Kathleen Hogan**  Ellen Burstyn

## Characters

**Jacob Brackish**, *80(ish); a Yankee Jew, Gloucester native*
**Kathleen Hogan**, *40(ish); an Irish Catholic Yankee, Gloucester native*

## Place

The action of the play is set in the upstairs and downstairs rooms of the home of Jacob Brackish, East Gloucester, Massachusetts: a small 1850s wooden-framed, two-story Victorian house, with slightly Gothic pretensions.

## Time

From one winter to the next: the final year of Jacob Brackish's life.

## The Sequence of the Scenes of the Play

Sequence One – End of Winter
Sequence Two – Spring/Summer (Tourists in town)
Sequence Three – Autumn (Tourists gone from Town)
Sequence Four – Start of Winter

# One: The End of Winter

*The audience is seated. House lights remaining up in auditorium. We hear Vivaldi, Concerto in A Minor, played over auditorium loudspeaker.*

*The voice of* **Byron Weld** *interrupts the music to make a small announcement – a plea for money for his one-man fm-radio station. As* **Weld** *speaks, Vivaldi fades under.*

**Byron Weld***'s voice is the quintessential sound of North Shore Massachusetts speech. It is the very essence of 'wicked awful' . . . it hems and it haws. It is a veritable symphony of upper nasal croak and squeal, combined with splintery timbres of remarkably old age; years of poverty; a lifetime of frustration.*

**Byron Weld** (*over loudspeaker*)   This is Byron Weld, WGLO-FM, Gloucester, Massachusetts, on Cape Ann. If you think wint'ah's rough where you're sittin', try comin' 'round here by the transmitt'ah! You'll know what *rough* is! I got so many air leaks around the windows, every time the wind blows, the curtains shoot out straight, parallel to the floor and the ceilin' which, by the way, stopped leakin', finally, 'cause it's so cold in here, the water that was pouring through the holes *actually froze up* . . . but, you'll never hear *me* complain! (*New, solicitous attitude.*) Donations can be addressed to me, Byron Weld, WGLO-FM, Gloucester, Massachusetts, 01930. Don't hold back 'cause you think what you're sendin' is too small. I'll take anything . . .

*The auditorium lights are black by now, and we begin to hear the sounds of a winter's storm.*

**Byron Weld**   Antonio Vivaldi lived from 1678 to 1741. He wrote five gorgeous cello concerti. This one is his Concerto in A Minor, RV422, on an RCA Red Seal Recording featuring Ofra Hanroy, on the cello, with Paul Robinson conducting.

*We again hear the agonizing sound of the Andante of Vivaldi's
Concerto in A Minor, soft, Baroque. Additionally, we hear the storm
sounds, now increased.*

*Music to full.*

*Note: The season is winter. Any exterior foliage on set is without
greenery: absolutely bare.*

*Lights up in rooms of late nineteenth-century wood-framed 'Gothic
Victorian' house.*

*Upstairs, two bedrooms visible, but dimly lit in this first scene.
Downstairs, we see living room, dining area and kitchen alcove.
Overstuffed chair, center; sofa, bookshelves crammed with books, stereo
and speakers (prominent), substantial collection of records, CDs and
cassettes on bookcase.*

*It is February, deadly cold; night. In the distance, the wind howls, the
odd hound bays, the copious buoys sway, causing their warning bells to
chime; the lighthouse foghorn bleats its endless caution; a seagull
screeches out in hunger. A seasonal thunderclap claps.*

**Jacob Brackish** *and* **Kathleen Hogan** *stand near the door.*
**Brackish** *is ancient and frail of frame, but he is powerful and
immeasurably authoritative. By contrast,* **Kathleen** *is quiet and
mousey. She is a strong-backed woman, around the age of forty. Both
are quite tweedy.* **Brackish** *wears baggy trousers, dress shirt, necktie
and baggy wool coat-sweater.* **Kathleen** *wears wool skirt, black
tights and wool sweater. A swatch of black fabric is in evidence, pinned
to* **Kathleen**'s *sweater. She is in mourning.* **Brackish** *holds*
**Kathleen**'s *dripping wet raincoat and is about to find a hook on
which to hang it. She clutches dripping wet boots.*

*Note: Hearing aid in* **Brackish**'s *right ear prominent.*

**Kathleen** *stares at* **Brackish** *each time he looks away. When he
looks at her, she stares downward; frightened. He is animated. She is
paralysed. They are both intensely anxious. He goes to radio; turns off
music.*

**Brackish**    Kathleen I . . . I'm very happy you're here.

**Kathleen**   I . . . I'm very happy to be here, Mr Brackish.

**Brackish**   I'm very pleased that it was a person like you who answered my advertisement. (*Notices boots hugged in her arms.*) You wouldn't believe how few people replied. You think nobody needed work around these parts. Not that you wouldn't have landed the job if dozens had replied. I mean . . . you would have . . . (*Pause.*) It's not like I'll live for ever, you know . . . You'll still be young when this is over, Kathleen. I can promise you *that*.

**Kathleen**   I'm not complaining.

**Brackish**   No, no, you're not . . .

**Kathleen** (*laughs, nervously; sees puddle on carpet caused by her boots*)   Gawd! I made a wicked big puddle on your carpet! (*She bends down, quickly, tries to rub out the wetness with corner of her scarf. She looks up at* **Brackish***, laughs again nervously.*) Just rubbin' it up . . .

**Brackish**   Could you please let me take your *boots*, Kathleen?

**Kathleen** *removes a wadded packette of letters and money from her boot, pockets it.*

**Brackish**   Ohh, I see. Valuables . . .

**Kathleen**   Here. I'm really wicked sorry about yo'r carpet . . .

**Brackish** *goes to the doorway, hangs up coat and floors her boots.* **Kathleen** *stares about the room, intently. Her suitcase is near the door.* **Brackish** *lifts the same, returns to her proximity, smiles at her, nervously.* **Kathleen** *averts her eyes.*

**Brackish**   I imagine that your stomach's in knots, too, Kathleen . . . This isn't an everyday sort of occurrence.

**Kathleen**   I'm not complaining, Mr Brackish . . .

**Brackish**   Oh, I know you're not . . . (*Pauses.*) I've resisted having a housekeeper, but this last spell (I had) was a pip

... I saw Doctor Chandler, up Addison Gilbert. He was my student, two thousand years ago. He gives me six months to a year, if I turn myself into the hospital for total bed-rest. But, I prefer to live it out in luxury, thank you very much, right here in my own house. So, you've got yourself a job, and I've got myself an employee.

**Kathleen**    I'm not complaining, really ... What with my husband passin' on so sudden and leavin' me with next ta nothin', I mean, really, I'm happy ta be here ... ta be your housekeeper 'n all. Happy. (*Pauses nervously.*) Six months to a year is fine with me ...

**Brackish**    Yes. I see ... (*Hands suitcase to her.*) You're probably tired. You should go on up ... I hope the room's not gonna be too tiny for you ...

**Kathleen**    Oh, Gawd, no! First time I ever had a room on my own! I always had'da share with my sistahs kinda' thing ... Afta' I got married, a'course, I shared with my hus'bin. (*Smiles, nervously.*) This'll be my first room. My first bed, too ...

**Brackish**    You never had a *bed*?

**Kathleen**    On my *own*! I always had'da share beds ... before here.

**Brackish**    Ah, yes. I see what you mean ... I think ... Well, now ... The things you dropped off, yesterday, are up there, already ... I cleaned out four drawers for you. If you need more storage space, I can find the room, I'm sure.

**Kathleen**    Gawd, look at that! You've got about a million records. (*Smiles timidly; then looks directly at* **Brackish**.) I personally never saw the need for accumulation. It'll be fine.

**Brackish** (*looks up at her; confused*)    Accumulation of my records'll be 'fine'? Your antecedent is unclear.

**Kathleen**    Oh, gosh, no! Not y'or records. I just meant my *stuff*! Four drawers will be more than enough for my stuff!

**Brackish** (*senses* **Kathleen**'s *deep discomfort*)   We'll both be more relaxed with each other in short order. I know you're not complaining, Kathleen. It's just that the intimacy of the thing never occurred to me. These rooms have been mine, alone, for, well . . . (*Pauses, uncomfortably; crosses to his chair.*) This chair has been my closest friend . . . my comfort and my company . . . my sole *confidant*. It's a hell of a thing when a man comes to depend on his chair not only to hold up his backside but, also, to hold up the other side of the *conversation* . . . (*He pats chair, lovingly.*) I've come to love my chair, Kathleen . . . Me and my chair . . . the two of us . . . against the world! (*He sits in chair, picks up writing board, slots writing board across arms of chair: a perfect fit. He now pauses. His eyes turn in. He is still and silent, totally lost in a memory.* **Kathleen** *turns away, looks up staircase, or at records. When she looks at* **Brackish** *again, she thinks he's dead.*)

**Kathleen**   Mr Brackish? . . . Mr Brackish? . . . *Mr Brackish!*

**Brackish** ( *jostled out of his reverie*)   Hmmm?

**Kathleen**   I was just afraid maybe the doctor, you know, underestimated. I can bring the most wicked awful bad luck ta people! I got ta tell you: I have personally had all the death I can take for a while . . . (*Painfully embarrassed by what she's just said.*) I'd better go on up.

**Kathleen** *exits up the stairs.* **Brackish** *sits in his chair, looks out front, extremely worried.*

*We see* **Kathleen** *in her room, above. She goes to window, looks outside. She, too, is extremely worried. Note: Escape steps must be built into* **Kathleen**'s *bedroom, leading into kitchen. When lights dim down in* **Kathleen**'s *room, she immediately goes down escape steps into darkened kitchen. Continuous action must be felt.*

*Lights crossfade to* **Brackish**, *downstairs. He goes to the radio, turns it on. Bach emanates from the radio, filling the house. He then executes his morning routine, compulsively tidying living room straightening papers and furniture., etc., etc., precisely.*

*Bach is now interrupted by* **Byron Weld**, *who makes a second small plea for public funding.*

**Byron Weld** (*over lightly playing music*)   This is Byron Weld, WGLO-FM, Gloucester, Massachusetts, on Cape Ann. You are listening to Johann Sebastian Bach, music that's been played continuously by music lovers ever since it was first written in 1725. Imagine! Music that's held up more than two hundred and fifty years, when this music station won't hold up another twenty-five *days* if you don't send in some hard cold cash. This is a final warning!

**Brackish** (*calls out, loudly, to* **Kathleen**)   Kathleen? Hullooo?

**Kathleen** (*off*)   I'm in the pantry, Mr Brackish!

**Brackish**   *Still?*

**Kathleen** (*enters*)   I've got about a half-dozen more to go.

**Brackish**   Isn't it cold out there?

**Kathleen**   Oh, yuh, wickid . . . It's freezing.

**Brackish**   I don't want you to freeze to death on your first day! Finish up in here!

**Kathleen**   That'll be alright?

**Brackish**   What'll be alright? Freezing to death on your first day, or finishing up in here?

**Kathleen**   To iron . . . in with you!

**Brackish**   It'll be fine.

**Kathleen**   I'll get my stuff. (*She disappears, and quickly reappears, carrying ironing board. She knocks into furniture with ironing board; knocks pots off stove. She attempts to collapse ironing board. It won't. And then refuses to open. Finally, it explodes open. She sets up ironing board near desk in living room.*) Sorry for bangin' inta everything . . . A strange ironing board can kill a woman. (*She giggles, nervously.*) No problem . . . (*Giggles again.*) I'll get the iron . . . (*She does.*) I'll plug in here . . . (*She plugs it*

*in under desk; stands; touches iron; burns fingers.*) Oh, *Gawd*! It's
still hot! . . . No problem. (*She runs off, again, reappears with
laundry basket filled with white shirts about to be ironed, plus, an
armload of freshly ironed shirts; holds up shirts to iron.*) These are
the ones to do . . . (*She now holds up armload of freshly ironed
shirts, on wire hangers.*) These are the done ones . . . They'll be
much better over here by the grate where it's wa'm . . .
(*Begins to hang the shirts from bookshelves, above the fireplace grate.*)
They're still slightly dampish . . . The heat comin' out ta the
grate here will dry 'em nice. (*She now hangs freshly ironed white
shirts everywhere . . . The effect should be such that* **Kathleen***'s
enthusiastic labor – and her boundless energy – changes the look of the
room, absolutely.* **Brackish** *watches* **Kathleen***, bewildered.*) Are
you ready for another cup'pa tea yet?

**Brackish**    No more tea, Kathleen, please! I don't want to
hurt your feelings, but I don't want to drown in my own
living room, either! (*Suddenly, he whacks his hearing aid; yells at*
**Kathleen***.*) *What?*

**Kathleen** (*startled*)    What?

**Brackish**    My hearing aid died out! (*Points to his ear.*) I
can't hear you. I'm deaf as a haddock without this thing! (*He
taps hearing aid twice.*) Just a minute . . . (*He crosses to small
writing desk and rummages through drawers.*)

**Brackish**    I got ta change my battery. I went dead on you
. . . (*Searches for, and finds, a new battery.*) Wicked awful thing, to
hav' ta depend on the likes of the Radio Shack to make the
difference between hearing and not hearing. (*Changes battery.*)
Ahhh . . . That fixed it. (*Suddenly, he is aware of the music.*)
Ahhhh . . . Bach . . . Concerto Number 2 in E Major.

**Byron Weld** (*on radio*)    Bach Concerto Number 3 in D
Major played by the English Concert of London, under the
direction of Trevor Pinnock . . .

**Brackish** (*overlapping*)    Goddam it, Byron, that was
Number *2* in E Major!

**Byron Weld** (*overlapping*)    . . . This is Byron Weld, your host at radio station . . .

**Brackish** (*switches radio off, angrily; turns to* **Kathleen**) Number 2 in E Major! You can take my word for it, Kathleen. The man knows *nothing*! (*He goes to his chair; sits. The moment his bottom touches down,* **Kathleen** *screams out.*)

**Kathleen**    Whoa!

**Brackish**    Somethin' wrong?

**Kathleen**    Iron's a little leaky. No problem.

**Brackish** (*looks at shirts everywhere. Looks at* **Kathleen** *ironing more shirts*)    You're not overdoing it, are you? I mean, there's no need to iron *all my shirts* the first day . . . I don't have any active *plan* for dressing-up . . .

**Kathleen**    I don't mind, really. I like ironing.

**Brackish**    OK. Well, then. Iron. (*He starts reading his newspaper: obituary page.*) Oh, dear . . . 'Porker' Watson died. Scares me to open the paper, these days. 'Course, at my age, I'm runnin' out of possibilities. (*Reads a moment; looks up, again.*) Look at that! Crispy Franklin's son died. I'm so old now I've not only outlived my friends, I've outlived their *children*! (*Makes a noise.*) Ffffhhh . . . (*Puts down the newspaper: enough awfulness: speaks to* **Kathleen**.) You've seen some tragedy yourself? I don't mean to pry, but you did mention your husband's death . . .

**Kathleen**    Oh, well . . . no point in complaining, is there?

**Brackish**    Oh, well, I dunno . . . I complain all the *time*!

**Kathleen**    I mean, nothin's bringing him back, right? Once you're dead you're dead . . .

**Brackish**    I suppose . . .

**Kathleen**    The worms crawl in, the worms crawl out kinda thing . . . (**Brackish** *looks away disgusted.*) My Da use'ta say that . . . He also use'ta say that 'all the complainin' in

the world wasn't worth two-bits for a box'a clams, down
Woodman's . . .'

**Brackish**    Woodman's . . . You grow up local? On the
North Shore, I mean? I thought you were living down the
line in Woburn? Didn't you say you grew up in Woburn?
[*Pronounced 'Wooobin'*]

**Kathleen**    Oh, noo. I was just staying up my husband's
cousin's . . . She's married to a Woburn boy . . . McGrath . . .
(*Suddenly.*) *Gosh darn it!*

**Brackish** (*stands; goes to* **Kathleen***; inspects her labor*)    What
now?

**Kathleen**    Leaked on the shirts, again . . . it's been doin'
that on me all mornin' . . .

**Brackish**    Don't worry if you spoil a couple . . . I've got a
lifetime of white shirts. (*Looks around room.*) Looks like the
Marblehead Regatta in here. (*He sees her fiddling about with the
leaky iron.*) You can't fill it all the way. If you drain off some
of the water, you'll be fine . . . (*Makes small joke.*) I think I
bought that iron off President Taft . . .

**Kathleen**    Mmm . . . (*Thinks about* **Brackish***'s small joke.*)
Oh . . . Got'cha! (*She* doesn't *drain off any water. She continues to
iron.* **Brackish** *watches her.*)

**Brackish**    Say, aren't you gonna' . . . (*She looks up*) . . .
Drain it off?

**Kathleen**    No point in drainin' it *off* with just a couple of
shirts to go . . .

**Brackish**    It'll only leak . . .

**Kathleen**    It's goin' better . . .

**Brackish**    Suit yourself.

*He returns to his chair; sits.* **Kathleen** *completes ironing another
shirt, buttons it onto a wire clothes hanger, walks it past* **Brackish**
*into living room, hangs it on an inappropriate place in living room. She*

*manages to move furniture and papers, somehow undoing* **Brackish**'s *compulsive morning routine.* **Brackish**'s *space is (clearly) invaded. And he is (clearly) not happy.*

**Brackish** (*pauses; sighs deeply*)    This first day is probably the most difficult we'll ever have . . . together, I mean . . .

**Kathleen**    Oh, well, I guess, yuh . . . (*She crosses to get another shirt.*)

**Brackish** (*his most practiced, most charming smile*)    You mentioned you had sisters.

**Kathleen** (*she is relieved; chirps her answer*)    Oh, yuh . . . two, plus me, for three. Irish triplets. All three of us sistahs born in less than four years . . . They both went to Catholic school. I'm the only one got to go to public school. I'm the baby. (*Laughs.*) We're all 'eens'.

**Brackish**    I beg your pardon?

**Kathleen** (*steps forward to tell what is, possibly, the best joke she knows*)    Me and my sistahs . . . We're all 'eens' . . . Maureen, Doreen and Kathleen. (**Brackish** *doesn't laugh.* **Kathleen**'s *courage withers.*) I guess they didn't have a lot of time for thinkin' up imaginative names or nothin' . . . .

**Brackish**    It's quite difficult for me to follow the complexity of your sentences, Kathleen . . . the twistings and the turnings, so to speak *'We're* all "eens"' . . . '*They* didn't have a lot of time for thinkin' up names' . . . The antecedents to many of your pronouns are not precisely clear . . . not as clear as they should be . . . (*Sees he's hurt her feelings.*)

**Kathleen**    I guess I should finish . . . up. (*She stands, goes to ironing board. She picks up iron. Water gushes out onto shirt and onto floor.*) Goddamn it!

**Brackish**    What?

**Kathleen**    Oh, Lord! Sorry to be swearin' in the house!

**Brackish**    What happened?

**Kathleen** (*lifts the arm of the white shirt that she has been ironing. It is brown, stained, ruined*)    The iron leaks brown rusty water . . . It's all over the floor . . . I can bleach this out . . . (*She puts shirt into laundry basket; starts to iron another.*)

**Brackish**    Aren't you gonna mop it up? . . . The rusty water!

**Kathleen**    I'll get to it, later. No point in moppin' it up and havin' it leak again . . . moppin' it up, havin' it leak, moppin' it up, havin' it leak . . . over and over. I'll get to it later . . .

**Brackish**    It's your decision . . .

**Kathleen** (*after a few moments of thoughtful ironing*)    I don't speak well, do I, Mr Brackish? From a point of view of bein' understood quickly, or, you know, bein' a natural conversationalist kinda' thing . . . From a language point of view, I mean. (*Pauses; thinks.*) My husband cooked short order. He never had much of a mind for long sentences. Just quick little ideas. 'Hi. How's it goin'?' kinda' thing. 'I'm hot, I'm cold, I'm tired . . .' Those kinda' little quick ideas . . . I mean, the only thing he said to let me know the heart attack was comin' on was 'Heart!'

**Brackish**    'Heart!'?

**Kathleen**    That was it!

**Brackish**    Certainly not much warning there.

**Kathleen**    He was dead inside a minute. (*Irons; thinks.*) Coulda' be'n worse, I guess . . .

**Brackish**    I guess . . .

**Kathleen** (*she stares a moment, lost in a memory*)    He hated music.

**Brackish**    I actually *taught* music. Music Appreciation and English Literature . . .

**Kathleen**    'Course, you did! You taught my husband.

**Brackish**    I didn't know your *husband* was local . . . His name was . . . ?

**Kathleen**    Otto . . . Otto Hogan.

**Brackish**    Possibly . . . There were so many . . . Possibly . . .

**Kathleen**    Definitely! (His name was) Otto Hogan . . . We called him 'Princie' . . .

**Brackish** (*sincerely*)    I'm afraid I don't remember your Princie, Kathleen. I hope that doesn't hurt your feelings any . . .

**Kathleen**    Oh, no, Mr Brackish, really . . . it don't matter . . .

**Brackish**    Strictly speaking, I suppose it really doesn't.

**Kathleen**    I don't have any kinda' wicked serious regrets . . . if you get my message . . .

**Brackish**    I certainly do.

**Kathleen**    He was good to me.

**Brackish**    I'm sure of it . . .

**Kathleen**    We had our fun.

**Brackish**    No doubt of that . . .

**Kathleen** (*pauses; has a memory*)    He wore a bright orange shirt every day. Day and night. I don't even think they required it.

**Brackish**    I really don't get your message, this time, Kathleen. *Syntactical! Who* required the orange shirt?

**Kathleen**    Bob's Clam Shack. Princie cooked short order for 'em.

**Brackish** (*he's had enough. He rolls his eyes to Heaven*)    Why should I want to remember this 'Princie' person? . . .

(*Realizes his gaffe.*) . . . Your *husband*, I mean . . . Was there anything unusual about him . . . ?

**Kathleen**   He saved your life.

**Brackish**   In what sense, Kathleen?

**Kathleen**   It was years back, when you use'ta work summers givin' lectures on the tourist boat, in the harbor . . . the *Dixie Bell* . . . Princie was havin' a cigarette out back'a Bob's, and he saw ya' flip over and he swam out . . .

**Brackish**   My God!

**Kathleen**   You were trapped under the boat with three tourists.

**Brackish**   Labor Day Weekend . . . *YES*! I was in a stupor from their endless questions about cheap lobsters and early Americana. A former student . . . swam out . . . saved us . . . and thank the Lord he did, they woulda' buried me with *tourists*! . . . I remember that he wore an odd uniform . . . orange . . .

**Kathleen**   That's what I've be'n tellin' ya!

**Brackish**   . . . He wasn't one of the good ones . . . students . . . I remember that. He wasn't one of the good students.

**Kathleen**   You flunked him in English and gave him a D-plus in Music Appreciation.

**Brackish**   Really? I suppose I had to . . .

**Kathleen** (*moves to collect shirts from shelves*)   It wasn't like he was dumb . . . retarded, or nothin' . . .

**Brackish**   Some were, Kathleen . . . some of them actually *were* . . . dumb, retarded. My memory system has set up a kind of magical defense against remembering the failures: they fail, I forget. If 'To err is human' then 'to forget is *divine*' . . . Forgiving is forgetting! . . . *Je ne me souviens pas donc içi suis! Non momento ergo sum!*

*He laughs heartily at his own arcane joke. On hearing his laugh,*
**Kathleen** *wheels about and [accidently?] drops armload of*
**Brackish***'s freshly ironed white shirts, floorward, into the rusty*
*water. An instant of shocked silence.*

**Brackish**   You've dropped them in the muddy water! Oh,
Kathleen, I told you six times to mop it up! Oh, Kathleen!
What a shame! What a waste of effort! Oh, dear . . . Oh,
dear . . .

*He turns and goes to the radio, switches it on.* **Kathleen** *swishes*
*stack of shirts around on wet floor, mops up water.* **Brackish***,*
*satisfied that he's found* **Byron***'s station, goes to chair, finds*
*newspaper, opens same; sits; reads.* **Kathleen***, in the meantime, has*
*placed the soiled shirts in a saucepan to which she adds some bleach.*
*Note: Aroma of bleach wanted.* **Brackish** *sniffs the air; looks over at*
**Kathleen***, smugly.*

**Brackish**   Brahms. Notice the contrapuntal shading . . .
(*Hums along with music.*) Dah dee dah dummm . . . (*Calls to*
**Kathleen***.*) *A* composer of great sobriety. Don't you agree?
(**Kathleen** *is nervously bleaching out the shirts. She fakes paying*
*attention with false admiration for Brahms.*)

**Kathleen**   Me? Oh, yuh . . . Marvelous.

**Brackish**   What the hell's that smell?

**Kathleen**   Bleach water. I could do it outside.

**Brackish**   In the snow?

**Kathleen**   I guess I won't . . . (*Nervous giggle.*) I forgot about
the snow . . .

**Brackish**   It smells like more than just bleach . . .

**Kathleen** (*suddenly realizes that pan on stove is on open flame,*
*empty, burnt*)   Ah, shoot! The pot's burnt! (*She leaps to stove,*
*burns her hand, She screams out.*) Ahhhh! (*She tries to pretend that*
*she hasn't burnt her hand.*) No problem! (*She does a little dance*
*around kitchen after chucking hot pot loudly into sink and running cold*
*water on to the thing, causing steam and sizzling sound in room.*)

**Brackish** (*watches the entire sketch in astonishment*)   You OK?

**Kathleen**   Oh, yuh, perfect.

**Brackish**   It was an old pot. Not to worry . . .

**Kathleen**   Oh, no . . . pot's OK. It was only bleach water . . .

**Brackish**   In the pot?

**Kathleen**   Mmmm . . .

**Brackish**   In the pot that boiled away?

**Kathleen**   That's all. Nothin' black . . .

**Brackish**   Bleach was boiling away all that time . . . evaporating into the air we breathe?

**Kathleen**   I s'pose. Yuh . . .

**Brackish**   That's chlorine . . .

**Kathleen** (*corrects* **Brackish**, *lightly*)   Chlorox . . .

**Brackish**   When chlorine evaporates into the air, it is deadly, Kathleen, *deadly* . . .

**Kathleen**   I'll crack the window . . . (*She opens kitchen window.*) There. That should be better . . .

**Brackish**   The German nation was censured by the entire *world* for using chlorine gas in World War I . . .

**Kathleen**   You can hardly smell it now . . .

**Brackish**   Chlorine gas causes a slow, devastatingly painful death.

**Kathleen**   I'll crack open the back door, too (*She cracks open the back door. She smiles.*) Smell's all gone in here. Really . . . (**Brackish** *coughs.* **Kathleen** *begins to scrub pot enthusiastically.*) I'll have this shining like a baby's beehind in no time at all.

(**Brackish** *rolls his eyes to heaven. He reopens his* Boston Globe; *reads. The Brahms piece has concluded and now Bach's Chaconne fills*

*the world, brilliantly.* **Brackish** *listens to the music a moment. He is
embarrassed by his behavior toward* **Kathleen**. *He looks over at her;
watches her labor a moment, silently. He tries to make calming small
talk, speaks.*)

**Brackish**   I don't know why the *Globe* gives so much
attention to the marathon runners. The sport requires no
brains at all. It's just left, right, left, right. I mean what *is* the
big deal, I ask you?

**Kathleen** (*absently, barely looking up*)   Hmmm?

**Brackish**   The Boston Marathon . . .

**Kathleen**   Mmm?

**Brackish**   It's weeks off, and they're already startin' to
tout the thing . . .

**Kathleen** (*displays clean pot*)   See? Good as new.

**Brackish**   Why don't you take a break now, Kathleen . . .
(*Pauses.*) You don't hav'ta work day and night . . . It isn't as if
we're goin' against any kind of *deadline*, here . . . (*Pauses.*) Sit
down, Kathleen . . . Take a break . . .

**Kathleen** *smiles. She enters the living room, nervously. She takes her
quilting basket, sits on sofa, in corner of seat at furthermost possible
distance from* **Brackish**. *Bach's Chaconne plays on, in spite of all.*
**Brackish** *looks over at* **Kathleen**, *who is now sitting on the sofa,
intently working on a patchwork quilt. She is deciding among various
patches which to appliqué and which to discard.*

**Brackish** (*aware of the music; smiles*)   You hear this piece,
Kathleen?

**Kathleen** (*intent on choosing quilting patches, doesn't look up. She
fakes an interest; smiles and grunts, lightly*)   Mm.

**Brackish**   Bach. The Chaconne.

**Kathleen**   Mmmmmm.

**Brackish**   The same few notes are repeated in different
variations. Twenty-nine of them in all: variations. The

untrained ear would never hear the repetition, but I do. I hear 'em all. And they scare me silly . . .

**Kathleen**    Mmm.

**Brackish**    Over and over, nothing changes, sometimes faster, sometimes slower, sometimes broken into bits and pieces that accumulate in the memory and one day shock you with the realization 'I've heard all this before!' . . . It honestly does scare me silly . . .

*Following speeches overlap.*

**Kathleen**    That's what scares me, too . . . the repetition . . . (*Pauses;* **Brackish** *barely looks at her.*) The waking up one morning and the realizing 'I've done all this before . . . over and over again . . .'

**Brackish**    Even the beautiful parts of it irk and irritate . . . irk and irritate.

**Kathleen**    The seagulls screaming and screeching . . . The bed getting made and unmade . . . the food shopped, cooked, eaten, shopped, cooked, eaten . . .

**Brackish**    Twenty-nine variations in all . . . twenty-nine variations.

**Kathleen**    Huh? (*She looks at* **Brackish**, *absently.*)

**Brackish**    The Chaconne, Kathleen . . . (*Annoyed.*) This Bach piece . . . (*Shakes head in schoolteacherish fashion; scolds her.*) Don't you *ever* pay attention, Kathleen?

**Kathleen** *is devastated. She stands, takes her quilting basket and runs upstairs to her room. She sits on her bed. She is unhappy. Downstairs,* **Brackish** *is thoughtful after* **Kathleen**'s *exit from the room. He feels guilty. Upstairs,* **Kathleen** *sits on her bed; unhappy. The Chaconne concludes.* **Brackish** *goes from his chair to the staircase. He pauses a while, as though looking upstairs. He listens, as well. He goes to bookcase and removes hearing aid batteries from where he hid them earlier; depositing same in wastebasket beside desk. He then covers them with waste paper.* **Brackish** *goes to the radio,*

*carrying hearing aid in his hand. On the radio, we hear: Beethoven's*
Diabelli Variations. *He turns the volume up full blast, deliberately.*
**Kathleen** *hears the change; perks up her ears.*

**Brackish**    Damn it, damn it, damn it! (*He moves to foot of
stairs; screams up to* **Kathleen**.) Could you come down here?
Hello? Helloooo? (*He now crosses to writing desk; begins fishing
through drawers. He continues to call* **Kathleen** *as he searches for
fresh batteries.*)

**Kathleen** (*appears; top of stairs*)    Did you call me? (*No
response; she screams over Beethoven blasting from radio.*) Did . . . you
. . . call . . . me. Mr Brackish? (*No response.*) MR BRACKISH!

**Brackish**    I'll have to ask you to go out and buy some
batteries for me . . .

**Kathleen**    *Now?* It's freezing out there!

**Brackish**    *What?*

**Kathleen**    Yuh, sure, why not . . .

**Brackish**    Be an angel, will you, and fire down to Radio
Shack . . . Better still, try Tru-Value . . . yes, Tru-Value . . .
(*Reaches into pocket, produces wallet and cash.*) Better buy two.

**Kathleen** (*makes an 'OK' sign with her thumb and forefinger, three
remaining fingers in the air above the circle*)    Fine. I'll buy two . . .
right away . . . (*She takes overcoat from clothes tree, puts it on. Takes
hat from hook.*)

**Brackish**    Bundle up, now, young lady . . . I wouldn't
want your catching your death on my conscience . . .
(**Kathleen** *smiles.* **Brackish** *thinks she has spoken to him.*)
What?

**Kathleen** *puts her cap atop her head; en route to door, sneaks to
radio; switches the station. We hear: jazz station, Miles Davis being
played.* **Kathleen** *allows the music to play for a moment; checks*
**Brackish**. *He doesn't hear: no reaction. She switches station,
again, settling now on a raucous, caustic rap song . . . MC Hammer
or Ice T.* **Brackish** *does not seem to hear the music – thus, does not*

*at all react to it.* **Kathleen** *smiles; exits, quickly, never looking back.* **Brackish***, alone, engulfed in the dreaded music, sinks low in his seat. Dreaded music swells and then concludes. The lights fade out.*

# Two: Spring / Summer

*In darkness, we hear* **Byron Weld***'s voice, on radio.*

**Byron Weld**    This is Byron Weld, WGLO-FM,
Gloucester, Massachusetts, on Cape Ann. You're in your
wa'm house, with your heat turned back on, again, against
this Memorial Day cold snap . . . no doubt toasty-warm,
while I'm sittin' here on a metal stool, by the transmitt'ah,
half frozen ta death for the want of heat. If you don't send in
your contributions, this station's closin' down. No ifs, ands
or buts. This next selection is on a Musical Heritage Society
recording, Symphony No. 40 in G Minor, K550, Wolfgang
Amadeus Mozart . . .

**Brackish** *is at the stove, fussing with a hot pot of soup, bowls,
cooking utensils. We hear: Kathleen coughing, upstairs, off – three
substantial coughs.*

**Brackish** (*calls upstairs to* **Kathleen**)    Are the vapors
helping?

**Kathleen** (*calls from bathroom, off* )    I'm just now fillin' the
bowl with hot water. (*She coughs; then sneezes.*)

*Lights up in* **Kathleen***'s bedroom. Note: Season is now
spring / summer. Exterior foliage now lush green.* **Kathleen** *enters
bedroom; sits atop bed. She is bundled in gathering of bathrobes, towels,
scarves; wears heavy stockings on her feet, over which are jammed
slippers of the 'mule' variety. She is a veritable symphony of pastels.
Her head is swathed in terry-cloth pastel toweling. There is a large
steaming pot on her lap, producing vapors, which she inhales from time
to time by means of an intricate system of toweling connecting the pot to
her headdress. Chutes of toweling are employed to convey the vapors
from pot to nostril. She coughs, six times.*

**Brackish** (*calls upstairs*)    A Memorial Day cold snap is just
God's way of telling us that the tourists are coming, and that
makes everybody sick. And that's no doubt why the good
Lord invented chickens. So there'd be a cure. (*Burns his hand;
screams out.*) Owwwwwwww! I burned my hand!

**Kathleen** (*calling downstairs; worried*)    Oh, God! Are you OK?

**Brackish** (*he does a little dance, whisking his hand, flailing his arm. He calls out, enraged. A new voice: gentlemanly*)    You'll have to excuse this, Kathleen . . . (*He throws back his head, bellows.*) HO'SSSSSSSSSSSSSSSS-SHHHHHHHHHIIIIIIITTTTT!

**Kathleen** (*after a short silence*)    Is your hand better?

**Brackish** (*calls upstairs*)    It feels just fine, now. 'There's nothing so far gone that a little ho'ss-shit can't make it better.' (**Brackish** *walks upstairs to her room carrying tray with soup etc. Calls out, while on staircase.*) My father use'ta say that. My father use'ta say lots more than that, too. (*Enters* **Kathleen***'s room.*) If this old house could talk. What it's seen, huh? (*Pours chicken soup into cup, crosses to* **Kathleen**. *She coughs.*) My mother's secret potion. Many a chicken died so that you might live, Kathleen. I suggest that you drink this slowly and reverentially . . . It tastes like what it is . . .

**Kathleen** (*samples soup*)    Uggggggggghhh! . . . Dead chickens.

**Brackish** (*smiling his agreement*)    Dead chickens . . . 'Even honey tastes like medicine when it's medicine . . .' My mother used to say that . . . (*Looks around room.*) This was my room. (*Smiles.*) This house was built by a stevedore . . . a lumper. It's a poor house. I imagine the original owner spent his life workin' the docks . . .

**Kathleen**    My father was a lumper . . .

**Brackish**    Hmmm?

**Kathleen**    Nothin' . . . Not important, really, go on . . . 'This house, built by a lumper . . .'

**Brackish**    It's tiny, really, but me bein' an only child and all . . . it was spacious . . . a perfection. Imagine . . . living an entire life in one house . . . My father bought this house when he was twenty-two years old, with money he earned, sellin' books and magazines, door-to-door, off a horse-and-buggy. He was born over in Plum Cove – God! – over a hundred years ago! He was a Yankee Jew. Quite a rare breed. He spent his last cent educating me . . . wanted the best for me. (*Pauses.*) I always figured I'd move from here one day, when I married and had children, but, I didn't: none of those things. (*Pauses: another memory.*) Forgive me if you've told me this, before, Kathleen, but did you and your husband have children?

**Kathleen**   Us? No. We never did.

**Brackish**   Understandable. It's already such a crowded planet.

**Kathleen**   I guess. All my friends were havin' 'em . . . Use ta trouble me, at first, worryin' why we were, you know, bein' *passed over.*

**Brackish**   I myself never wanted any . . .

**Kathleen**   Yuh, well, you weren't *married*, were you?

**Brackish**   Still and all, the choice is a basic human right.

**Kathleen**   Yuh, well, life's a lot different for Catholics.

**Brackish**   I suppose.

**Kathleen**   Princie was never bothered. He said he was glad to never bring any kid of his inta *this* mess.

**Brackish**   My sentiments, precisely . . .

**Kathleen**   Sittin' with his body down ta Pike's, I couldn't help but wonderin' if it might'a be'n different if we'd had 'em: kids . . .

**Brackish**   Only natural to wonder.

**Kathleen**   He was laid out four extra days, on account a' the ground froze up solid and they couldn't get a bite with the bulldozer ta get his grave dug. I had a lot of time alone with him ta think.

**Brackish**   Must've been grim.

**Kathleen**   Wasn't so bad. It was kinda' like havin' him asleep in front of the TV, only there was no TV. (*She shrugs.*) This cold is getting me mentally depressed. (*She smiles. Silence.*)

**Brackish**   I regret, Kathleen, that we have this odd coincidence between us . . . that your late husband was my student and that he . . . failed . . .

**Kathleen**   It wasn't like he was dumb or nuthin' . . . He was wicked unhappy when he found out he'd flunked English. He was supposed ta repeat, in order ta graduate, but he didn't . . . he dropped out. Since he didn't finish high school, college was out ta the question . . .

**Brackish**   And you?

**Kathleen** (*looks up*)   College? Me? No.

**Brackish**   What held you back?

**Kathleen** (*stares* **Brackish** *straight in the shoes*)   I'd have to say, more than anything, it was the grades.

**Brackish**   'The grades' in what sense, Kathleen? Antecedents.

**Kathleen** (*screws up her courage, as best she can*)   The grades you gave me in Music and English. They ruined any chance I had for a scholarship.

**Brackish**   You were my *student*?

**Kathleen**   Both subjects, yuh . . .

**Brackish**   But, I . . . My God, Kathleen! Why didn't you mention this *before*!?

**Kathleen**   No point . . .

**Brackish**   Of course, there was a *point*! I . . . I had no idea! (*He is shaken by this news.*) It's so *perverse*, Kathleen . . . *really*! You should have mentioned this to me, specifically . . . during our interview . . . You just let me ramble on and on and you never once mentioned this to me . . . My God!

**Kathleen**   I guess my feelin's got hurt, 'cause you forgot me kinda' thing . . .

**Brackish**   Kathleen, *really*. Do you have any idea of how many students passed through my life in fifty years of teaching two completely different subjects?

**Kathleen**   Lots, I guess . . .

**Brackish**   'Lots, you *guess*'? Tens of thousands, Kathleen. Tens of thousands . . . (*Pauses.*) Did you fail?

**Kathleen**   Fail? Me? Oh, I wouldn't so much say I failed as I would say I was failed. Object versus subject kinda' thing . . . You gave me a C in English IV, and a D-plus in Music Appreciation, which, a'course, pulled my Senior average down too low for a scholarship, anywhere. I didn't even bother applyin', finally . . .

**Brackish**   Oh, Kathleen . . . I *am* sorry . . .

**Kathleen**   Doesn't bother me, Mr Brackish, really. No sweat . . .

**Brackish**   Oh, no, really, I am sorry . . . I don't really remember: that's the worst: I don't really remember. I'm sure I had my reasons . . . I was fair. I was *demanding* . . . hard, strict, but I was fair! . . .

**Kathleen**   I said that it didn't bother me, OK?

**Brackish**   There were so many . . .

**Kathleen**   Yuh. There were. In my family alone, there was a number. You might even say an *astonishin'* number . . . Mother, father, husbin' . . .

**Brackish**   That I taught?

**Kathleen**   That you failed. Good thing Maureen and Doreen went to Sistah school! You probably woulda' nailed them, too! (*She smiles at an astonished* **Brackish**.) You were the toughest teacher in Gloucester, Mr Brackish. Practically no one got away . . . from *you.*

**Brackish**    I was strict. It's true.

**Kathleen**    Listen, it's really no bother to me at all. Really. I hardly think about it. And I do understand. There are tests and kids either flunk or they don't. It just happens that most of the people in Gloucester that I was connected to, did: flunk. That's just the way it happened . . . the past is the past, right. Nothin's gonna change it.

**Brackish**    What was your maiden name, Kathleen?

**Kathleen**    O'Hara.

**Brackish** (*stands; stunned*)    Was it?

**Kathleen**    My father was Jebbie O'Hara and my mother was Francine Flynn . . . I'm in the Flicker with the green cover, tenth from the end, second shelf down, if you ever wanna' check it out . . . (**Brackish** *moves into window, bends forward, terribly upset.* **Kathleen** *is suddenly aware of his upset. Foghorn sounds.*) Mr Brackish . . .

**Brackish** (*turns to her; suddenly*)    You lied to me! . . . What are you doing in my house? (*She turns away, terrified.*) Don't you turn away from me, Francine Flynn! . . .

**Kathleen**    *What?*

*Foghorn sounds again.*

**Brackish**    . . . Lying to me about who you are . . . tricking me into pleasant chat . . . (*He shivers.*) I feel cold. (*Tries to calm himself down.*) I will not have this terrible upset in my house! I never have and I never will . . . not here . . . not in this house. I simply will *not*! I'm going to my room. I want to be alone now. I should like to regain the sanctity of my home . . . I'm going to my room.

(*A distant foghorn groans.* **Brackish** *moves quickly to his room, sits atop his bed, facing front, sadly. Foghorn groans in distance, again.*

**Brackish** *and* **Kathleen** *sit in their separate rooms, each facing front, each alone, but inexorably connected to one another by their similar pride, similar guilts, their similar anger, their similar regrets.*

*Light fades down to spotlights on both . . . one moment . . . then, lights to black. In black, tea kettle's whistle whistles.*

*Lights fade up again in* **Brackish**'s *room. He is looking out of the window. He moves to his bedside chair, sits; reads. His hearing aid sits atop bedside table, out of use. He has a headache.*

*Lights fade up in kitchen . . . and* **Kathleen** *is there, removing kettle from flame.* **Kathleen** *puts teapot and aspirin bottle on to a tray, along with cup and saucer, glass, silver, etc. She sticks dust rags and feather duster under her arm; calls up stairs to* **Brackish**.

**Kathleen**    I'm bringin' your tea up! . . . (*No reply.*) Hullo? (*She climbs the stairs to* **Brackish**'s *room, pauses at the door, seemingly unnoticed by* **Brackish**, *who continues reading, his back to* **Kathleen**. *She tests his deafness.*) Hullo? Your hearin' aid in or out or what? Hullo? (*No reply.*) Hullooooo! (*She enters* **Brackish**'s *room. She slams door closed to test his hearing. He doesn't respond at all. She pauses, directly behind him, out of his line of vision. She stares at him, silently, five count. Satisfied that he cannot hear her,* **Kathleen** *speaks into his deafness.*) Sometimes, I am just amazed to think that I'm standing here and you're just there, within striking distance and all. You're like a legend to me, really . . . If my father could see me now. Wouldn't he'd a'b'en the jealous one, huh? I mean, he use'ta dream a'bein' this close ta you . . . and havin' a rock in his hand, a'course! . . . He was interested in marine biology, my father. He loved the sea and the boats and all. He always loved ta point out the different kindsa' weeds and name the fish and all especially down the marshes. You'd think you were listenin' to some kinda' *Hav'id professor,* or some such. It really pisses me off ta think that he spent his life, workin' the docks, lumpin', as he did. It killed him young, carryin' crates in wintah, and all. Deadhead stupid labor. Stupid, stupid, useless! . . . He use'ta get tanked up, wickid, down ta Sherm's . . . he'd come home and beat my mother . . . I know he woulda' loved to have beaten *you,* Brackish, but the closest he could ever come was ta beat my mother. The three of us girls cowerin' in the corner . . . like mice, scared shit so wickid bad . . . Nobody havin' a life worth livin' . . .

Every time I heard your name out loud, Brackish, it was in connection with somebody like my father gettin' their hearts broken, gettin' flunked, gettin' creamed. Nobody was ever good enough . . . smart enough . . . worth sendin' on inta the world . . . You musta' hated passin' the ones you had ta pass: the John Connors and the Annie Bells . . . the naturally-smart-student-types. Mosta' us scared little bastids, us poor lumpers' kids, we didn't stand a chance, did we? Not a chance!

**Brackish** (*whirls around, faces her; suddenly aware of her presence in his room*)    There you are! I was wonderin' if you'd taken a walk . . . forgotten me . . . my aspirin . . .

**Kathleen**    I didn't forget nothin' . . .

**Brackish** (*points to hearing aid on table*)    I'm keepin' my hearing aid out . . . Better for my headache.

**Kathleen** (*mouths the words, broadly*)    Fresh tea . . . your aspirin . . . (*She starts to pour a fresh cup of tea for* **Brackish**. *He pulls back, frightened.*)

**Brackish**    Careful! You're gonna scald me!

**Kathleen**    Wouldn't I love ta, huh?

**Brackish**    Excuse me, are you saying something?

**Kathleen** (*startled; stiffens*)    Me? Nope. (**Brackish** *returns to his reading; deliberately ignoring* **Kathleen**. *Hostility abounds.* **Kathleen** *straightens* **Brackish***'s bed. He glances at her; returns to reading. She resumes talking to his back . . . to his deafness.*) I'm gonna' keep you alive until you apologize to us all . . . me, mother, father, husbin' . . . And after you do . . . then you can kick off . . . and I can kick off, too . . . 'cause there won't be any reason for us two pathetic bastids not to . . . (*She goes to* **Brackish**, *touches his arm; gesticulates widely as she talks.*) I'm goin' back downstairs . . .

**Brackish**    Fine.

**Kathleen** *turns and exits his room, carrying tea kettle, tray, etc. She walks downstairs and into kitchen; begins chopping vegetables for a soup.* **Brackish** *sits alone a while, worried. He puts down his reading, and, curiosity having gotten the best of him, replaces his hearing aid in his ear; goes downstairs. He stops at radio, finds* **Byron Weld**'s *station. A Bach cantata fills the room. Satisfied,* **Brackish** *goes to his chair; sits. He looks over at* **Kathleen**, *who is busying herself with the cutting and slicing of soup vegetables.* **Brackish** *listens to the music a moment, smiles, takes his book, again; reads, again. Suddenly,* **Brackish** *looks up startled.*

**Brackish**   *Oh my God!* I just went completely dead! It was cracklin' with static when I put it in. Now, there's *nothin'*! (*He whacks his battery pack.*) I'm taking this machine out of my ear, once and for all. (*Pops the hearing aid earpiece out of ear; places battery pack on table; looks at* **Kathleen**.) Much better. (*Suddenly, yells out.*) *What!*

**Kathleen** (*rolls eyes heavenward*)   Oh, sweet Jesus! (*Yells to* **Brackish**, *pantomiming her message.*) I'll go downtown and get'cha some new batteries as soon as I finish my soup! (**Brackish** *stares dumbly.*) As soon as I finish my soup! (*Panto, with screams.*) As soon as I finish . . . the soup . . . (*Whacks pot with wooden spoon.*) *The soup!* Lemme finish the soup, *first!*

**Brackish**   No, no, dammit! You finish your soup, *first*, and *then* head downtown for the batteries. No trouble ta me ta wait a coupla' extra minutes. (*Looks at* **Kathleen**; *sees her frustration.*) I'm a hard man to please, aren't I, Kathleen?

**Kathleen**   Sayin' you're 'a hard man ta please' is kinda' like sayin' 'a rattlesnake's a hard animal ta hug'!

**Brackish** (*looks up, suddenly, feelings hurt. Has he heard her?*)   I beg your pardon, young lady?

**Kathleen** (*alarmed*)   I didn't say nothin' . . . (*Mouths the words, carefully.*) I didn't say nothin', Mr Brackish . . .

**Brackish**   Got'cha!

**Kathleen** *smiles.* **Brackish** *smiles.* **Kathleen** *chops the final vegetables and adds them to the soup stock. She smiles again.* **Brackish** *smiles again. She will now speak to him, into his deafness, simply, clearly, perversely . . . and without fear or hesitation.*

**Kathleen**    Well, that's it! Add some . . . fire and water . . . and, by magic, in three hours we shall have . . . *seagull shit!* (*She smiles at him again, as though she's just said something expected, such as 'soup'.*) I love it when you're stone deaf, Jake!

**Brackish**    It's no use, Kathleen.

**Kathleen** (*smiling deeply; sweetly*)    That's probably the hot roasted goat shit . . . We're talkin' hot roasted goat shit on a bed of clam shells, seasoned with the seagull dung that I just mentioned, and topped off, Mister stone-deaf-and-dumb Brackish, with hound's pubic hair! (*She pats the pot atop the stove.*) . . . *That* is lunch, dearie!

**Brackish**    What's that you've got cookin'? Smells good . . . *Looks* good, too!

**Kathleen** (*smiles and nods*)    I live for these moments, Mr Bricklips, I truly do . . .

**Brackish** (*samples soup*)    *Tastes* even better! (*Sees and returns* **Kathleen**'s *smile and nod.*) I'm delighted by your mood, Kathleen. Your spirits have lifted, haven't they?

**Kathleen** (*nods and smiles again*)    Goat shit, rat shit and my grandfather's leather boot up your arse, Brackish . . .

**Brackish** (*returns smile and nod, again*)    This does my old heart good.

**Kathleen** (*returning his nod and smile with still another nod and a smile*)    Oh, you are a foolish-lookin' turd, you are!

**Brackish**    While you're in such a jolly mood . . . Could I take up your offer to fire on down to Tru-Value?

**Kathleen**    I'll fire on down, alright. An hour away from you is worth more ta me than a whole fuckin' day at the beach!

**Brackish**    Yes? Or no?

**Kathleen** (*nodding affirmatively; broadly*) Oh, yes . . . Oh, yes
. . . ohhhh, *yesssssss!*

**Brackish**    Oh, that's good of you! I'll be waiting right
here.

**Brackish** *faces front, smiling.* **Kathleen** *seems to be leaving. She
goes behind his back to the radio and switches the station. This time,
she settles on a popular rap song such as the Beastie Boys might sing.*

**Kathleen**    Yuh, right, Mr Backlash . . . You wait. I'll be
back.

**Kathleen** *stops at the door; gloats.* **Brackish** *looks across room to*
**Kathleen**. *She smiles, blows a kiss to him. He smiles, returns the
blown kiss. She exits.* **Brackish** *sits a moment, not reacting to the
music, which is loud and frenzied. He now rises from his chair and
crosses to the radio. He picks up his hearing aid from the table, tosses it
in the air a few times, sets it back down on the table top, in easy view
of the audience. A moment passes. He wipes his forehead, bringing his
palm over his eyes, which he cups for a moment, masking his face. He
switches dial . . . rap song magically changes to Bach* Jesu Meine
Freude. *We hear: male singer singing sweetly. After listening a
moment,* **Brackish** *sings along with the recording, in perfect
German, word for word. We are now certain that* **Brackish** *is not at
all deaf. He has heard everything we have heard.*

**Singer** *and* **Brackish**    'Duld ich schon hier Spott und
Hohn, dennoch Bleibst du auch im Leide, Jesu, meine
Freude . . .'

**Brackish** *has sung in perfect harmony with recording. The motet
ends. Music fades. After a brief silence,* **Brackish** *bows his head.
The lights fade to black.*

*Note: Author suggests play be done without intermission.*

# Three: Autumn

*The auditorium is dark.* **Byron Weld**'s *voice is heard in darkness.*

**Byron Weld** (*on radio*)    It's just gorgeous out there, isn't it?
. . . Could you ask for a better autumn weekend? 'Course
not. Perfect football weather. Or, perfect for just takin' a
brisk walk along the Back Shore. But, a'course, I'm locked
up here alone at the transmitt'ah . . .

*Lights up now in downstairs rooms.* **Kathleen** *is in the kitchen,
cooking jelly. Fruit baskets and jelly pots, all around. Two huge corn
pots steam away on the stove. Odor of jelly wanted in auditorium.
Note: Foliage blazen color: reds, yellows, browns, oranges. Some leaves
already on ground.*

**Byron Weld**    . . . I'm cooped up here like a man in
prison, so's I can play for you the work of composers who
are all deeply gifted . . . and this station better be gifted, too,
and quick, 'cause without your gifts, we're gonna fold faster
than you can say 'Wolfgang Amadeus Mozart' . . . speaking
of which [sic], this is a Columbia Masterworks recording,
K172 . . . Mozart Quartet in E Flat . . .

*Music up (on radio): Mozart Quartet in E Flat.*

**Brackish** *appears outside of kitchen window, presses nose against
glass, peers inside; sees* **Kathleen**, *smiles. He disappears,
momentarily, then, enters house through kitchen door. He is a symphony
of fall colors, plaids and tweeds. His trouser cuffs are tucked into his
argyle socks, creating the effect of 'plus-fours'. There is a pith helmet
atop his head, for private reasons. He carries a basket of beach plums
and rose hips in one arm and a fat, neutered male cat in the other. Note:
Cat should be absurdly fat, friendly: no question of safety near the beast
wanted.*

**Brackish** (*chirping gaily*)    There isn't a tourist left on the
entire beach. It is a marvelous, marvelous, *marvelous* thing,
the way the seasons change. It restores faith in the Deity.
(*Smiles.*) March: the snow melts. April: the cellar floods.
June, July and August: the cars all sport New York and New

Jersey plates, and they weave from side to side, takin' in all the sights, threatening life and limb. (*Smiles, and pontificates.*) But, then, by God, Labor Day comes, and the tourists all pack up their dreadful greasy hot-dog-colored bodies, and their Godawful charcoal sketches of Motif No. 1 . . . and they vanish! Like Greenheads and Mosquitoes: mystically, magically, they are . . . simply . . . *gone* . . . and it is a marvelous, *marvelous* thing (*Nuzzles cat; sighs.*) Ah, it does please me: autumn. I don't know why people insist on calling autumn 'fall' . . . Autumn is autumn . . . Fall is what you do from Grace!

**Kathleen**    Who's your friend?

**Brackish**    Ohhh. The cat's name is Nathaniel Hawthorne. Say 'Hello', Nathaniel. The girl's name is Kathleen Hogan. (*Pretends to be the cat's voice.*) 'Hello, Kathleen . . .' (*Laughs.*) Oh, did I get a phone call while I was out?

**Kathleen**    This phone? *Ring?* Uh uh.

**Brackish**    I thought maybe Nobby Ellis called. Nathaniel's Nobby's cat. I bumped into him . . . Nathaniel . . . back of Good Harbor Beach, near where Nobby and I use'ta pitch our ho'ss-shoes . . . so I thought maybe Nobby was back home, seein' the cat and all . . . (*Pauses.*) We took a walk up to Nobby's house, up Brier Neck, but, it was still boarded up. (*Pauses.*) Kinda' a worrisome thing . . . (*Smiles; nuzzles Nathaniel absently.*) He'll be callin' me . . . If it were bad news, I would have heard it by now. Nothin' spreads faster than bad news and cheap oleomargarine . . .

**Kathleen**    Are we gonna boil Nathaniel down, too? Or, are we just gonna eat him in the rough?

*Nathaniel squirms.*

**Brackish**    Oh, dear, I think Nathaniel heard you, Kathleen. (*Strokes cat.*) Easy, easy, easy, Nathaniel! Kathleen was just joking. She would never boil a wonderful cat like you. The girl just has a warped sense of humor! (*Nuzzles cat.*)

I've known this beast for fourteen years . . . each human
year is worth eight cat years . . . eight fourteens is a hundred
and two . . . Nathaniel's a hundred and two, Kathleen. I'm
just a kid, next to this old codger . . . (**Brackish** *first sets
down milk, then cat. Cat knows exactly what to do with milk; does.*)

**Kathleen**    A hundred and twelve . . .

**Brackish**    What's that?

**Kathleen**    A hundred and twelve. You said Nathaniel was
a hundred and two . . . Eight fourteens is a hundred and
twelve. You got it wrong . . .

**Brackish** (*after a long pause*)    Well, my God! . . . You're
quite right, Kathleen . . .

**Kathleen**    Yuh, I guess I am, yuh . . .

**Brackish** (*harumphs*)    Harumph . . .

**Kathleen** *turns away; giggles.* **Brackish** *flashes a play-acted,
over-acted, look of annoyance at* **Kathleen** *who giggles again.*

**Brackish** (*stops; worries*)    Where was I? (*Remembers;
continues.*)

**Kathleen**    We'd both counted up Nathaniel's age. You
got it wrong and I got it right.

**Brackish**    C'mon, Nathaniel, walk me to the mailbox.
I'm gonna get my paper.

**Brackish** *exits.* **Kathleen** *goes, immediately, to radio, switches it
on, tries a few stations before settling on a sentimental 'Easy Listenin''
song. She lip-synchs and dances to music.* **Brackish** *re-enters,
without Nathaniel, carrying newspaper. He catches her dancing. She
blushes, runs into kitchen, mortified.*

**Brackish**    Weather's changin'. I think we're in for it . . .
(*Goes to the radio.*) What an odor comin' from the fish plant.
Hard to believe the stuff they're bakin' is gonna' *be* food,
instead'a havin' already *been* food!

**Kathleen** (*shrugs*)    Makes a lot of jobs.

**Brackish**    I s'pose. (*He switches station, finding* **Byron Weld***'s WGLO-FM.*)

**Byron Weld** (*has caught the cold of his life!*)    . . . and it'll be yo'r fault, not mine. (*Coughs.*) This is Johann Pachelbel . . . (*Coughs.*) Canon in D Major with Jean-François Paillard conducting his Chamber Orchestra . . . (*Coughs.*) . . . recorded in 1972 at Albert Hall . . . (*Coughs.*) I've got a wickid cold . . . coughin' . . . the chills.

*The music begins.* **Brackish** *sits in chair, reading* Gloucester Daily Times. *He suddenly yells aloud, middle of a thought, height of a rage.*

**Brackish**    *Scabrous son of a bitch!* I knew when I saw his cat on the beach he'd pulled something like this! Nobby Ellis was a scabrous son of a bitch, from the day I met him! I was five years old, Kathleen . . . five years old . . . and I could tell! He was competitive! To the point of somethin' very nearly illegal! *Competitive!* I would get an A, he would get an A-plus! I would buy a bike, he would buy a red bike. 'Course, as I knew he was pathologically competitive, it didn't really bother me when he beat me out for Valedictorian . . . 'cause I understood the psychology of the situation: He, being from a broken home and all, and me, bein' from a wonderful family-oriented family . . . But, when he went into *graduate* school . . . *graduate school* . . . well . . . I knew he was directly competing with me. I mean, I got my BA from the finest, right? As did he? Two Gloucester boys goin' off to Harvard like we did? Hell, as far as I was concerned, the competition was finished: dead tie. Dead tie . . . But, no, not Nobby Ellis . . . He hadda keep competin' . . . MA from Yale in English Literature: isn't that just the most goddamn absurd thing you ever heard of? I pick up the *Gloucester Daily Times* and I cannot believe my eyes! 'Norbert Alvin Ellis the 2nd will leave tomorrow for New Haven, Connecticut, where he will begin his studies for a Masters Degree in English Literature . . .' (**Kathleen** *tries to pour his tea.*) I didn't ask for that, did I? (**Kathleen** *backs off.*) I shoulda' let it go. I shouldn't a' got down to his sick level

and competed . . . BUT . . . I went back ta Harvard . . . two
miserable years of takin' the heart and soul out ta the likes a'
Byron and Keats and Shelley . . . learnin' lists of what Dr
Johnson had for breakfast on his two-hundred-mile walk
with Boswell . . . makin' maps of goddamn Wordsworth's
goddamn walks around the Lake District . . . I mean, really,
is this the stuff that's gonna' get the fire lit on a cold winter's
morning? (*Pauses; disgusted.*) No sooner do I get back ta
Gloucester and back ta teachin' . . . bang! I pick up the
*Times* and there's Nobby . . . off to Trinity College, Toronto,
Canada, for a Ph.D. in guess what? Right! *English Goddamn
Literature* . . . This still gets my nipples up, Kathleen, if you'll
pardon my anatomical reference . . . Ph.D. in E.L. . . .
Great! Back I go into Harvard. You'd think I was working
for the MTA, I rode it so often . . . Back I come ta
Gloucester . . . four years older, carryin' more letters after
my name than a postman could fit in his goddamn sack! A
Jewish Ph.D. teachin' High School Music and English in
Gloucester, Massachusetts. What I was, was something that
happens every *two hundred* or *three hundred million* years! And
Nobby Ellis goes off ta England, to Oxford University, to
teach English to the English! . . . Isn't that a kettle  of fish
you'd call 'just fine'? . . . It never ended, Kathleen! . . .
Never! They retire the son of a bitch at age sixty-five, same
as they retired me, but where does he come for his twilight
years? Does he stay in Merry Olde You-know-where? You
know he doesn't! Right back ta Merry Olde Gloucester,
where I have ta pitch horseshoes against him at Good
Harbor Beach every wa'm day, and play gin rummy against
him every cold day, right here in my own dining room . . .
for eighteen years, until they take the stupid bastid away ta
Rattray's Old Age Home down Wakefield, because Nobby
ain't got the brains, nor the guts, ta simply say, 'No, I ain't
goin' ta any old-age home, anywhere, under any condition!'
His halfwit son-in-law speaks and he obeys, like he was still
in goddamn graduate school. I begged the pencil-brain ta
move in here with me . . . I offered free rent, the works . . .
We were practically even in gin games and I was way, way

up pitchin' horseshoes . . . but he went. He goddamn went
. . . (*He is desolate now.*) Over a year and not a single word . . .
until this . . . (*He picks up* Gloucester Times *and slams it down.*)
First-ta-Die Award. Nobby wins it, huh? The stupid bastid,
leavin' me like this. He was two months and a week older'n
me, Kathleen, so, you know what that makes me now, huh?
I am officially the oldest livin' man in Gloucester,
Massachusetts, US of A. Nobby was it, but now, it's me. I
outlasted him. I took the title. I . . . win.

**Kathleen** *re-offers cup of tea to* **Brackish**. *This time, he picks up
cup, sips. Note: Pachelbel piece must be timed out to conclude precisely
as speech concludes with '*I . . . win*'. Repetition of small section of
music needs to be added just prior to ending to achieve perfect timing.*

*The lights fade to black.*

*Lights up in kitchen.* **Kathleen** *has prepared a tray with 'vapors'
. . . bowl, toweling, etc.* **Brackish** *pulls on bathrobe, puts
thermometer under tongue. She calls over to* **Brackish** *softly, gently.*)

**Kathleen**   We're ready for you . . . (*She sets vapors bowl and
toweling at table.* **Brackish** *has thermometer in his mouth.*)

**Brackish**   You'd better check on Nathaniel. Make sure
he's peeing in his box instead of in my bed, again . . .

**Kathleen**   Don't talk with the thermometer in your
mouth . . .

**Brackish**   What's hell's the difference? We know I've got
a fever! A thermometer's a waste of time, if you ask me! (*He
goes to calendar.*) Same damn thing as a calendar! If you don't
know what date it is already, a calendar's no use at all! I
mean, really, try starin' at one when you really don't know
the date! All a calendar will give you is 365 guesses! (*Turns on
radio, flips through stations, finds* **Byron Weld**, *who is also ill.*)

**Byron Weld** (*on radio; coughs twice*)   Robert Schumann
lived from 1810 to 1856 . . . (*Coughs twice, again.*) Excuse me,
I'm sweatin'. I'm wickid sick . . .

**Brackish**   You hear that? Byron's sick, too . . . (*To* **Kathleen**.) This sickness you caused is goin' through the town like wildfire! I'm one foot in the grave . . . Nathaniel's up there, half dead . . . sweating away, incontinent . . .

*Music in: Schumann's* Bach – *Op. 60.*

**Brackish** *walks, slowly, to the dining table, under* **Kathleen***'s watchful eye over-acting his illness, badly, as might a child. He stops en route to the table and sticks a finger in the frosting of a partly eaten Halloween cupcake, orange frosting, samples same; doesn't respond to the taste. He hands thermometer to* **Kathleen***; sits.* **Kathleen** *moves the vapors bowl in front of him.*

**Brackish**   We'd better use the blackboard. Last time I took the vapors with my hearing aid in, the steam rusted the damn thing brown . . . Get the blackboard (*He takes hearing aid out of ear, places it on table.*) What?

**Kathleen** *fetches a largish blackboard from kitchen, sets it up, propping same against slack of books.*

*Music continues, under.*

**Kathleen**   Get under the towels.

**Brackish**   What?

**Kathleen** (*pantomimes his getting under toweling*)   Go under . . . towels.

**Brackish**   What's my temp?

**Kathleen** (*under her breath*)   I thought you weren't interested. (*Reads thermometer.*) Ninety-nine-one . . .

**Brackish**   I can't hear you, dammit. Write it!

**Kathleen** (*writes same on blackboard*)   Ninety-nine-point-one . . .

**Brackish**   Ninety-nine-one? That's *nothing*! I'm burning up! I'm way over a hundred! Goddamn thermometer's useless!

**Kathleen**    Go under the towels . . .

**Brackish**    That s'pose ta be *funny?* . . . Talkin' ta me when I can't hear?

**Kathleen** (*exasperated; pantomimes*) Go under . . . the *towels!* . . .

**Brackish** (*goes under and comes right back up; glasses steamed opaque*)    Great! My glasses steamed up! Now, I can't see what I can't hear . . . (*Rubs glasses, puts them on.*) Did you say something?

**Kathleen**    Nothin'. I didn't say nothin' . . .

**Brackish** (*from under towel*)    I cannot bear this.

**Kathleen**    Yuh, well, tough luck. (*She walks to radio and switches it off; pops in cassette of an 'Easy Listenin'' tune such as Phoebe Snow might sing. She allows music to play in room, softly. She returns to kitchen and work.* **Brackish** *continues his complaint, sans fin.*)

**Brackish** (*pops out from under towel*)    Philosophically speaking, the ultimate danger for a deaf man in not hearing a tree fall in the forest isn't that the sound doesn't *exist!* It's that the goddamn tree will fall on your *head!* (*Goes under the towels, again; pops out, again.*) Where the *hell* is United Parcel with my records? Did you call them?

**Kathleen** (*nods an enormous nod*)    Yes, I did . . . (*Holds up three fingers*) Three times, three . . . one, two, three times . . . (*She writes '3 TIMES' on the blackboard.*)

**Brackish**    There's no need to write *that!* I counted your fingers, dammit! I'm not blind, ya' know! I'm *deaf.* (*Sneezes; coughs.*)

**Kathleen** (*exaggerated bowing and scraping*)    Sorry, sorry, sorry . . . SORRRY! (*Writes word on blackboard*)

**Brackish**    Don't act mousey with me, Kathleen. (*She shoves him under the towels.*) I hate this. Dammit! I am an educated man! I don't want to die face down in a bowl of

Vick's Vapo-Rub! (*Pops out from under.*) This is your fault,
really. All that damned opening and closing of the door for
trick-or-treaters. That's what did me in . . . One of their
horrid little killer snot-noses brought us the trick and the
treat of this virus, that's what. (*Sips tea.*) Encouraging them
with *cupcakes*! Gimme one of those! . . .

**Kathleen** *places cupcakes on table.*

**Brackish** (*fingers frosting; tastes*)    Why's this frosting orange?
What did you use to color it? It tastes weird.

**Kathleen**    Carrot juice.

**Brackish**    What?

**Kathleen**    Carrot juice!

**Brackish**    I can't hear you. You forget?

**Kathleen** (*writes 'CARROT JUICE' on blackboard*)    Carr . . .
*ott* fucking *jooooosss*! (*Picks up hearing aid.*) Will you please put
yo'r goddamn hearing aid back in!

**Brackish**    Carrot juice? Carrots are vegetables! (*He shoves
cupcake aside in disgust.*) You feed 'em carrots, they'll be able to
see in the dark! They'll be comin' around every night!
(*Coughs; listens to music a moment, forgetting his alleged deafness.*) Is
this your idea of music? This isn't music!

**Brackish** *stands, walks to cassette deck; switches Music off.*
**Kathleen** *stares at hearing aid in her hand, and then at*
**Brackish**. *She is amazed to catch him hearing without his hearing
aid.*

**Kathleen** (*a voiceless whisper*)    Oh my God . . .

**Brackish** (*snaps at her; meanly*)    I'm talking to you, young
lady! (**Kathleen** *turns and faces him.*) I need some tea. What
you put in front of me is cold . . . You have a simple job to
do here, young lady . . . to keep things hot . . . (**Kathleen**
*doesn't move.*) I must insist that you keep your half of the
bargain, I provide wages and a place for you to hang your

hat; and you provide *assistance . . . as I need it . . . And I need it now, please! (Yells, full voice.) Now, please! (There is a silence.)*

**Kathleen**    Lemme just put on a record first, Mr Brackish . . . One a' your favorites . . . a'course, you won't be able to hear nothin', what with your hearin' aid out ta your ear . . . Right? (*Walks to phonograph, pulls out an album, at random.*) 'Pablo Casals . . . Bach, "Suite for Unaccompanied Cello" . . . 1936 to 1939 . . .'

**Kathleen** *puts phonograph record on turntable, starts the music, lightly. It is indeed Casals playing Bach's 'Suite for Unaccompanied Cello. We hear the gentle sound of Casals' cello . . . until . . .* **Kathleen** *pulls the arm of the record player and needle across the record. A terrible scratching sound is produced.* **Brackish** *looks away. Another pull, another scratch. Another and another.* **Brackish** *finally talks to* **Kathleen** *through clenched teeth.*

**Brackish**    Stop it . . . stop . . . STOP . . . STOP THAT!

**Kathleen**    Kinda' a miracle your hearin' improved so much . . . ain't it? *Ain't it?*

**Brackish** (*mortified*)    I'd better check on Nathaniel.

*He stands; gets away from* **Kathleen** *as quickly as he can . . . up the stairs, switches on stair light, then radio, goes up into his room. He is beyond embarrassment: mortified. We hear: Beethoven's Symphony No. 1 in C Major, Opus 21.* **Kathleen** *goes to kitchen, sits at table, begins writing a letter. The music stops, suddenly. The lighting dims. We hear* **Byron Weld**. *His voice is incredibly weak, near death.*

**Byron Weld** (*on radio*)    I'm sorry ta hav'ta shut down shop for a while . . . (*Coughs.*) . . . I'm sick as a dog . . . (*Coughs.*) . . . I'm just gonna hop up ta Addison Gilbert and get myself looked at . . . (*Coughs. Coughs again.*) . . . This is Byron Weld, signin' off . . . (*Coughs.*) . . . WGLO-FM, Gloucester, Massachusetts, on Cape Ann . . .

*Suddenly, dead air: Silence. In his room,* **Brackish** *hears this, stands, alarmed. We hear: Voice of young man replacing* **Byron Weld**.

**New Voice** (*on radio*)    This is Arnold Weld, Byron Weld's nephew. Uncle Byron died last night, up Addison-Gilbert. Before he died, he told me to tell ya's that he thanks none of ya's. I'm takin' over the station, for the moment, and WGLO-FM, Gloucester, Mass., is gonna be playin' more 60s-70s-80s-and-90s rock 'n' roll than any other station north of Boston. From the 70s, here come the Buzzcocks . . .

*Music in: A nasty rock tune.* **Brackish**, *without cat, rushes downstairs, shuts off radio.*

**Brackish**    I sent the bastid six dollars a week, fifty-two weeks a year for forty-one years in a row, you know that? And do you think he ever once mentioned my name on the radio?! Even just once?! I cannot tolerate his ingratitude! . . . I cannot tolerate the ingratitude of my former students, either! Not a one of them calls, comes around. Not a one of them. I never married because of my students, you know . . . I mean, did I have need for children? I had thousands, right? (**Kathleen** *ignores him; doesn't answer. Instead, she sits at kitchen table, writing letter, intently.*) Don't you know that non-verbal noncommunication reveals an *ignorance*? If you have a thought to express, express it in language . . . Speak English words! (**Kathleen** *ignores him; continues writing letter.*) So? Here I sit, alone, except for the likes of you, Kathleen O'Hara, and Nathaniel Hawthorne, a fat, half-blind, half-dead, neutered male housecat! So? What added up? What *accumulated?* What . . . mattered? (*With self-pity, but aimed at* **Kathleen**.) *A* lifetime of teaching in Gloucester High School. A *lifetime*! Thousands of students and not a single one of 'em can come around and say a 'Hello'. *Not a single one of 'em!*

**Kathleen** (*speaks without looking up*)    You oughta be thankful nobody come around and stuck a knife in your heart. You oughta be thankful. Thankkkfulll.

**Brackish**    I might remind you that my hearing is working just fine, young lady. Your obscenities are coming in loud and clear. *Loud and clear!*

**Kathleen**    Really?

**Brackish**    Really.

**Kathleen**    Kathleen O'Hara shoulda' gone ta college and be'n somebody, but you crapped it up!

**Brackish**    Jacob Brackish shoulda' stayed at Ha'vid and taught some real students . . . but you crapped it up! (*Screams.*) Who are you writing to, Goddamn it! Sittin' in that mousey way, scratchin' . . . scratchin' . . . Who? Who? WHO?

**Kathleen**    None of your damn bis'ness!

**Brackish**    I don't wanna sit in this chair! (*He throws his leg blanket onto floor, leaps up, enraged.*) I don't want these terrible flashing pains inside my head . . . under my arms . . . I don't want my gums pulling back and my teeth falling out in the sink! And I don't want you sitting there in that mousey way, scratching those letters in my house. (*He moves to her and raises his hand; strikes her. She pulls back from him, stunned.*)

**Kathleen**    *Oh my God! You hit me. You old bastid! You hit meee!* (*Leaps up.*) I'm writing to my mother and father!

**Brackish**    They're dead!

**Kathleen**    I'm still writin' to them! I'm writin' to my husband, Princie, too . . . all of 'em, Brackish! I'm tellin' all a'them!

**Brackish**    You're squealin' on me, Kathleen?

**Kathleen**    I am! I'm tellin' 'em everything I know . . . every goddamn thing about you I've picked up . . . and I seen it all, Brackish, *I seen it all!* (*She runs upstairs and into her room.*)

**Brackish**    You don't know a thing about me!

**Kathleen** (*screams to him, downstairs*)    Lonely, miserable old fuck! Lives alone with a half-dead cat, and a Scrooge-voice that drops dead on the radio! They're all leavin' you,

Brackish! Every last one of 'em! Same way I'm gonna be cuttin' out ta here, myself!

**Brackish**    Ungrateful little bitch! You deserve to flunk!

**Kathleen**    Yuh, sure! I deserve ta flunk and so did Mama and Da and Princie and Josie Evangelism and Floey Rizzo and Fast Eddie Ryan and Ruthie Flynn! . . . You wanna hear the whole list? I got it all written down! Every last one of us you ruined!

**Brackish**    You know what a sick waste of your time it's been makin' a list like that?

**Kathleen** (*runs downstairs; confronts* **Brackish**)    Ohhh, you're really som'body ta be talkin' ta *me* about a 'Sick waste'a'time'! How's about the sick waste'a yo'r time never marryin', huh? Nobody in this town was never good enough for you, Brackish? You were too *smart,* too *sophisticated,* too *worldly* for any of the local crop, right? *So,* you coop yo'rself up in this pathetic hovel for fifty-sixty-seventy years! You coop yo'rself up, pissed off and gutless, and you flunk the whole goddamn Town of Gloucester . . . and *you* talk to *meee* about 'a sick waste of time'? What are you? *Crazy?*

**Brackish**    I did not, young lady, flunk the 'whole Town of Gloucester'. I did nothing of the kind!

**Kathleen** (*counting on her fingers*)    Mother, Father, Hus'bin, me . . .

**Brackish**    *You failed! Your family failed!* I may not be proud of much else in my life, but I am pretty goddamn proud of my teachin' record, so don't you attack it! And don't you attack the way I lived, my life, either! I've got no regrets! Not *one!* All's I hate is the bein'-old part of it . . . bein' trapped inside a body that doesn't work. *I hate it!* But most of all, I hate bein' trapped inside a house with the likes of you! *I just hate it!*

**Kathleen**    Then what did ya' beg me ta come here for?

**Brackish**    You answered an ad . . . for *money*! I have never begged anybody for anything in my life!

**Kathleen**    *THEN TRY IT! IT'LL DO YA' SOME GOOD!* Try sayin' 'Thank you' and 'You're welcome' and 'You ain't so smart, but you ain't *nothin'* . . . you ain't a piece'a tossed-out goddamn lobstah shell on the beach!' *TRY SAYIN' THAT, BRACKISH!* Try sayin', 'You ain't Einstein, but, you certainly do deserve a pat on the back for gettin' through the wintah,' 'cause, it's miserable wicked awful cold and lonely . . . and it's *tough . . . It's TOUGH!* (*Chokes back her tears.*) I ain't gonna cry I ain't gonna cry I ain't gonna cry! I ain't gonna *mouse out ta this*! (*Looks up at* **Brackish***. Square in the eye, now, no tears.*) I may've be'n a D-plus dodo in Music Appreciation, Mr Brackish, but I knew how'ta give a hug and a kiss and I knew how to get a hug and a kiss . . . and you didn't! Now look at you! You got no friends at all. Cooped up alone with the goddamn radio, and this half-blind neutered cat, who, by the way, ain't fakin' his blindness, Brackish. He ain't fakin' a handicap like some *sickos* I know, tryin' to win sympathy stead'a love, hidin' behind fake deafness, spyin'! Pretty fuckin' pathetic, if ya' ask me! I'll give you another dose of the truth: I came here to watch you die. I came here to enjoy your death. I open the paper ta see the obituary I phoned in for my Princie and it ain't there, Brackish. It ain't in the paper! I call Nan Cobbey, who I've known since Girl Scouts and she's now some kinda' deal down the *Times* and she don't know and she calls back an hour later and says the *Times* is '. . . sorry they left it out . . .', that the little blank hole on the page is where it was s'pose'ta be, but after the paper was pasted up, Princie's ahhhticle fell off, somehow . . . Princie fell off the goddamn page! She asks me did I know 'A white hole on a newspaper page is called a "widow"?' And isn't this a '"gross irony"?' And then she gives me her 'sympathy' . . . The next thing I see in the paper is your ad, which stuck ta the page like God Himself glued it down. And I knew I hadda take your job. I knew I hadda do it . . . There was nobody at Princie's wake, down Pike's Funeral Home, Mr

Brackish. Just me and nutso Buster Sheehan, who'll sit with
anybody's body overnight, so long as you give him the
Guinea Red . . . I felt relief when Princie died, Mr Brackish.
I did. I felt relief. He wasn't very nice ta me. (*Sobs openly.*)
They start you out in fifth grade with a nickname like
'Titmouse' and it don't do a whole lot for your spine. They
tell you when you're seven that 'you'd better learn ta
typewrite, KO, 'cause you ain't goin' ta no college, or endin'
up intellectual or even hopeful'! (*Ruefully.*) KO. Great little
set of initials ta start out with, huh? KO'd at birth! KO'd
right at the first-round *bell*!

**Brackish**   I've never heard such self-pitying paranoic
ho'ss-shit in my entire life! The world was out to get
Kathleen O'Hara, right? Even me: out ta get'cha', right? I
gave you a D-plus, not because it was what you earned, but,
because I was perverse . . . vindictive . . . whimsical! It had
nothin' whatsoever to do with your actual achievement
right? (**Kathleen** *starts to run upstairs.* **Brackish** *stops her with
his voice.*) Am I correct? Am I correct? AM I CORRECT?

**Kathleen**   (*covers her ears: as might a child. She turns, screams at*
**Brackish***; and to the world*)   I did it all ta myself: me! (*She
slaps her own face, three times, powerfully.*) I did it myself, OK?
(*She now punches her own hip to punctuate her guilt.*) I only got
myself ta blame. Okayyy? (*Punch.*) I been my own worst
enemy. Okayyyy? (*Punch.*) OK? OK? OKAYY? (*Final punch.
She weeps, turning her face away from* **Brackish***. She leaps into
chair and buries her face in pillow on the chair-back, so as to muffle her
sobs.* **Brackish** *chokes back his own tears, now. He speaks to her,
compassionately.*)

**Brackish**   Oh, Kathleen . . . Kathleen, please . . . tell me
what I can do for you. I want very much to help you. I want
to know that this time you've spent with me was *worthwhile*.
Please . . . tell me what I can do . . . for you.

**Kathleen**   (*looks up at him: front*)   A make-up test in Music
Appreciation. I want private tutoring and I want another

chance . . . to raise my grade. A make-up test in Music
Appreciation. That's what I want.

*Lights suddenly bump up to day lighting: hot, bright, alive. Music in:
lights build as music by Strauss fades in . . . swells.* **Kathleen** *runs
upstairs. She appears in bedroom wearing Walkman earphones:
studying sheet-music.* **Brackish** *goes to desk, gets his bluebook,
crosses to bookcase, arranges albums for test, then puts one record on to
turntable. The Strauss piece is the first of a medley of Bach, Debussy,
Brahms, Chopin selections, ending with Mendelssohn's Symphony No.
4 in A Major.* **Kathleen** *runs downstairs carrying bluebook and
pencil. She goes to coffee table, writes her answers in bluebook. When
final piece (Mendelssohn) in medley has played,* **Brackish** *drops the
needle arm of the phonograph onto the record. The lights come up to
scene level. Schubert's* Unfinished Symphony *is heard. The make-
up test is under way.)*

**Brackish**    There's a time limit.

**Kathleen**    I know, I know . . .

**Brackish**    Enough?

**Kathleen** (*panic*)    One sec, one sec . . . Oh, God . . . (*Yells,
relieved.*) OK! OK! Got it!

**Brackish**    Three to go . . . (*He plays a snippet of Mozart.*
**Kathleen** *bites her pencil and, suddenly, remembers. She writes an
answer, stops, thinks better of it, punches fist down on table top, three
sharp blows.*) Ready?

**Kathleen**    One sec, one sec . . . Oh, God, oh, God, oh,
God . . . (*She writes her answer into her notebook.*) OK. Ready . . .

**Brackish**    The final pair . . . Here's the penultimate . . .
(*He places arm of record player into groove and Bach's Chaconne,
played by Nathan Milstein, plays in room. After a few moments,
during which* **Kathleen** *smiles and writes her answer,* **Brackish**
*switches the record and plays a final piece. Last one.* **Brackish**
*allows the arm of the phonograph onto the record and Rachmaninoff's
Symphony No. 2 in E Minor fills the room.*)

**Kathleen** (*worried*)   Oh, God, oh, God, oh, God, God, God . . . (*She thinks she's got it. She writes her answer into her book.*) Done.

**Brackish** (*turns from stereo and faces her*)   Done.

**Kathleen**   My brain's inside out . . .

**Brackish**   You wanna check over any of 'em?

**Kathleen**   I heard 'em once. Fair's fair . . .

**Brackish**   Would you like a cup of tea before you turn 'em in?

**Kathleen**   What are you so nervous about?

**Brackish**   Ready when you are, Mrs Hogan . . .

**Kathleen**   Number one was Strauss . . . definitely . . . late-Romantic period . . . Strauss . . . Number two is Bach . . . Baroque . . . G Major . . . The Brandenberg concertos . . . Number three was hard . . . Impressionistic. Debussy. My guess is one of the Nocturnes . . . I'll go with that: Debussy Nocturnes. Number four was Romantic . . . Brahms . . . fairly easy. Number five was a gift, thank you very much for the birthday present, Chopin Ballade in F Minor . . . Six was Romantic, I'll have ta say Mendelssohn . . . Number seven was another piece of cake, thank you for the birthday present, Schubert *Unfinished Symphony* . . . number eight was sneaky, but I'm gonna go with Mozart, and I think it was No. 40 in G Minor . . . I dunno, but I'm relatively certain it was Mozart, so that's my answer: classical period, Mozart . . . number eight. And number nine was Baroque: Bach's Chaconne. No doubt about it. And number ten was a wicked awful sneaky thing for you to pull on me 'cause you know I don't really know much about Rachmaninoff, I would say Rachmaninoff . . . Maybe not, but my hunch is Rachmaninoff . . . No. 2 in E Minor . . . And that's it. Oh, and I'm wicked awful sorry I scratched your Casals record . . . How'd I do?

**Brackish**    That was precisely the ID section of my Freshman General Music 'drop the needle' midterm at Harvard. I got six out of ten, which was good enough to pass, but just. I saved my bluebook. Here . . . (*He opens a dog-eared 'bluebook'; reads.*) I missed Rachmaninoff. I also missed Mendelssohn, Bach's Chaconne, and that piece of cake: Chopin Ballade in F Minor, thank you very much . . . You didn't miss anything. You went ten for ten.

**Kathleen**    I did. Yuh. I knew I did.

**Brackish**    The ID section counted only fifty per cent.

**Kathleen**    What?

**Brackish**    The other fifty per cent is all on Section Two which I have decided to make oral: one question. You ready?

**Kathleen**    I am. Yuh.

**Brackish**    Here goes, then. Final question . . . worth fifty per cent. This is probably the most important question you'll ever hav'ta answer in your entire life about classical music! . . . Ready?

**Kathleen**    Yes. I'm ready.

**Brackish**    Did you enjoy the music, Kathleen?

**Kathleen**    I did. Very much, Mr Brackish. I did.

**Brackish** (*pause*)    Congratulations. A perfect score.

**Kathleen**    Oh, my God! That was the *question*?!

**Brackish**    Oh, yes, as you suggested, I listened to your Miss Phoebe Snow singing the Paul Simon song, 'Something So Right', and I do see what you mean . . . homophonic . . . romantic . . . reminiscent of English Court ballads . . . in the sonata form . . . lyrically quite sound, really. (*Smiles, simply.*) I . . . liked . . . it.

*The lights fade.*

# Four: The Start of Winter

*Music in: Albinoni Adagio for flute and strings plays under entire scene. The season has returned to winter; foliage is, again, barren, bare. Snow is falling, heavily.*

*Lights fade up in downstairs rooms again. It is Christmas time. Christmas lights, hidden in bookshelves, around room, around window frames, etc., now twinkle, gaily.* **Kathleen** *hangs a string of Christmas lights over the mantle.* **Brackish** *reclines on the sofa. At his feet are stacks of papers that have come from a storage trunk, old-fashioned variety, that has probably been in evidence, throughout the play, upstage. There is also a large wastebasket, overflowing with papers, nearby the trunk.* **Brackish** *takes sheet music and book written in Greek from trunk; considers them.*

**Brackish**   I regret never having the vision, the talent, or the discipline to compose beautiful music. I also regret never learning to read ancient Greek . . . This is Euripides . . . (*He tosses sheet music and book into wastebasket. He finds Chinese primer.*) Or Chinese . . . (*He tosses primer in wastebasket. He finds a small oil-painting kit and palette.*) I also regret never having an ounce of talent as a painter. Winslow Homer's paintings of Niles Pond and Brace's Cove still thrill me silly! (*He tosses kit and palette into wastebasket.*)

**Kathleen**   I was conceived on the Niles Pond sand bar . . . I'm blushin' . . . I must be beet-red . . .

**Brackish**   No need to be embarrassed . . . Not with me.

**Kathleen**   My mother told me that toward the end, just before she passed on . . . I was dozin' off beside her bed . . . She was sleepin' all the time . . . all's a'sudden I hears her say, 'Kathy, you were started inta life on the Niles Pond sand bar. Your father and I lay together there and I knew a child would come of it, and you did . . . I had a lotta trouble goin' over there after I found out . . . Took me maybe a year, but I went there . . . Two big dogs, Labrador retrievers, were, uh, well, they were . . .

**Brackish**    . . . Doin' it?

**Kathleen**    Doin' it! They were! Right there on the same spot . . . Well, *relatively* the same spot! It made me laugh! Oh, God, it made me feel good! (*She chortles, then, suddenly, she sobs.*)

**Brackish** (*watches her weep for a moment, then he speaks to her, soothingly*)    It's the worst thing in life, Kathleen . . . outlivin' the ones you love. It's the worst thing. It strikes a terrible loneliness, and a terrible fear of dyin' . . . I always loved takin' morning walks across the Niles Pond sand bar . . . especially in summer . . . wearing shorts . . . feeling the tall wet Goldenrod and Angelica against my naked legs . . . smellin' the wild roses, the Honeysuckle . . . Nuns and priests from the Catholic Retreat on their dreamlike prayer walks, scarin' the piss out ta the birds and the berries with all that spooky holiness . . . (*Watches* **Kathleen** *regain her composure.*) Let your memories make you happy, girl . . . Otherwise, they'll cripple you . . . turn you to stone.

**Kathleen** (*wipes eyes dry; looks up at* **Brackish**, *smiles*)    Any other regrets to chuck out?

**Brackish** (*pauses; thinks*)    Yup. I regret never sleeping with certain women.

**Kathleen**    Which women, specifically?

**Brackish**    Oh, uh, well, Grace Kelly, the movie actress. I've seen *High Society* nine times. And Agnes Virgilio, from the bread store. She married Cosmo who'sis . . .

**Kathleen**    She's about eighty!

**Brackish**    This is not a recent regret. We're talking about a *lifetime* of regret! Agnes Virgilio had eyes that stopped you from thinkin' . . . deep, happy, full of promise . . . And breasts that stopped your breath. Agnes would walk into my class and I would turn, look at her, and within the countin' from one to six, I would suffer the loss of vision, of logic, of all pulmonary functions!

**Kathleen**    You ever sleep with her? . . . Oh, no, right.
This is a regret list.

**Brackish**    And right at the top of my list, Princess Grace
Kelly and Agnes Virgilio.

**Kathleen**    What held you back? From sleepin' with her?

**Brackish**    She married Ranier!

**Kathleen**    I mean Agnes Virgilio.

**Brackish**    She saw through my hearing aid, same as you
. . . *Both* my mother and my father went deaf, early on . . . I
was so sure *I* was going deaf, I started to wear my father's
hearing aid. I started wearing it to school. I could hear a pin
drop! . . . One day, in front of my sophomore English class,
it fell out. I said, 'I'm deaf without my hearing aid, class. I
can't hear a thing!', and one of the little sons-a-bitches up
the back of the room yells, 'You're a wicked arsehole,
Brackish!' . . . From that day forward, I had my own secret
way of knowin' exactly what was on my students' minds . . .
They told me themselves . . . same as *you*!

**Kathleen**    Oh, God, I'm sorry about my swearin' and my
sayin' bad things about you and all . . . (*Remembers things she's
said.*) Oh, Godddddd!

**Brackish**    Don't apologize. I deserved every word of it.
Any man who peeks through a keyhole deserves ta get a key
in his eye . . . (*He laughs, she laughs. There is a pause.*)

**Kathleen**    I have a regret. I regret never asking my
mother about something before she died. I remember bein'
home alone and getting a call from Sherm's, the bar, down
by the head of the harbor . . . My father had caused a
commotion . . . a fight . . .

**Brackish**    He'd . . . struck somebody?

**Kathleen**    Opposite. He'd got himself creamed by some
big 'mukka'.

**Brackish**    Oh.

**Kathleen**   They called for Mama to come get him . . .
Mama wasn't in the house and I felt panicked somethin'
wicked. I rode my bike down there in about a minute flat
. . . down over your hill. We were living top of Mount
Pleasant, just near here . . .

**Brackish**   Yes . . .

**Kathleen**   Papa was layin' on the floor, drunk . . . all
bloody . . . singing 'Red Roses for a Blue Lady' . . . I can't
ever forget it . . . me comin' inta this dark pit of a bar room,
seven y'ars old, wearin' a powder-blue dress with little tulips
printed on it . . . findin' my Da singin' away, drippin' his
blood, nobody payin' the slightest attention ta'either of us. I
don't think Papa knew who I was. I try ta lift him but I can't
and he keeps singin' the very same words over and over
again. (*Sings.*) 'I got some red roses, for a blue lady . . . I got
some red roses, for a blue lady.' (*Speaks.*) The cops came in
. . . Papa stood up and started walkin' . . . I followed him. Up
Haskell Street hill here . . . He just kept singing the same
words, over and over 'til we got ta your yard here . . . Mama
had taken our car, and it was parked out at the end here . . .
(*She screws up her courage. She will now, for the first time in her life,
admit to a connection between* **Brackish** *and her mother.*) Mama
parked her car in yo'r yard, Mr Brackish! (**Brackish** *looks
away,* **Kathleen** *watches him, she continues speaking, again, softly.*)
Papa walked up to our car, face still all bloody, and he rubs
his fingers in his own blood, after spittin' on 'em, and he
takes his hands and does like fingerpainting, on the
windshield . . . (*Pauses.*) He painted red roses . . . all in his
blood . . . about a half-dozen of 'em, maybe . . . Then, Papa
walked off home. I cleaned off the windshield so's Mama
wouldn't get scared when she got into the car and all . . .
(**Kathleen** *and* **Brackish** *allow their eyes to meet, for a moment.*)
Mama parked her car in yo'r yard, Mr Brackish. (*Pause.*) Did
you sleep with my mother a lot?

**Brackish** (*nods*)   Yes, I would have to say 'a lot'. Francine
and I began seeing each other long after you and your
sisters were born. Your father had hit her, and for some

reason she came here to me. After that I was here whenever
she needed me. (*Pauses.*) Being with your mother was the
most terrifying and exciting thing I've done in my (entire)
life.

**Kathleen**    Poor Da . . .

**Brackish** (*pauses*)    Poor Da . . . poor everybody. He was
bellowing his song about the roses out by my gate . . . Your
mother and I went to my window, looked down, and there
he was . . . You, too . . . tiny little thing, off to one side, as
scared as we were . . . (*He pauses.*) She never came back to
me after that day . . . I never saw her again. (*Sighs.*) I adored
your mother, Kathleen . . .

**Kathleen** (*goes to* **Brackish**, *hugs him*)    So, why'd you flunk
her?

**Brackish**    Why'd I flunk Francine Flynn? Are you
kidding? Your mother was a terrible student, Kathleen.
How could I pass a student like Francine Flynn? Just
because I would choke for oxygen when she walked into my
class? Just because my vision darkened and dimmed when I
tried to *look at her*? These are not reasons to pass a poor
student. A man's got to have some *standards*! (*Laughs.*) Oh,
God! If the man I *am* met the man I *was*, there would be a
fist fight! (*They share a laugh.*)

**Kathleen**    If I walked into your class today, would ya' . . .
you know . . . feel a little blind and dumb? Hard ta breathe
kind of thing. Would ya'?

**Brackish**    Oh, Kathleen . . . if I could live my life over, I
would have you walk into my class and I would behave like
an *animal*! I would choke for oxygen . . . You would cause a
spontaneous pneumothorax . . . blindness, deafness, mental
lapse . . . I would deliquesce: melt . . . (*There is a substantial
silence.*) Ah, Kathleen . . . Gloucester! I've got to get some
rest, now. (*He stands, bracing himself against* **Kathleen**'s *arm.
He recites a schoolboy poem, softly.*) Gloss-tah bo'hn . . . Gloss-
tah bred . . . Couple'a days, I'll be Gloss-tah dead. (*Looks at*

**Kathleen**. *His accent is now exactly like* **Kathleen***'s accent.*)
I'm wicked awful tired. (*Starts up stairs, falters; falls.*)

**Kathleen** (*runs to him*)   Mr Brackish . . . ?

**Brackish**   I went weak. I'm short of breath . . . maybe my
chair . . .

*The lights dim down.* **Kathleen** *goes to* **Brackish** *and leads him
slowly, painfully, to his chair. He sits. Albinoni Adagio swells to
conclusion, and Pachelbel Canon in D Major plays softly. Lights swell
to full.* **Kathleen** *is discovered at the phone, ending conversation. She
hangs up; goes to* **Brackish***. He is incredibly weak; obviously near
death.* **Kathleen** *chirps, happily, as if to pump strength into*
**Brackish***'s failing spirit.*

**Kathleen**   I had some really great news from Mrs Dallin
down at the High School. They're naming a prize for you.
It's official: The Jacob Brackish Prize for Outstanding
Scholarship in English Literature and Music Appreciation.
Mrs Dallin is workin' out the final details with Mick Verga,
who's president of the Gloucester National Bank, now. (Do
ya' ba-leeeve that?) If the graduate goes ta Ha'vid, he (or,
she) gets double. Great news, huh? (*She softly sings the first four
lines of the 'Easy Listenin'' song previously heard on the radio.*
**Brackish** *is unresponsive. Her smile fades.*) They've all be'n
callin', from ten towns around. You'd think it was the Pope
himself that was sick, honest ta God! Some of them wanted
ta run right over here now and give ya' their get-well-quick
wishes in person, but I told 'em all ta wait till you're feelin' a
bit less punk . . . (*Pause.*) Maybe I better call Dr Chandler,
huh? I won't let 'em take you to any hospital. I'll keep my
promise on that, but maybe he better come over and just
have a look, huh? (*She stands and starts to the telephone. The rattle
of Death rattles.* **Brackish** *dies.* **Kathleen** *turns around, in a
sudden, looks across to him.*) You say som'pin'? (*She goes to*
**Brackish***; stares a while before realizing that he is dead. She
'crosses' herself.*) Oh, God. Oh, God. Oh, God. Oh, God . . .
(*She removes his glasses, 'closes his eyes'. She talks to* **Brackish** *as if
to comfort him.*) You remember Snoddy Timmons from my

year? He called. They all called: August Amoré, Franny and Evvie Farina, Harry and Margaret Budd, John Sharp, the Shimmas . . . God! *Everybody!* You're really respected around these parts, Jacob. You can't imagine. (*She sits holding his hand, watching him, waiting. They are both at peace. She smiles at* **Brackish**. *She holds his hand. She looks at him admiringly. She removes her locket.*) This was Mama's locket. My baby-picture's in one side. Mama, herself, is in the other . . . from when she was, ya' know, young. I was thinkin' you might want it. I've got other stuff of hers ta keep for myself . . . (*Presses locket into his hand.*) Thanks, Mr Brackish . . . Jacob. I'll always be grateful. (*She stands, listens to the music, just one brief moment; She speaks, softly, to a world.*) Pachelbel . . . Canon in D Major . . . eighteenth century . . . Baroque . . . Beautiful. (*She walks to the telephone, dials the police station.*) Hullo . . . I wanna report a death.

*The lights fade to black.*

**Cat Lady**

*Cat Lady* had its USA premiere at the Boston Theatre Marathon on 18 April 2004. It was produced by the Gloucester Stage Company and directed by M. Lynda Robinson. The cast was as follows:

**Cat Lady**     Nancy E. Carroll

*In darkness, We hear . . .*

**Cat Lady**  Here, puss! Here, puss-puss-puss!

*Music in . . . Bach, played by a single cello, loud, elegant, terrifying . . .*

*Single spotlight fades up on . . . old lady, on beach, calling out to her missing cat.*

**Cat Lady**  Here, puss! Here, puss-puss-puss! (*She blinks in the sunlight, sees audience, speaks . . .*) You cannot trust a cat. They have too many lives. There is no ultimate threat to a cat. You can't threaten to kill them, unless you threaten to kill them nine times, because they've got nine lives, so they couldn't care less. And if you actually kill them, they just come back. Of course, if you hang around through seven or eight of their lives, they only have a couple left, and they start to get a little nervous, but not really.

*Beat.*

Many people think that cats having nine lives is a myth – an old wives' tale – but it's true. I've seen it. I *lived* it.

*Beat.*

My cat – Cabbage – ran away, two days after I found her. I say *found her,* but I didn't actually find her. She found me. She walked through my bedroom window. Somebody had abandoned her, I suppose. Anyway, she chose me. I was sleeping. It was summer, hot, I was in my bed with the window open. I was dreaming and I had this sense of somebody staring at me. I opened my eye and Cabbage was on my pillow. Her nose was pressed right up against mine. She was tiny, all gray, like an old baby.

*Beat. She calls out to the missing cat . . .*

Here, puss-puss-puss! Here, puss-puss-puss!

*Beat.*

I called her Cabbage because she *ate* cabbage. I know cats aren't supposed to eat cabbage. They're supposed to eat fish. But my cat hated fish. Wouldn't touch the stuff. She loved *cabbage*. Cabbage stuffed with meatballs was her favorite, but she would also munch raw cabbage, and with great enthusiasm.

*Beat.*

I also love cabbage – cabbage, the vegetable, not Cabbage, the cat. I suppose I love Cabbage, the cat, as well. I don't *feel* a great deal of love for this particular cat, but I suppose I must *have* love for her, because she's been with me for so many years. I can't remember how many, exactly. A lot. I wasn't young when she came to me, but – well – I wasn't young forty years ago, was I?

*Beat.*

I suppose that I'm quite like a cat, myself. I've also had a lot of lives. I was first married when I was sixteen. I was actually *fifteen*, when I got pregnant, and sixteen when I got married. I was still sixteen when I got divorced. The baby was stillborn, a stillbirth. I went the full nine months, and delivered him in the normal fashion. A little boy . . . perfectly well formed, quite beautiful, but definitely dead. I felt him die, several days before he was born. He was kicking, furiously, and then, nothing. I went to the doctor for confirmation, but I had no doubt. My stomach had been full of life, large, robust – and then, it was just, you know, soft, lifeless, like a sack of bones.

*Beat. She calls out to the missing cat . . .*

Here, puss-puss-puss! Here, puss-puss-puss!

*Beat.*

My parents and my boyfriend's parents all celebrated the erasure of this sin. I said 'my boyfriend'. I meant to say 'my husband'. It's difficult to talk of a fourteen-year-old as 'my husband'. Especially, now, when I'm nearly a hundred. He

was only fourteen, when I got pregnant. I'm nearly eight
times older than that, now. Eight married-lives later, you
might say.

*Beat.*

I can't actually remember his name.

*Beat.*

Not my husband's. My husband's name was Billy. I mean
the son, the baby – the *dead* baby. Neal. We named him
Neal. It wasn't anything official, of course. You're not
allowed to name a dead baby anything. The name Neal was
just something between us – something we decided . . . my
husband and me. Officially, Neal was in the record books as
'The dead baby'.

*Beat.*

Our marriage was annulled, which is different from divorce.
Divorce is a legal division of a marriage – a legal closure.
Annulment is a legal trick. It takes the entire marriage from
the record books, dissolves it. It no longer exists in the
present, or in the past. As if it never happened. Billy and I
were annulled. Absolutely annulled.

*Beat. She calls out to the missing cat . . .*

Here, puss-puss-puss! Here, puss-puss-puss!

*Beat.*

I don't know what's become of Billy. I'd heard he'd moved
quite far away – to Europe or Asia. Perhaps, Africa,
although I would tend to doubt that.

*Beat.*

It takes courage to move far away.

*Beat.*

Think how far a cat moves from its natural habitat. Very
far. Very courageous, really.

*Beat.*

My second marriage didn't last much longer than my first. I was married to a bus driver. He left me, six months after we were married. Drove away, bus and all, never came back. It was a city bus. We were living in Boston, at the time. I was nineteen when I married him, and twenty when he drove away.

*Beat.*

The police couldn't believe I wasn't involved, implicated in his crime. I don't mean his leaving me was a crime. I mean the taking of the bus.

*Beat.*

I wonder who was on the bus with him? I'd never thought of that before. There might have been innocent people on the bus — shoppers, schoolchildren. Fancy that!

*Beat. She calls out to the missing cat . . .*

Here, puss-puss-puss! Here, puss-puss-puss!

*Beat.*

I didn't marry again until I was twenty-five. I wasn't allowed to. There was a court order, in fact, preventing me from marrying again – a sort of statute of limitation. The police never really believed he'd left me. They thought we were still partners – partners in crime. A team of bus thieves. After five years, they gave up looking for the bus and my husband. As did I.

*Beat.*

I turned twenty-five, and remarried, immediately. My new husband – Alfred – never learned to drive. That was fine with me. Alfred tried to learn. He went to many, many driving schools. He was desperate to learn, but he failed his driving test, seven or eight times. No motor skills, you might say. Poor Alfred was afflicted with a rare astigmatism. He was both far-sighted and near-sighted. He was far-sighted in his right eye and near-sighted in his left eye. On top of that, he was totally colorblind. Everything appeared blue to poor Alfred. Life was so difficult for him. It's difficult not to feel blue when everything else actually *is* blue. Alfred was constantly depressed. So much so, I couldn't stay married to him. I left him in our thirteenth month. I went into the bedroom to tell him I was going, but I found him crying. So, I said nothing. I just left.

*Beat. She calls out to the missing cat . . .*

Here, puss-puss-puss! Here, puss-puss-puss!

*Beat.*

It's upsetting, when you leave things you love, or when things you love leave you. Even things you don't love. It's always upsetting. Coupling and uncoupling. Both so difficult.

*Beat.*

My fourth and fifth marriages were catastrophic. Both husbands died, within a year of the wedding bells. George was the first. Well, the fourth, actually, but the first of the two who died. We never knew if he died of natural causes, or if there was foul play. There was a noose around his neck, which certainly opened the door of suspicion. Richie, my fifth husband, put his head in the oven. It was horrible. Electric stove. He was *roasted*!

*Beat. She calls out to the missing cat . . .*

Here, puss-puss-puss! Here, puss-puss-puss!

*Beat.*

My sixth husband Roger and I stayed in the throes of marital bliss for more than forty years, from the time I was twenty-six 'til I was sixty-six, nearly sixty-seven. We had two sets of twins and a set of triplets.

*Beat.*

That's two and two and three – seven kiddoes, in all, plus, of course, Cabbage.

*Beat.*

Roger's gone, the kiddoes are all gone, as well.

*Beat.*

It's not such a great thing to live as long as I've lived. You pay a terrible price.

*Beat.*

Two of the kiddoes went in a car wreck. Roger and the other kiddoes lived long lives and died. One of the triplets – Allen – he only went 'til forty-eight. Not really a long life. His brothers went 'til seventy, and died within two days of each other. Roger – my husband – was nearly ninety when his heart gave out.

*Beat.*

He left me alone with the cat. Many women are left alone with a cat. Men seem to be left alone with dogs and women with cats. This is a theory I would explore, if I were younger.

*Beat. She calls out to the missing cat . . .*

Here, puss-puss-puss! Here, puss-puss-puss!

*Beat.*

We stayed together, Cabbage and I, for nearly two years before the accident. It's difficult to know if the accident were my fault, or Cabbage's fault. Not important, I suppose. It seemed important, at the time.

*Beat.*

We often came to this beach, to take the air. I love the sea. Cats, I suppose, are not sea lovers like people. Let me be honest: I don't love the sea. I love the sea*side*. Here, Cabbage and I are in total accord. I never liked the sea, never liked the idea of waves lapping my legs. I never liked wet. But I've always adored the beach, the sand. And how could Cabbage not adore the sand, as well? It's a giant cat box, after all, totally liberating for a cat, I should imagine. I've relieved myself many a time in the sand. Most people relieve themselves in the sea, but I have always found that to be most unpleasant.

*Beat. She calls out to the missing cat . . .*

Here, puss-puss-puss! Here, puss-puss-puss!

*Beat.*

When we crossed the street from the beach to the bus, Cabbage bolted away from me. I tried to stop her, but she was a cat who could not be convinced of anything. Once her mind was set, she never wavered. She wanted to bolt, and she bolted. I saw the car hit her and it was horrible. First the front wheels, then the back wheels. And then, as if that weren't enough, the crazy bastard backed up to see what he'd done – rolled over her one more time. I was *dumbstruck*, really dumbstruck.

*Beat.*

And that's how it happened.

*Beat.*

I moved into the road, toward the poor flattened cat, and saw nothing of the bus but the bus driver's eyes, wide as saucers. I remember the thud of the bus hitting me. I remember my flight through the air to the sand. I remember thinking 'This is quite fun'. And then, nothing.

*Beat.*

Could I have been thrown so far that I've not yet reached the spot where the cat lay dead, or has she moved into her ninth life and run off again? It's so difficult to know.

*Beat. She calls out to the missing cat . . .*

Here, puss-puss-puss! Here, puss-puss-puss!

*Beat.*

I've been walking for days and days, calling and calling, but, there's no sign of her.

*Beat.*

She'll come back. She always comes back. She would never leave me alone. Never alone.

*Beat. She calls out to the missing cat . . .*

Here, puss-puss-puss! Here, puss-puss-puss! Here, puss-puss-puss! Here, puss-puss-puss!

*The lights fade out.*

www.ingramcontent.com/pod-product-compliance
Ingram Content Group UK Ltd.
Pitfield, Milton Keynes, MK11 3LW, UK
UKHW020717280225
455688UK00012B/398